Stories

of
NARRATIVE FEATURES OF ORGANIZATIONAL PERFORMANCE

Achievements

Stories
of
NARRATIVE FEATURES OF ORGANIZATIONAL PERFORMANCE
Achievements

HERVÉ
Corvellec

Transaction Publishers
New Brunswick (U.S.A.) and London (U.K.)

This book is printed on acid-free paper that meets the American National Standard for Permanence of Paper for Printed Library Materials.

Library of Congress Catalog Number: 96-49383
ISBN: 1-56000-282-4
Printed in the United States of America

Library of Congress Cataloging-in-Publication Data

Corvellec, Hervé.
    Stories of achievements : narrative features of organizational performance / Hervé Corvellec.
        p. cm.
    Revision of the author's thesis (doctoral)—Lund University, 1996.
    Includes bibliographical references and index.
    ISBN 1-56000-282-4 (cloth : alk. paper)
    1. Organizational effectiveness.   2. Performance.   3. Achievement motivation.   I. Title.
HD58.9.C674   1997
658.3'14—dc21   96-49383
                                                                              CIP

*En célébration
de ces heures passées plage Marquet
avec ma mère.*

Contents

Acknowledgments

This work has been financed in its major part by the Swedish Council for Planning and Coordination of Research (Forskningsrådsnämnden) and the Faculty of Social Science, Lund University. Additional financial support has been provided by the Chamber of Commerce of Southern Sweden (Sydsvenska Handelskammaren), the Helge Ax:son Johnsons Foundation, the Institute of Economic Research (Lund University), the Knut and Alice Wallenberg Foundation, the Jan Wallander Foundation for Research in Social Science, and the County Governor Per Westling Memorial Fund (Landshövding Per Westlings minnesfond).

I am sincerely indebted to my colleagues at the Department of Business Administration at the School of Economics and Management of Lund University. Throughout this work, Barbara Czarniawska-Joerges (now at the Gothenburg Research Institute) and Göran Widebäck have provided me with highly efficient help and support, as did Philippe Daudi (now at the University College of Kalmar, Sweden) and Claes Svensson at an earlier stage of my research. Karin Jonnergård and Hans Lindquist were particularly discerning readers of earlier drafts. Göran Alsén, Per Arvidson, Margareta Bernstad, Christine Blomquist, Sven-Olof Collin, Ulf Elg, Lennart Hansson, Ulf Isacsson, Ulf Johansson, Håkan Lagerquist, Allan T. Malm, Gert Paulsson (now at the Swedish National Audit Office [Riksrevisionsverket]) have all had the kindness to read and comment on the fragments I presented them with.

I would like to thank, as well, Mary Jo Hatch (Cranfield Business School, UK) and Richard J. Boland (Case Western Reserve University, Ohio) for their valuable and comprehensive comments on earlier drafts of this book. I would also like to acknowledge the circumscribed but none the less important support I have received from Timothy S. Doupnik (University of South Carolina), Seppo Ikäheimo (Turku School of Economics, Finland), Peter Miller (London School of Economics), Jan Mouritsen (Copenhagen Business School), Ingemar Oscarsson (Department of Comparative Literature, Lund University), and Gösta Widmark (Linköping University, Sweden).

x   Stories of Achievements

Numerous people from Swedish public libraries have devoted time
and efforts to guide me into the world of library management. Two of
them deserve my particular gratitude. Here I have in mind Anna-Lena
Höglund (Linköping County Library) and Greta Renborg, now retired,
whose receptiveness and kindness never failed.

Two more persons, finally, deserve my gratitude. These are Robert
Goldsmith, from the Department of Applied Psychology, Lund University, who, as a dedicated language corrector, excelled in putting into proper
English the ideas I formulated in my own Creole; and, most of all, Richard Sotto, from the Department of Business Administration, Stockholm
University, who never ever complained at my—at times pressing—demands for his opinion, and who unremittingly provided me with valuable
comments.

This book is a slightly revised version of a doctoral dissertation presented early in 1996 at the Department of Business Administration of the
School of Economics and Management, Lund University. Parts of this
work have also appeared elsewhere: Chapter 1 is a shortened version of
Hervé Corvellec, "Translating Management Accounting Terms—The
Case of 'Performance,'" in *Advances in International Accounting*, vol.
8, edited by Timothy S. Doupnik (Greenwich, Conn.; London, England:
JAI Press, Inc., 1995), 129–47; a previous version of chapter 2 appeared
in *Proceedings of the 13th Conference on Business Studies, August 14–
16, Copenhagen*, vol. 2, edited by J. K. Christiansen, J. Mouritsen, P.
Neergaard, and B. H. Jespen (Copenhagen: Copenhagen Business School),
525–45; parts of chapters 3 and 4 were published previously in Hervé
Corvellec, "Biblioteksprestationer sedda i ljuset av sportprestationer,"
in *Biblioteket som Serviceföretag—Kunden i Centrum*, edited by Göran
Widebäck (Rapport 4, Stockholm: FRN, 1992), 67–76; chapter 5 devel-
ops ideas featured originally in Hervé Corvellec, "Shaping an Activity
Indicator Set for a Public Library," paper presented at the *2nd International Conference on Arts Management*, Jouy-en-Josas, France, 23–25
June 1993; and chapter 6 has been published in part as Hervé Corvellec,
"Library Performance in Activity Reports," *Swedish Library Research*,
no. 3–4 (1994): 52–68. The author gratefully acknowledges the permis-
sion these publishers and publications gave for using previously published material.

H.C.

Introduction: Performance Stories

"C'est sur ce mot qu'on a fait ce livre."
—Victor Hugo[1]

What is it that fills a sports arena and excites stock brokers? What is it, likewise, that is of concern to the dean of a faculty as well as to the manager of a profit center? It is, in each case, performance—performance that permeates contemporary societies, breathes its spirit into them in a diffuse but penetrating way, and imprints its mark upon them.

Performance leads to the opening, the localization and the closing down of a factory, a post office or a hospital. Performance determines the existence, the nature, and the price of products, from bridges to green peas. Performance is the yardstick by which the quality of individual and collective human efforts is assessed. It is the key motif in sports shows, television games, and all the many works of fiction concerning those whose accomplishments are heralded, whether these be police officers, lawyers, doctors, or ordinary people. It accompanies want-to-see-all-in-a-week tourists, as well as terminal-state patients kept alive by life maintenance devices. It is found at the heart of debates regarding currency rates, possible reforms of public sectors, and mergers of companies or unions of states. Everywhere, performance shapes the lives of people and organizations in accordance with its logic and its demands.

The concern for performance has spread to an ever-increasing range of contexts, into a quest that societies have adopted—"a new cult," as the French sociologist Alain Ehrenberg (1991) claims. It has successfully invaded the whole of our contemporary imagination and become one of its most recurrent signs of recognition. We have all, regardless of whether as employees, sports practitioners, car drivers, or holiday makers, become susceptible to falling under the influence of performance in our ways of looking at things and people as well as our ways of behaving. The notion of performance has become of central importance for our perception of our activities and our understanding of the world.

1

Such importance calls for reflection, at least if scholarship is to be a matter of inquiry into the conditions of our existence, and it is particularly important for at least two reasons that this reflection be located within the context of organizations. First, as Perrow (1986:vii) observes, it is now widely acknowledged that "all important social processes either have their origin in formal organizations or are strongly mediated by them," and it is also increasingly accepted that "the study of organizations must be at the core of all social science" (ibid.). Not only do we spend most of our time interacting in and with organizations, but organizations today form the very conditions of our existence and thus our ways of apprehending the world around us.

Another decisive argument in favor of the study of precisely the notion of performance in organizations is that this is a context where performance enjoys, so to speak, a commanding position. Together with sports and engineering, the management of organizations is a context that makes intensive use of the notion of performance. Most managers, for example, would agree that performance is one of their central concerns. Accordingly, management literature on performance is abundant and covers seemingly all aspects of business and nonbusiness administration. Performance indeed has a major role in how organizations are managed and how they behave. These are two of many reasons, then, that make the study of the meaning assigned to the notion of performance in organizations an important matter for the social sciences of today.

The major question then—and the question to which this book attempts to provide answers—is: What is performance? I believe answers to this lie in the uses that are made of the performance notion. It is in these uses that one can learn what performance is and what it is not, what meanings organizational actors attach to it, and what is embedded in the assumptions, conditions, and consequences of performance being used as an element of the managerial discourse conducted in English. The meaning of performance rests, for example, on how management literature describes the way that specific organizations work with the notion. Its meaning lies, as well, in how performance is connected with related notions such as efficiency and competition, and how these notions borrow from, resemble, and differ from each other. To investigate the notion of performance is to explore the uses to which it is put.

The study of these uses of the notion of performance leads me to claim that performance is a story about the achievements of an organization. The implausibility of the idea that performance might be some intrinsic attribute of the organization, or of the idea that an organization's performance is what the organization does—the action itself—leads me to claim that performance is a tale affixed to an organization by managerial discourse. The arbitrariness with which authors within management literature choose their indicators of performance, the way in which accountants translate an organization's activity into performance measures, the way organizational actors account for an organization's activity in annual reports, and the way the feat of an athlete is encoded into discourse on sports—I will later show how relevant the latter analogy is—are all indications that performance is something narrated. An organization's performance is a series of meaningful statements recounting what has been achieved in and by the organization within a given period of time, for example, "the marketing department was effective at introducing our new product, allowing us to meet our budget." As an account of organizational activity, the performance of an organization is a tale, a narrative.

When speaking of story, tale, and narrative I refer to the literary tradition in which a story stands for "a chronological sequence of propositions consisting of actions and attributions that are invoked by a text" (*Columbia Dictionary of Modern Literary and Cultural Criticism* 1995). Thus, tales, stories, and narratives designate here textual chains of statements aimed at representing something.

Such a view is less encompassing than Bruner's (1986) for whom narrative designates a mode of knowing and argumentation based on lifelikeness and verisimilitude, as opposed to a paradigmatic or logico-scientific one based on procedures for establishing formal and empirical proof, and on logical argumentation. My view of tales is, likewise, of more limited reach than is Fisher's (1987) claim that stories and narratives are the basis of all human communication. These views can be seen as an appendage to Lyotard's (1979) use of stories and narratives as an epistemological way of challenging the modern generation of knowledge. This is where the inspiration for my perspective comes from: to say that performance is a story—in a literary sense—is a way of challenging the traditional view of performance as an ontological trait of organizations. It is a way of emphasizing that management consists in the production of small local narratives, which, for that matter, constitutes just another illustration of the communicative qualities of storytelling.

What I aim at in claiming that performances are narrative constructions is to qualify the nature of these constructions, indicating that, like any other tales, performances are the product of narration. My claim is that performances are organizational stories, or more specifically, stories of achievements. Accordingly, I propose to answer the question "what is performance?" by listing some of the central features of organizational performance stories. Listening to what organizational actors refer to when they speak of performance, my objective in this book is to explore, present, and discuss the distinctive features of performance stories, such as what they deal with, how they deal with it, where they come from, how they are constructed, and how they function as stories.

This study of the features of performance stories starts, in chapter 1, within the broadest and most basic context in which words and notions acquire a meaning, namely, language. In an imaginary meeting between three division managers who speak of performance, I find reasons to look in dictionaries for the meanings of performance. Dictionaries propose a wide array of meanings for the term, all depending upon the context in which the word appears. This contextuality is convincingly illustrated by the difficulties one encounters whenever one tries to translate the term from English, where it was coined, into a foreign language, for example French or Swedish. The first chapter provides a sense of performance as a word. It points to the multiplicity of meanings the term can take, and underlines the ambiguity this results in. The chapter emphasizes, in particular, the tension that exists between performance understood as an ongoing action, captured by the idea of performing, and performance understood as a result.

Chapter 2 is a contextualization of dictionary meanings in the context of management literature. Various sets of texts taken from the performance literature are queried regarding how they conceive of their core notion, the answers they give being presented. These answers turn out to be not only considerable in volume, but also quite diverse. Textbooks in accounting, for example, emphasize performance being a matter of results and control. Academic management journals see in performance an imperative that encompasses all aspects of organizational life, one to be used as a universal yardstick of validity. Public management literature, driven by managerialism, mimics its private counterpart and likewise views performance as an imperative, though less in the name of earnings than in that of improvements of and accountability for public services. The overall picture one acquires from reading performance literature, however, is confusing; definitions abound, contradictory claims cohabit in mute ignorance of each other. Performance emerges as a matter that involves varying criteria. What is considered as being the performance of an organization seems to depend entirely on the measurement procedures applied in the case at hand.

In order to avoid the reduction of performance to mere measurement, the two chapters thereafter carry the reasoning outside of management into sports. The aim of this detour is to investigate the narrative features of performance by taking advantage of the visibility and readability of these features in the sports context. Chapter 3 focuses on sports, going through sports history to provide insights into the historical background of the notion, and describing how one can actually read a performance. The chapter emphasizes the possibilities for multiple tellings and multiple readings of performance stories, and restates in this regard the importance of context for understanding what is meant by organizational performance. Chapter 4, in turn, discusses parallels between sports and organizations. It describes the fascination that contemporary organizations have with professional sports and details similarities and differences between the notion of performance and notions such as competition and hierarchy.

Chapter 5, which returns to the context of organizations, is concerned with the practice of performance measurement as considered within the light of insights gained in the two previous chapters. The chapter recounts the case of the creation of a set of performance indicators in a public library, tracing the creation of it from the initial manifestations of an interest in performance indicators to the constituting of a performance measurement set as a managerial tool. The chapter attempts to provide an understanding of how these indicators were selected rather than others. The case shows clearly how the performance indicators that were chosen are associated with a complex of individual intentions, collective representations, technical feasibilities, and narrative concerns. The case also illustrates the role of performance indicators in the construction of an organization's performance. The creation and use of performance indicators amounts to a textualization of the organization's activity, that is to say, the framing of this activity within a text. In specifying the series of historical contingencies that have shaped performance indicators, chapter 5 reveals the contingent character of the conditions that shape the process of the textualization of an organization's activity.

Chapter 6 then scrutinizes a specific form of textualization of an organization's activity: annual and activity reports. The focus is on how these texts narratively compose the organization's performance. On the basis of an examination of annual and activity reports of public libraries, the chapter describes who speaks in these reports (the narrator), to whom (the audience), and how (style, rhetoric, and arrangement). Three major traits of the stories delivered by activity reports are singled out—that they are mostly positive stories, that they are multiplot stories, and that they are stories by installments. Also analyzed is how these traits influence the way in which activity reports construct an organization's performance being discussed. It is proposed in the end section of the chapter that activity reports be regarded as a genre in itself: the administrative serial.

The concluding chapter restates the central argument of performances being tales and recaps the principal observations made in the previous chapters concerning the specific features of performance stories. If, as I argue, performance is the product of a narration, then there are as many performances as there are ways of narrating an organization. The endless possibilities of recounting an event and of reading an account of an event mean there are countless forms of performance in the world. Virtually any event, provided it is recounted in an adequate manner, can be made into a performance. This explains why performance stories abound—an abundance that fits particularly well the need of our time to be reassured of our capacity to achieve.

The study combines interpretations issued from the use of various methodologies in various contexts. Each chapter is situated within a specific context, and each covers particular aspects of the performance notion—linguistic, semantic, theoretical, logical, historical and narrative aspects. Such a construction of the study demands that each chapter follow a specific methodology that corresponds to the central issues the chapter raises and the type of material it features. Chapter 1, for example, consists of a lexical study based on dictionaries and a limited corpus of uses. Chapters 2 and 3 are literature studies. Chapter 4 combines cultural studies and traditional comparative methodology. Chapter 5 is a case study based on interviews, participation, and organizational texts. Chapter 6 makes use of a theoretical framework and a methodology of systematic questioning of texts borrowed from narratology. What unites these chapters is a common interest in the meanings attached to the notion of performance. Each chapter undertakes to examine how these meanings are constructed and constituted in the context at hand. Each chapter represents, therefore, a smaller study on how the notion is manifested in a particular context. Together, the chapters provide a general presentation of how the performance notion is utilized in organizations, where it comes from, and what is meant by performance in managerial discourse generally, raising the important issue of how an organization's performance is objectified.

Note

1. *Notre Dame de Paris,* 1831 Preface. "This is the word about which this book has been written" (translation Robert Goldsmith).

1

Polysemy and Contextuality: *Performance* as a Term

> *"Every sign* by itself *seems dead.*
> *What gives it life?*
> *– In use it is* alive.
> *Is life breathed into it here?*
> *– Or is the* use *its life?"*
>
> —Ludwig Wittgenstein[1]

Imagine an international meeting between an English, a French, and a Swedish manager, all division heads in a large multinational company. The conversation takes place in English, which is the company language. All of them are well acquainted with the others' functions and the activity within their divisions, and they share a common experience in the company reporting system. Competition in their sector is intense. The headquarters is very demanding, and performance is at the heart of their concerns. The discussion has gone on now for some time. Its most technical part is over. Tables and charts lie strewn out on the meeting table, and the discussion becomes less formal. The managers deliberate over the need for an ongoing focus on continuous improvement, quality management, re-engineering and lean management. They like the idea of continually comparing what their divisions do and benchmarking good practices, methods, and processes, though not without pondering on whether success is really the same thing for all the divisions and for all the companies. One of them mentions, regarding the integration of financial and nonfinancial measures, a presentation at a conference he attended that Robert Eccle made of Kaplan and Norton's (1992) balanced scorecard concept, a scheme that integrates innovation, quality, customer relationships, and the company's financial situation.[2] Another of them complains of the inadequacies of available methodologies for measuring nonfinancial performance and emphasizes the need of developing an effective information and measurement system, one that would effectively link business strategy with operational performance. Their talks are filled with such statements as: "this term, the financial performance of the division has only been moderately satisfactory," "our distribution performed extremely well," "we need to improve our manufacturing performance," "we have already introduced the new performance review procedure," and "we may have to pay more attention to environmental performance in the future." The discussion goes on in this way.

The issue is what these persons mean by *performance* and what they understand from each other while discussing it. This is an important issue since the meaning they attach to the term is likely to have decisive consequences for their own behavior and that of their organizations, the meaning seldom being straightforward.

I propose to approach this issue in two stages: in this chapter I will look into dictionaries for the lexical content of the term; in the next chapter I will then look at the meaning that management literature on performance attaches to its core notion. Dictionaries constitute an adequate starting point in that they describe the meanings that terms are given in what must be considered the most basic and important context of these meanings: that of language. Regarding the dictionaries, I use not only English ones, but also English-French, French-English, French, English-Swedish, Swedish-English, and Swedish ones. I do this to emphasize that even if English is indisputably the linguistic medium of international business, the way international managers apprehend words cannot be totally disconnected from their sometimes being non-native English speakers. Internationalization, in this regard, is just as much needed in academic business studies as it is for business activities. This chapter provides a comprehensive account of the meanings given to performance in English, as well as an account of how the term can be translated to French or to Swedish. Thus, the linguistic features of the term *performance* are dealt with before turning to the use which management literature makes of the notion—which is the subject of the next chapter.

Performance (English): A Lexical Study

Performance was formed from the English word *perform* and the suffix *-ance* somewhere around 1500, yielding a word meaning either a performing or a thing performed. Perform stems from the medieval English word *parfourmen* and later *performen,* which meant to do, to carry out, to go through, or to render. Still earlier, *parfourmen* came from the old French word *parfornir* or *parfournir,* meaning to finish or to accomplish, which stems from the Latin *performare,* which meant to form thoroughly. The understanding of performance as a public exhibition or as entertainment seems to have been recorded first in 1709 (*Barnhart Dictionary of Etymology* 1988; *A Comprehensive Etymological Dictionary of the English Language* 1967; see also *The Oxford English Dictionary* 1989).[3]

The authors of the 1955 edition of the *New Practical Standard Dictionary of the English Language* list two main meanings of performance. The first is that of the execution, the completion, the action, or the achievement of something. The second meaning is that of a representation before spectators, an exhibition of feats, any entertainment. Roughly contemporary with that, the *Dictionary of Contemporary American Usage* (1957) reported the word to have quite a different meaning, the entry performance referring one further to the entry *rendition,* the latter being the act of rendering, the action of restoring, surrendering, yielding; rendering, especially in America, meaning the translation of a text and performance itself being regarded there as a term for singing or acting.

Somewhat more contemporary, *Webster's Third New International Dictionary* of 1966 provides a richer array of meanings than the two sources above. Its authors list for the word the same meanings as those appearing in the *New Practical Standard Dictionary:* on the one hand, both the act or process of carrying out something, the execution of an action and something accomplished or carried out, accomplishment, feat, and, on the other hand, both a literary or artistic composition and the action of representing a character in a dramatic work. Moreover, though, *Webster's Dictionary* also indicates that performance can be the fulfillment of a claim, promise or request, implementation, and mentions too its being the capacity to achieve a desired result, efficiency. In addition, this source refers to those factors (as speed, rate of climb, ceiling) influencing such capacity in an airplane or an automobile and the acceleration, power, and speed of an automobile, as well as to its meaning the manner of reacting to various stimuli, behavior. It likewise notes that performance can mean the rate of sale of a product.

More recent dictionaries attach similar meanings to the term. The second edition of the *Random House Dictionary* of 1987, for example, starts with the public exhibition or entertainment component of the word and then continues with the achievement component, including the efficiency with which something reacts or fulfills its intended purpose. In addition, the *Random House Dictionary* indicates that in transformational grammar performance stands for the actual use of language in real situations, which may or may not fully reflect a speaker's competence, being subject to such nonlinguistic factors as inattention, distraction, memory lapses, fatigue, and emotional states.

The *Collins English Dictionary* (1991) and the *Oxford Advanced Learner's Dictionary of Current English* (1992), for their part, state additionally that in informal use the term can stand for a mode of conduct or behavior, especially distasteful or irregular, or any tiresome procedure. The *Oxford Advanced Learners Dictionary* also specifies that the term may denote an ability to move quickly, which is an interesting linking of the notion of performance to that of speed.

To summarize, performance appears to cover a wide and diversified semantic array in current English. The term can depict both an act and the result of an act. It can mean both the process of carrying something out and that which has been accomplished or carried out. This is an ambivalence that is particularly evident in relation to the performing arts. There, performance is the act of presenting a ceremony, play, music, or the like, or a musical, dramatic, or other form of entertainment. These are meanings that stem from the oldest definitions assigned the word. In more recent years, the term has evolved in the direction of referring to the idea of an accomplishment, of something desired or intended, or which has taken place within a planned situation, such as when one speaks of a performance test, the performance of a car or an airplane or of a performance in sports. In addition, the word, in most cases value-neutral, sometimes means, in a somewhat ambivalent way, not only some outstanding result, something showing high capability, or the ability to operate efficiently, but also, quite in contrast to this, some ridiculous or disgraceful behavior, the latter, to be sure, in informal use only.

These are the senses in which the word is used in current English. Academic English, as well, has invested the word with many meanings. Literary studies, for example, have approached performance as "the mode of assessment of the 'textual/character/actor' interaction," as Thompson (1985:78) states; "Performance is...placed at the intersection of the text, the actor/character and the audience" (ibid.). Performance is given in this regard the meaning of representation or signification, particularly the former of these, as, for example, on the stage or in films. It is thus very closely allied with acting. In this sense, performance is predominantly analyzed in terms of the creation or construction and the presentation of character and characters, where the latter are the constructed representation or representations of persons. Performance thus stands for an event which supplements the structure/text: the text produces an outline of meaning and of sense, the role of performance being to fill this outline or supplement this text with the necessary richness. This, as Thompson points out, is a meaning close to that in the works of Erving Goffman (e.g., Goffman 1959), in which performance is approached as being enacted through "interaction rituals" and thus as being tied to the *mise en scène* of customs.

My purpose here, however, is not to discuss the meanings given to the term in social sciences at large, but instead to focus on accounting, management, and organizational studies and the specific uses of the term which these disciplines have prompted. The *Dictionary of Scientific and Technical Terms* (1974) contains the following ten entries involving performance: performance bond, -characteristic, -chart, -curve, -data, -evaluation, -index, -number, -rating, and -sampling. Still, it does not have a specific entry for performance itself. A similar lack of any entry for performance per se can be observed in the *International Dictionary of Management* (1986) (containing seven entries involving performance, namely performance appraisal, -index, -linked pay, -measurement, -objectives, -reviews and -tolerance), in the *Management Glossary* (1968) (three entries: performance appraisal, -rating and -sampling), and in the *New Palgrave Dictionary of Money and Finance* (1992) (two entries: performance evaluation and performance-related fees).[4]

The authors of specialized dictionaries tend to leave the term undetermined. Instead of explaining what is specific to a performance bond as a bond or to a performance chart as a chart, they generally provide circular and nearly tautological definitions. The *International Dictionary of Management* (1986), for example, defines performance appraisal as the systematic assessment of an individual performance; in the same style it defines a performance index as a technique for measuring management performance according to certain agreed indices. Informing one that an appraisal is an assessment or that an index is one of several indices tells one very little about what performance itself means. Caught in the trap of circular reasoning, technical dictionaries fail to clarify the term.

A similar indeterminacy of meaning is also to be found in how authors in management use the term. Several conceptions of performance cohabit in management literature (the next chapter will discuss this point at greater length). For Miner, Singleton, and Luchsinger (1985:114), for example, performance is what the actor of an organizational role does: "performance...is what one does within the limits of a position created by an organization to achieve goals." Their overall position is that performance is a behavioral matter, a matter, as Hannabuss put it (1987:150), of "doing something in a particular way with a particular end in view."

Insisting even more on the behavioral aspect of the term, Trujillo (1985:201) studies managerial work as performances "conceptualized not in the 'bottom line' sense of organizationally productive behaviour but in the 'dramaturgical' and 'cultural' sense of those situationally variable interactions in which managers and others members [of the organization] construct senses of organizational identity and reality." Such a use of the term unmistakably refers to the term's performing art component.

Others consider an organization's performance to be the result of its activity. Such a view can be ascribed, for example, to the numerous authors who choose to measure performance using such indicators as accounting profit, return on investment, residual income or sales revenue. Performance, then, can also be a synonym for efficiency or effectiveness. The Local Government Training Board and the Audit Commission (UK) stated, for example, that "one useful way of thinking about performance is to consider it as having two distinct elements: service *efficiency* and service *effectiveness*" (1985:59, emphasis original).

Meyer and Zucker (1989:67) advocate still another view. To them, an organization's performance is how the organization attains its official objectives: "We construe performance narrowly, as measuring attainment of official objectives however imperfect."

As Emmanuel, Otley, and Merchant have observed (1990:31), in the context of organizational behavior the term performance is indeed highly ambiguous, its meaning changing from one work to the next, and even, one could say, from one page to another. So, if one wishes to experience the lack of clarity that is often concealed by the use of the term, one can simply, as the latter three authors suggest, try to substitute a synonym of a more precise nature whenever the term is encountered.

To summarize, as Hannabuss (1987:149) put it:

The concept of performance is...a pluralistic concept, consisting of several levels of interpretation, from the literal meaning of the "doing of something" or "an activity" to more complex meanings. Among these might be included the notion of dramatic performance, a set of actions displayed by an individual for effect, or the execution of such actions with a degree of efficiency and success.

And for corporate managers, as Jackall (1988:62) observed, performance is not simply "hitting your numbers"—that is, hitting your targets. It is, as well, performing right on the organization's scene—that is, fitting the social rules that commend clothing or vocabulary, being perceived as a reliable team member, or endorsing the official organizational reality as the only reality. In the corporate world, performance is as much producing results as it is acting correctly.

History has progressively endowed the term with more and more significations and taken it into more and more contexts. Today, its semantic register is broad and changing, encompassing many contexts that have only little to do with each other. The meanings attached to the use of the term in an organizational context are, in this regard, only the latest in a long series.

Performance represents the central motif of a multitude of small stories. Enjoying a greater than usual mobility, as Hannabuss (1987:150) indicates, performance is a *keyword* in the sense of that term intended by Williams (1976:13), to denote a word employed both in a general way and in a wide range of specific fields of knowledge, a word that is significant in playing a nonnegligible role in the practices and institutions we group as culture and society. Taken into the web of significations of English vocabulary, it is a word expressing a certain perception of the world and certain sociocultural norms. The term is crisscrossed by meanings that stretch and echo each other from one use to another, and, as with any other term, the meaning of performance *is* this network of meanings.

The various associations the term is susceptible to generating introduce a certain ambiguity as to which meaning(s) the term takes in particular uses. This ambiguity appears all the greater when one is to translate performance (English) into other languages. Translation makes it conspicuous how the meaning of the term, depending upon the context of its use, is oriented in different directions. This is why the next sections are concerned with depicting how laborious and nevertheless imperfect the translation of performance (English) into French and Swedish can prove to be.

Translating *Performance* (English) into French

There is no unequivocal translation of performance (English) into French. Instead, there are a dozen and a half or so words that can serve as alternative translations, depending upon the particular meaning and the context involved: *accomplissement, exécution, résultat, acte, action, exploit, record, performance, rendement, marche, fonctionnement, efficacité, célébration, interprétation, représentation, séance, numéro, allure, session, prestation*. None of these, however, can pretend to translate performance (English) in an indisputable way though all do it in part.

Few of them render the idea of both a process and a result. Most of them lean to the one side or the other. *Accomplissement* (French) and *représentation* (French) may be the only two that are somewhat balanced in this regard. Yet they are far from being such broad terms as performance (English) is. The former is strongly attached to the idea of something being fully achieved, its meaning excluding all sorts of imperfect or incomplete results. The latter, for its part, refers to the action of presenting something to the mind so that it becomes concrete in some way, for example, through an image, a symbol, a sign, or a play. Although both words can serve as translations of performance (English), they cover only a part of the semantic register involved.

Acte (French) and *action* (French) are other candidates. Both render adequately the idea of something being done, but these are terms that possess a philosophical undertone of the realization of the will. This undertone places them at a different linguistic level than performance (English): they tend, as terms, to have a higher dignity than the English term and can in this respect fit only occasionally.

Exploit (French) would indicate more bravery than the performance (English) term usually denotes. Likewise *prestation* (French) or *record* (French) would only be appropriate within the context of sports. The point is that no French word can express the whole semantic register of performance (English). Each French term renders a particular nuance in a particular context of what a performance (English) can be. Choosing a translation word thus involves carefully identifying the context at hand, and then selecting which nuance of the English term is to be rendered.

Even with such precautions though, translation will remain approximate. Take the economic context. A common translation of performance

(English), for example, is *rendement* (French). Yet *rendement* is quite an imprecise word. It can, for example, be translated into English as yield, output, productivity, return or efficiency (*Collins and Robert Dictionary* 1987), which, for an economist, refer to quite differing concepts. To then translate performance (English) as *rendement* (French) is to respond to ambiguity with still further ambiguity. Basically the same is true for *résultat* (French), a term that is both broader and narrower than the English term, not unlike result (English).

Faced with such difficulties, French-speaking writers might be tempted to use the French word performance. *Performance* (French) indeed has good qualifications to be an adequate translation for performance (English), not the least thanks to its seductive interlinguistic homophony and to the reasonable assumption that the French reader might have some acquaintance with the English term. The word was actually borrowed from English about 150 years ago, originally to designate horse race results. By progressive extensions it came to depict all kinds of sports results and also the manner in which something is done. In the 1920s it also came to designate the optimal possibilities of a machine. (The latter signification was condemned, apparently without effect, by the French Academy of Science in 1955.) More recently, the word has become a standard in psychology and linguistics. In its most recent evolution, the adjective *performant* (French) has become a challenging synonym for *compétitif* (French), which approximates competitive (English). (*Trésor de la langue française* 1988; *Dictionnaire historique de la langue française* 1992).

Performance (French), however, is not totally satisfying as a translation. First, performance in French has hardly ever been used to depict a theater play or the execution of a piece of dance or music. Historically, the term was only used in this way by Victor Hugo, on a single occasion in 1869; more recently, it has occasionally been used as a synonym for happening (French, borrowed without modification from English). It thus communicates poorly the idea that a performance (English), even in an economic context, is something displayed for an audience (e.g., a superior, or the stockholders), or that a performance is a unit of communication imbedded within institutionalized rules of presentation (e.g., performance review procedures).

Although such a discrepancy between the sense of the English and the French term might appear to many economists as negligible, a second discrepancy proves to be more problematic. The French term does not cover, as does its English counterpart, what is going on within the organization, what the organization has achieved, or the organization's efficacy. As used by French authors (e.g., Richard 1989; Crozier 1990; Terny 1990), and especially in its plural form as Bourguignon (1994) points out, *performance(s)* (French) is more limited to the notion of result(s)—in absolute or relative terms—than is the English term.[5] Performance in French is not what people do. A performance (French) is not a behavior. The reference to action that is found in the English term is absent from the French one.

Third, *performance* tends in French to have a positive connotation which it does not necessarily possess in English, especially in its singular form. Technical French seems to have been much influenced in this respect by common French, where performance is a praise word nearly synonymous with *exploit* (French) (see, e.g., Ehrenberg 1991). The value connotations of the two terms *performance* (French) and performance (English) thus differ significantly—so significantly that one cannot pass from one to the other without, again, taking careful precautions.

Translating *Performance* (English) into Swedish

Translating performance (English) into Swedish raises the same issues as in the case of French. No single word exists covering the whole semantic field of the English term. Again, translation involves choosing some word that only imperfectly matches the English word, and what is more, does so in some of its meanings only.

The action component of the term can be rendered, for example, by *utförande* (Swedish) or *verkställande* (Swedish). Both of the latter terms express something being carried out. However, as present participles used here as substantives, they indicate more a process than a result. Neither term can be used to refer to performing arts.

It is with the words *framförande*, *föreställning*, *uppträdande*, and *framställning* (Swedish) that the sense of a theater play or the execution of a piece of music can be rendered. These are words that all have meanings broader than the mere performing of a play, however. *Framförande* (Swedish) renders the presentation of something such as a drama, a poem, or a song for an audience, with an undertone of seriousness and dignity. *Föreställning* (Swedish) can signify a mental image, something that someone represents in one's mind. *Uppträdande* (Swedish) is a general term that expresses how one behaves in all sorts of situations, being on stage representing only a particular case of this. *Framställning* (Swedish), finally, has an undertone of something that is done in a systematic manner.

In engineering, performance (English) in the sense of the potential power or effect of an engine is rendered by *prestanda* (Swedish). *Utfall* (Swedish) renders the idea of result. For a sports result, though, one would use *prestation* (Swedish) instead. *Prestation* (Swedish) is a very interesting term. It can be used in many different situations, for example, to express how students perform their studies, how people perform their tasks at work, or even how actors behave on stage. In all these contexts, it can depict both what is currently happening and what has already been achieved. However, in contrast to performance (English), it is a word that has strong positive connotations. Not unlike *performance* (French), it suggests the idea of something, most often a result, that is above average. The result achieved is one that evokes an intensive use of one's capacities. Often too, it suggests an achievement that has occurred under unfavorable conditions. *Prestation* in everyday Swedish is thus something a little bit outside of what is normally done.

The term *prestation* (Swedish) is, for that matter, frequently used in an economic context. Expressions such as *prestationsmätning* (Swedish) for performance measurement, *arbetsprestation* (Swedish) for work performance, and *prestationsbaserad ersättning* (Swedish) for performance-based pay are common uses within the Swedish public sector. These uses differ slightly, however, from those employed in everyday conversation. For example, they are not necessarily colored with the same positive connotation, they do not necessarily evoke something outstanding, and they tend to emphasize the material aspect of what is done, thus making *prestation* (Swedish) close in meaning to *produktion* (Swedish) ("production") (e.g., Anell 1991). *Prestation* (Swedish) possesses qualities, then, which make it of interest in providing a translation of performance (English) in the economic context. However, this does not preclude other terms being able to serve quite adequately as well. *Effektivitet* (Swedish) ("efficacy") is one such term (e.g., Bengtsson 1993:5). *Resultat* (Swedish) ("result") is another (e.g., Didriksson and Mogensen 1993:17).

For the record, *Nordstedts Comprehensive English-Swedish Dictionary* (1992) also mentions the word *performans* (Swedish) being used in linguistics.

In French or in Swedish, many different terms can serve as a translation of performance (English), depending upon the context. However, none of them cover all the meanings of the English term. Moreover, most of them have other meanings as well that do not correspond to performance. Translating performance (English) thus represents a matter of adequately intervening in both languages so as to establish a nonobvious link between a term in each. It implies first that one decide which selected meanings of the English term one wishes to express. Moreover, it frequently implies that one choose a specific (range of) meaning(s) of the French or Swedish word that is employed, since most of the words that can serve to translate the English term prove to encompass meaning that are absent in the latter. It implies, third, that one keep careful track of what meaning is gained or lost when the translational link between the two words—performance (English) and the target term in French or Swedish—is established.

All of this depends upon context and situation, and requires careful observance of how the term in each language relates to nearby terms. In this creative endeavor, translators enjoy considerable freedom. It is indeterminable beforehand which aspect of the French term should be assigned to which aspect of the English one. Entering into a translation involves entering a game of meanings—a game that gains from being openly endorsed and made explicit—where one unties the dynamic ambiguity that exists in the English term and arbitrarily replaces this ambiguity with another, one that pertains to another term, in another language.

Conclusion: Context-Bound Meanings

Returning to the fictitious story again, the company's manual for economic reporting does not provide any specific guidelines for how performance is to be conceived. The meaning of the term is an individual matter, providing a certain leeway for creativity. This leeway is all the broader in that the situation is one involving a translation situation, there being the risk of subtle but far from negligible misinterpretations being injected into the communication between interlocutors. Here are three examples.

- Example one: the French manager comprehends the term in a more positive way than the English manager does. In accordance with how the term performance sounds in French, the French manager uses it with something like an achievement which is of outstanding character in mind. To the

French manager, therefore, a performance, a *good* performance and a *remarkable* performance all become stronger expressions than what her or his English counterpart understands them to be. Conversely, when the latter speaks of a *bad* performance, the former thinks this to mean more serious failure than the latter intends. Diverging value judgments have thus surreptitiously introduced themselves into the conversation.

- Example two: thinking of *prestation* (Swedish), the Swedish manager refers to the division's result. The French manager, familiar with the meaning of performance in French, shares the Swede's view. Without being aware of it, both reduce the English term to the same meaning, arriving at this by different routes. Without things being made precise, however, nothing provides the English manager with the basis for sharing this understanding of the statement with them. They could easily talk at cross-purposes, at least for a while, without noticing it.
- Example three: The Englishman allusively, and not without irony, evokes the theatrical dimension of an investment decision. This derision goes unnoticed by the other two, who miss the point and associate the investment in question with some exceptional result only.

Misunderstandings have intruded into the discussions, reminding us that the three managers differ in their linguistic background.[6]

The misunderstandings selected for these fictitious examples are by intention rather slight. Thus, they might pass unnoticed. The speakers themselves would also have difficulty in pointing them out. Far more obvious are examples of words with radically differing connotations in different cultures, such as *red,* which in Chinese is associated with ceremonies and happiness and in English with cruelty and fear (Newark 1991:74), also, at least in recent decades in the United States, with political power (red and black as power colors) or with political peril (red as communism) (Hatch 1995). One can assume (and hope) that the persons here have much in common in terms of education, life, and business experience, and that this precludes particularly grave misunderstandings. If the conversation continues, this suggests some degree of understanding to have occurred through conversational sense-making.

Even minor misunderstandings, however, can be of major significance, since they concern a construct for which objectivity is widely assumed—a company's performance. Such misunderstandings intervene in communication by way of the person involved believing that the organization's performance is accounted for in an objective way (e.g., that effects of institutional differences have been neutralized). Misunderstandings arise when it is assumed that a common and nonproblematic code of communication is actually functioning. To use a boxing metaphor, these misunderstandings pass the defenses of the reporting system and attack it when its guard is low. Cultural misunderstandings of this kind thrive on the assumption of objectivity that surrounds the notion of performance (as expressed, for example, by the abundant use of figures and charts). The more a performance measure is considered to be adequate, precise, informative, and the like, the greater the effect is of linguistic imprecision, especially when the interlocutors firmly believe that they understand each other perfectly. Paradoxically, it is the very assumption that performance is an objective feature of organizations that, through inflating the misunderstandings that can occur when one speaks of performance, radically undermine the validity of this assumption of objectivity.

These misunderstandings differ in origin from the contextual and institutional differences that reporting systems usually try to account for (e.g., Schoenfeld 1994). They have their roots in words being not only vectors of expression but also vectors of representation. Each word alludes to a referent of its own, defined by proximity to other words, and contrasting with them. Words are not only the written representations of ideas but also the conditions for these ideas' existence. Belonging to specific cultural ambiences, words are the bearers of language-specific thought habits and language-specific visions of the world.

The lexical study of the English term performance has unfolded the diversity of the images the term can evoke in that language. Far from belonging to technical terminology, performance is hardly neat and precise as a term. Its significations stretch along an extended and moving semantic register that basically goes from behavior to results and from performing arts to achievements. The difficulties in finding adequate terms in French or Swedish have demonstrated how even fine distinctions of contexts and denotations can have a decisive impact on connotations.

Contexts have a decisive impact upon which images the term performance can evoke. Depending upon the context, the word can be understood in radically different ways. The choice of context is thus a critical matter in the study of the meaning attached to the notion of performance. The concern of this book being how performance is understood in organizations, the next chapter focuses on how the notion of performance is approached in management literature. Whereas language is the prime context of any word and is thus a decisive context when it comes to meaning, management literature—especially if by this term is meant both popular and academic productions—is a context with a decisive impact upon how managers comprehend the notions they use. Management literature on performance is, in this regard, a context of principal interest for understanding what organizational actors mean when they speak of performance.

Notes

1. *Philosophical Investigations,* translation G.E.M. Anscombe, § 432 (Oxford, United Kingdom: Blackwell Publishers) (emphasis original).
2. *Integrating Financial and Non-financial Corporate Performance Measurement and Management,* Hotel Vier Jahrzeiten, München, Germany, 27th and 28th January 1994. Organized by ICBI (London, UK), in collaboration with Arthur Andersen, and Ernst and Young, this conference gathered presentators and an audience, mostly top-level practitioners, coming out from the most prominent companies in the world. My account of this imaginary meeting is largely based upon the proceedings of the conference.
3. A list of all dictionaries consulted in this chapter is contained in Appendix 1.
4. The *Longman Dictionary of Business English* (1982) does have a specific entry for performance, but defined as a law term only, signifying the act of carrying out the duties contained in a contract and that the contract is discharged (completed and ended) once these duties have been performed.
5. It is interesting to note, in this regard, that a singular form in English can be rendered by a plural one in French. Such is the case, for example, in the title of a publication by OCDE/OECD (1994) which was published simultaneously in English as *Performance Management in Government: Performance Measurement and Results-Oriented Management* and in French as *La gestion des performances dans l'administration: Mesure des performances et gestion axée sur les résultats.*
6. The two speakers who do not have English as their mother tongue indeed run the risk of getting caught in a linguistic no-man's-land in which words are disembedded from their cultural contexts and thus deprived of their evocative values. In this no-man's-land, words have a tasteless and soundless character. Anyone found there runs the risk of being linguistically dispossessed, systematically degraded socially, and, to use Kristeva's expression (1988), of becoming a foreigner to oneself. Conversely, Hatch (1995) noted that persons who do not have English as their mother tongue also have opportunities for enhanced richness of meanings through access to even greater polysemy.

2

A Measurement Construct: Performance in Management Literature

> *"Toute la foi et la bonne foi occidentale se sont engagées dans ce pari de la représentation: qu'un signe puisse renvoyer à la profondeur du sens, qu'un signe puisse s'échanger contre du sens et que quelque chose serve de caution à cet échange—Dieu bien sûr."*
>
> —Jean Baudrillard [1]

The present chapter describes how the notion of performance is used in textbooks on management accounting and control, in academic management journals, and in public management literature. These are three domains of management literature that cover the disciplines of management accounting as well as of strategy, and also deal with both private and public organizations. They represent, as the chapter will detail, a significant share of what management literature says on performance. Texts in these three domains analyze the performance of specific organizations; depict theories, operationalizations, and prescriptions regarding performance measurement; and describe how to design and use performance reports. Here are also texts that reach a large share of the people interested in performance since they are compulsory readings for students, are published in major academic journals on management, or are successfully marketed to practitioners.

Textbooks, academic management journals, and public management literature describe with precision the ought-to's and should-be's of performance management. These three domains of management literature constitute a major locus of elaboration on the notion of organizational performance and thus strongly influence how both individuals and organizations perceive the notion. My rationale in this chapter is to describe how the notion of performance is conceived within these domains with the aim of producing insight into the meanings that management literature attaches to the notion. This involves delving into the bewildering richness that one encounters in management literature on performance and rendering how the notion of performance is conceived, presented, operationalized, and understood in texts that have made it one of their core notions. The aim is to get closer to how performance literature endows the notion of performance with meaning.

The chapter takes us through the various meanings performance can take in management studies. A first section introduces several definitions that have been given of performance and highlights the variety of these definitions. The next section takes up specific subsets of management literature on performance—management accounting textbooks, academic management journals, and public management literature—and describes, for each, with the use of selected examples, how performance is apprehended, how it is endowed with meaning, and how it is used. A third section concentrates upon the measurement of performance. Performance appears to coincide with what authors measure as being the organization's performance, and I accordingly present organizational performance as being the collective creation of those who write about it.

The circular structure of the chapter follows the self-referring character of performance literature. Starting with the observation that the numerous definitions that have been given of performance are impossible to reconcile, the chapter moves into the content ascribed to the notion when used in management literature; then it closes the loop with the claim that every piece of work within performance literature indeed produces its own definition of what performance is. This claim is first an explanation of the initial observation concerning the existence of many, though irreconcilable, definitions of performance. It is also an invitation to break through this self-referentiality of management literature through moving outside the context of management studies, for example, into the context of sports.

Reading Performance Literature

As Meyer and Zucker (1989:65) have pointed out, "the underlying definition of performance is rarely explicit in research studies." Still, as performance literature is so large, it is possible to find a glut of definitions. Baguley (1994:3), for example, argues that "the typical dictionary defines performance as the act of carrying out an action"; this is a broad definition that hardly commits its author and that represents only a part of what dictionaries actually say regarding this word. Other authors are more specific. Voicing stockholders' interests, Gomez-Mejia et al. (1987:58) declare that performance is "a composite of [the firm's] financial success and the extent to which it maximize[s] the welfare of its stockholders." Others do not share this commitment to a financial approach. Among them, Meyer and Zucker claim that organizational performance is a function of the attainment of objectives or goals (1989:47), a view echoed by Schefczyk's (1993:303) claim that "performance analysis is the measurement and comparison of actual levels of achievement of specific objectives." Achieving one's goals, however, is only a part of what performance is, at least if one is to agree with Caves (1980:64 n. 2), for whom the economic performance of a firm is its "efficiency (measured by the divergence of its input-output relation from the best attainable), its profitability relative to comparable competitors, or some other operational test of efficiency." A related position is that of Venkatraman and Ramanujam, for whom business performance is a subset of the overall concept of organizational effectiveness (1986:803). Even if most works lack clear definitions of what is meant by performance, there are numerous definitions of performance in any case, definitions which can be considered, for the most part, to live side by side in utter ignorance of their divergence, nay, of their contradictions. Readers of performance literature falter: How is performance to be understood? Is performance the same as efficiency? Is it to be seen as effectiveness, output, or outcome? Can it be a result? Is it a return? Is it a composite of all these notions?

Few, indeed, have tried to answer such questions, Ford and Schellenberg (1982:50) being a noticeable exception. These authors suggest that three identifiable perspectives pervade the organizational performance literature. One of these, the goal approach, assumes that organizations pursue ultimate and identifiable goals; this perspective, accordingly, defines performance in terms of goal achievement. A second one, the system resource approach, stresses the relationships between an organization and its environment; it defines performance in terms of the organization's ability to secure scarce and valued resources. Finally, the process approach defines performance in terms of the behavior of the organization's participants.

Ford and Schellenberg's typology is worthy of attention. This is, first of all, because it has largely gone unnoticed that they do try to produce some degree of order, where most authors either simply ignore the issue, regret the absence of agreement, or list a few of the many different definitions that exist. Second, it is because their typology respects the word's polysemy—rendering the two central meanings of the word as described in chapter 1: achievement and behavior—which is a praiseworthy effort to preserve the evocative capacity and the dynamic ambiguity of the term. Third, this is because they try to relate performance literature to a theoretical mainland, that of organization theory.

This relating of performance literature to organization theory, however, is where Ford and Schellenberg's typology fails. What the authors tell us is that if one views an organization as a tool aimed at serving goals, then performance is the success in achieving these goals, whereas if one views an organization as a resource-organizing device, then performance is the success in securing these resources. What the authors do is to twice present the reader with the same idea, that an organization's performance is its capacity to achieve what it is supposed to do: two of their categories rely upon the same metaphor of success.[2]

However, one can overcome the theoretical weakness of these two categories' referring to the same principle and reduce Ford and Schellenberg's typology from encompassing three categories to two: a first one, dealing with internal performance, which says that performance is a behavior, and a second one, dealing with external performance, that considers performance to be an unspecified function of the success attached to whatever metaphorical views of organizations one entertains. Most metaphors that one can use in viewing organizations will do. If, for example, one views an organization as a locus of (patriarchal) oppression, then the organization's performance is its capacity to oppress (women). Likewise, if one chooses to view organizational life as the sharing of values and the exchange of signs, then performance is successful communication. The possible choices available are as wide as imagination itself.

When redesigned as a behavior, on the one hand, and as a function of success, on the other, Ford and Schellenberg's typology does organize many texts within management literature on performance. It is nevertheless of little help for those faced with the voluminous task of collecting statements that performance literature produces—concerning, for ex-

ample, what performance is, how good or bad it is for a given organization, why one should measure it, how this measurement is to be achieved
or carried out, or how to write and make use of performance reports—
and also who attempts to understand how these statements, in their richness and diversity, end up influencing individual and collective activity.

Comprehending the richness and diversity of performance literature
requires a finer approach, an approach that traces how performance literature endows its core notion with meaning and is concerned not with establishing who is right or who is wrong and not with stating that
performance is this or that, but that instead attempts to reveal how
performance is designed both in and by means of language practices in
those instances that result in utterances about it, an approach focusing
less upon what performance is than upon how it has become what it is
currently taken to be.[3]

Domains of Management Performance Literature

Let us now consider how accounting and control textbooks, articles in
academic management journals, and works on public management conceive of the notion of organizational performance. In accordance with
the patterns of reading just outlined, I will describe how these texts en-
dow the notion of performance with meaning, giving priority to the voices
of original authors.

Comparisons, Control and Results

A major textbook on management control will provide our entry into
the performance literature: Robert N. Anthony, John Dearden, and Norton
M. Bedford's *Management Control Systems*. Twenty-five years old when
the sixth edition came out, the book is a milestone, as Lowe and Puxty
(1989) put it, in the modern development of management control.

Obviously Anthony et al. consider performance an important notion.
They use it in numerous expressions, such as "actual performance" (Anthony et al. 1989:534), "budget performance" (ibid., 535), "cost performance" (ibid.), "economic performance" (ibid., 377), "financial
performance" (ibid., 250), "managerial performance" (ibid., 584), and
"performance of sales" (ibid., 250). The authors elevate the notion of
performance to the status of being one of the most important notions in

management accounting. As they state, "Performance measurement is *the key* to effective management supervision and control of people in organizations" (ibid., 142, emphasis added).

One searches in vain, however, for any clear assertion of what these authors mean by performance. In contrast to their defining control (ibid., 6), efficiency, and effectiveness (ibid., 13), they make no effort to define or clarify what they mean by performance. Only some form of inductive reasoning based on the uses they make of the term can tell the reader what meaning they assign it. From the examples above it seems that they use the term performance as some sort of synonym for the term result or outcome. Performance appears for them to be a situation reached as the effect of an activity and as a consequence of it.

Most obvious about the result aspect is that it is approached through comparisons. Anthony, Dearden, and Bedford list several types of comparisons, for example, actual compared with budgeted expenses (ibid., 191) and actual compared with budgeted outcomes, these being assessed by use of variance analysis (ibid., 534) and the results being compared with some sort of standards of performance (ibid., 597). The authors leave the reader with little doubt that if performance is a form of result, its assessment requires some form of comparison.

Consequently, performance pertains to the sphere of control, more precisely to the evaluative stage of the control process.[4] Here, for example, is the first occurrence of the term in their text: "An assessing device that evaluates the performance of an activity or organization, usually relative to some standard or expectation of what should be, and identifies out-of-control activities and conditions. The term for this component is *evaluator, assessor* or *selector*" (ibid., 7, emphasis original). Performance belongs, in this view, to the phase of management control in which one keeps records of the resources actually consumed, structures and classifies these records in terms of program or of responsibility, and uses these records both for future programming and for assessments (ibid., 28). This is reflected in the statement: "Performance measurement is the key to effective management *supervision* and *control* of people in organizations" (ibid., 142, emphasis added). To sum up, Anthony et al. view performance as a form of result assessed through comparison, as an element of the evaluation phase of the control process. Such a view could be said to be representative of most management control and management accounting textbooks. It is expressed in very similar terms, for example, by Michael W. Maher, Clyde P. Stickney, and Roman L. Weil in their fifth edition of *Managerial Accounting—An Introduction to Concepts, Methods and Uses* (1994). These authors too use the term performance for outcomes or results and associate the notion of performance with evaluation and control (e.g., ibid., 6). Similarly enough, they too suggest an approach in which results are assessed by means of comparisons, by use of variance analysis (e.g., ibid., 511). Likewise, Clive Emmanuel, David Otley, and Kenneth Merchant, though representing another tradition of textbook writing, insist in their *Accounting for Management Control*, 2d ed. (1990) that the measurement of actual performance is "a vital part of the control process," carried out "so that it may be compared with what is desired, expected or hoped for" (ibid., 31), and pointing out that "the assessment of organizational performance requires both the ability to measure actual outcomes and a predictive model to generate an appropriate standard of comparison" (ibid., 30).

Two main dimensions thus emerge from what management accounting textbooks say of organizational performance: control and results. Being under continual supervision by the organization's information system, and being tuned to comparisons, performance is considered in accounting textbooks as a pivotal element in planning and decision making, as well as in the organization's system of rewards and penalties. Control and results are the nodes around which accounting textbooks organize their view of performance. Connected to the notion of control are the notions of planning and strategy, as well as the notions of command and submission. Connected to the notion of results are the notions of outcome and output, efficiency and effectiveness, as well as of evaluation and value. The idea of control connotes the apprehending of behaviors, behaviors that have resulted from past accomplishments.

Many publications aimed at practitioners build upon textbook views of performance. Such publications usually emphasize their authors' having had long experience as consultants, possibly combined with teaching experience as well. Typically, they introduce performance management as a process and present what they describe as effective step-by-step guidance for improvement in organizational performance. Here, for example, are the twelve steps in performance management featured in Roger Moores' *Managing for High Performance* (1994 :10):[5]

1. Develop the mission statement.
2. Establish corporate objectives.
3. Formulate strategies and lower level goals.
4. Establish key measures for the goal, and start setting individual targets.

5. Set up the practice of reviewing performance against the key measures.
6. Set up team performance reviews.
7. At the same time, discover and develop competencies.
8. Cross-reference these competencies with key measures.
9. Check that regular one-to-one and team meetings are taking place.
10. Establish a management development program.
11. Throughout the process, carry out the necessary training and coaching.
12. If appropriate, design the reward scheme.

Moores' book consists of recommendations, all of them delivered in a straightforward and authoritative manner. Some of them are quite standard, for example, "[the mission statement] must be truthful and credible" (ibid., 19). Others are somewhat more original: "managers do *not* have to wait until their targets have been set before setting them for others lower down" (ibid., 29, emphasis original). The purpose of the literature of which Moores' book is a part is to provide a direct guide for action. Balancing commonsense statements with alert inspired-by-practice advice is probably one of the mainsprings of the commercial success of such publications. No issue is left open and the author has an answer to every point that is raised. The nonacademic character of the book and others like it is obvious, *made* obvious. Discussions are kept brief and references are scarce. As compared with academic textbooks, the rhetoric is deliberately more compact and simplistic.

Basically, though, popularization literature of this sort delivers a message on performance akin to that of management accounting or management control textbooks: performance is a matter of comparing results so as to monitor and control the organization's activity.

A Yardstick and an Imperative

Academic management journals display a somewhat different view of performance. In contrast to management control and management accounting textbooks, which locate performance in the well-delimited domain of control, academic management journals relate performance to virtually *any* aspects of organizational life. The list of organizational and managerial matters that academic management journals have studied in terms of performance is impressive. A small sample of these will illustrate the point: ownership; firm's location; firm quality; national, organizational, and business cultures; organizational learning; organizational change; competitive inertia; strategic sense making; strategic planning; multidivisionalization; diversification; concentration; downscoping; corporate divestment; organizational size; risk taking; entrepreneurial and conservative strategic postures; scanning, interpretation, and action; top management compensation; management turnover; labor force quality; technology; time; manufacturing practice; flexible automation; types of innovation; management control systems design; information use; budgetary information; and performance reporting systems.[6] Most of the basic organizational issues that have been studied within management and business administration are represented here.

The majority of performance studies presented in management journals follow the same rationale. Studies examine how one, two, three or as many as four management variables—any of the managerial tools or organizational features just listed—correlate with a company's performance. The study by Lubatkin and Chatterjee (1991:251), for example, "examines the stability of the *relationship* between diversification and shareholder value across contiguous time periods" (emphasis added). Datta et al. (1991:529) "review existing empirical research on the diversification-performance *relationship* along three different streams which have studied this relationship" (emphasis added). One can investigate, like Gordon and DiTomaso (1992:783), "the *relationships* of culture strength and two substantive cultural values with corporate performance" (emphasis added), or can hypothesize, like Gordon and Smith (1992:741), "that the *relationship* between firm performance and control (postauditing) of capital investments is dependent on the following firm-related variables: asymmetric information, capital intensity, level of capital expenditures, and insider ownership" (emphasis added).

Relationship is the key word used in many studies for describing their purpose. Even when the term relationship itself is absent, that idea is a central one. Bromiley (1991:37), for example, addresses the question of "how past performance and other factors *influence* risk taking and how risk taking and other factors influence future performance" (emphasis added). Hitchens and O'Farell (1988:429) compare "the specific dimensions of the performance and characteristics of a matched sample of small manufacturing firms in South Wales and Northern Ireland" to conclude that "the slower growth could not *be traced to* comparative Irish disadvantages arising from differences in cost or availability of capital equipment or designated labor force skills or premises, but to differences in the competitiveness of Northern Irish firms arising from the inferior quality of products produced" (emphasis added).

The rationale is to assess how given management variables influence an organization's overall achievements. The controlled variable—for example, the formalism of strategic planning, the sensitivity of incentive schemes to net earnings, or the company's age—is increased stepwise and one measures how variations in it affect the organization's performance taken as the dependent variable. The focus is on the controlled variable(s) at hand and if there are several on their interactions.[7]

If studies of performance as a dependent variable are to be interesting, one has to make the general assumption that performance of the parts will affect performance of the whole, and, conversely, that performance of the whole will be indicative of performance of the parts. It would otherwise make no sense to, for example, evaluate the quality of a specific planning procedure by looking at the organization's overall performance; for the quality of a planning procedure being evaluated by the organization's overall performance, one has to assume that the two in some way directly depend upon and index each other. Yet this is a highly disputable starting point for reasoning. It is textbook knowledge that wholes are not simply sums of parts. Surprisingly enough, nevertheless, this assumption is seldom questioned, is hardly expressed, and is tested even less.

As a dependent variable, performance is the yardstick along which one tests the quality of these tools. Considering the comprehensiveness of the topics dealt with under such premises, performance emerges in academic management journals as the standard along which all intellectual creations in management are evaluated. Performance stands as the gauge, the critical test of management tools and of managerial invention.

To use it as a gauge, one has to assume that an organization's performance is not something problematical, or at least that it is not so problematical that it cannot be used as a benchmark. Only few studies show a concern for possible bias introduced by the measurement procedures. The mere fact that—in review articles—one can compare the performance of an organization with that of another, assessed by use of measures that differ, indicates that measurement is assumed to be a technique lacking in effects upon that which it measures; variations in the performance one measures are assumed to be due to variations of the variables, not to variations induced by the measuring technique. For such an argumentation to hold logically, measurement has to be neutral as regards performance; performance may vary, but should only do so in relationship to the controlled variables, not as a result of the features of the characteristics of the measurement technique employed. No room is provided for the social, technical, or rhetorical features of indicators so as to let them deviate from this ideal. Indicators may be many, and may vary, yet they have to be of a neutral technical texture, which, as the following section on performance measurement will show, is a highly disputable assumption.

Academic management journals, to summarize, place the imperative of performance upon all aspects of organizational life. It is an imperative that concerns all the cogwheels of the machine. No space is to be left unattended. Performance—and, as one could maliciously ask: Performance only?—is presented as a necessity for the whole organization. One could argue about whether this is a moral imperative, a technical imperative, or an ideological imperative. Performance is characterized, in any case, as an ineluctable necessity to which all organizational preferences, decisions, and behaviors have to be bent and submitted.

Not unlike what Lyotard (1979:69) has found for contemporary scientific knowledge, management knowledge makes "performativity"—basically, the fact of being in a state of performance—its favorite legitimizing principle. All claims are evaluated on the basis of their performance, more precisely of their potential contribution to the organization's overall performance. This is true of each of the aspects of organizational life listed above. This is true as well of management research itself, as clearly shown for strategy research by Miles et al. (1993:176), who declared that "the ultimate purpose of the strategic management literature is to help firms improve their performance," to steer for performance!

Organizations are commanded to be performant in their smallest details, and management literature views as its mission to provide them with the tools this requires. Performance is both the yardstick and the imperative of management research. What is performant is good, and what is good is performant, and management research considers its role to be that of showing organizational actors how to enter the virtuous circularity of performativity.

Trait of Managerialism

The obsession with performance is not reserved for private companies alone. If the claim made by Osborne and Gaebler (1992) in the subtitle of their book *Reinventing Government* is true, "The Entrepreneurial Spirit is Transforming the Public Sector," then performance seems indeed to have made a pervasive entry into the agenda of politicians and public administrators.

As Steve Rogers (1994:1) observes, regarding developments that have taken place during the past decade in local government in the United Kingdom, there is a new focus on performance:

> The changes which have and are taking place have created considerable interest in the concept of performance, and as a consequence the vocabulary of local government management has been filled with phrases beginning with that word— performance review, performance appraisal and performance indicators being but a few examples. This is in stark contrast to the situation which existed in the past when the only time the word "performance" appeared on a committee agenda was when a council had its periodic debate on whether or not it should have a Performance Review Sub-Committee.

One can observe at the national governmental level, too, as a recent publication of the Organization for Economic Co-Operation and Development's (OECD) Public Management Committee states, "vigorous attempts in many OECD Member countries to shift from an administrative or compliance culture to a *managerial or performance culture* in the public sector" (OCDE/OECD 1994:15, emphasis added).

If one takes public management performance literature at face value, then performance today represents as strong an imperative for public organizations as it does for privately owned companies. As the author of a French textbook on management control for municipal public services writes, "in all systems of production, including the production of municipal public services, performance is for the organization an ontological imperative that pertains to its essence" (Rey 1991:18, my translation). Performance is presented by managerial authors as a universal imperative applicable to all organizational forms, independent of their belonging to the private or to the public sector.

There are strong indications in the literature that the fortune of the notion of performance in the public sector is a recent phenomenon, more recent, for example, than the public sector's interest in evaluation, and that this fortune has gone hand in hand with the fortune of managerialism. As Politt defines it "managerialism is a set of beliefs and practices, at the core of which burns the seldom-tested assumption that better management will prove an effective solvent for a wide range of economic and social ills" (1993:1).

Managerialism is a set of ideas that postulate that for social progress there is a crucial centrality of economically defined productivity, of related managerial knowledge and technologies, of an adequately disciplined labor force, and of the right and ability of public administrators to manage. It is an affirmation of not only the importance but also the value of management, seen as a value in itself, and a glorification of (private) managers, elevated to the rank of heroes (ibid.). It is also a reformulating of public life into an economic language of outputs, efficiency, effectiveness, value for money, and, not the least, performance.

The ideology of managerialism, Politt continues, has invaded the public sector during the past decade or two, where it has been propagating specific models of organizational functioning. These are models that rest upon only a limited set of ideas (for discussion of them see, e.g., Guthrie 1993; Isaac-Henry 1993). First, there is the idea that public services should adopt a "business-like" approach to management, as based on practices in the private sector, instead of professional ethos and values as traditionally conceived. This involves, among other things, a move away from consensus and bargaining modes of decision making. Second, there is the idea that management be made more accountable. This involves large organizations being broken down into smaller, more manageable units. Third, there is the idea, quite apart from that of privatization, that market forces, market mechanisms, market vocabulary, and market habits should, to an increasing degree, be introduced into the public sector. This presupposes the view, as Loveday (1993:145) noted, that democracy based upon consumer power is a more reliable agent of popular will than the ballot box. Fourth and last, there is the idea that greater emphasis should be placed on performance management, for example through reducing waste and improving efficiency, effectiveness and quality, so that new practices—eloquently qualified as "good" (Isaac-Henry 1993:11)—replace those inspired by traditional administrative cultures.

Managerialism, like other -isms, presents itself as a vector of change. Margaret Thatcher came to power in 1979 with a firm commitment to reform the British public sector from what she deemed was mismanagement, inefficiency, collectivism, and unacceptable oversizing (see Johnson 1993; Metcalfe and Richards, 1990). These are themes used again by the Democratic U.S. vice president Al Gore in his report to the National Performance Review Commission for the newly elected president Bill Clinton entitled *From Red Tape to Results—Creating a Government that Works Better and Costs Less* (1993), expressing in particular the theme of the necessity of reducing the size of the public sector (cost, staff, and percentage of the gross national product).

Ideas belonging to a classical and noncritical view of management, much indebted to a rational analysis of collective behavior, constitute the engine of change here. Politt (1993:4) notes, for example, the similarity of that which inspired the traditional POSDCORB (Planning, Organizing, Staffing, Directing, Co-ordinating, Reporting, Budgeting), on the one hand, and the recommendations issued in Margaret Thatcher's Financial Management Initiative (FMI), one of the milestone documents of the British public sector reform, on the other.

Performance occupies a central position among these various ideas that are supposed to lead to change. Alongside statements of mission, strategic planning, management by objectives, program budgeting, zero-base budgeting, evaluation procedures, staff motivation programs, decentralization programs, formalized lines of responsibility, quality programs, and the like, performance is one of the notions that have become particularly "hot" in the present heyday of the so-called efficiency paradigm. Indeed, that performance is measurable and can be reported by means of indicators is a requirement for many of the techniques of managerialism to function, as Guthrie (1993:70) judiciously observes. Conversely, the repetitive call for (more) performance evaluation, performance audits, performance appraisals, performance-related pay, performance management, and, of course, (better) performance measures that one hears in public organizations are clear expressions of managerialism.

Discussions of the performance of public organizations rely on implicit conceptions of such organizations. In public management literature on performance, a public organization is often conceived as being a production process by which a set of inputs is transformed into a set of outputs, which, in turn, result in a set of outcomes for the community. This conception of organizations has generated the so-called 3 E's model—economy, efficiency, effectiveness. Several versions of the model co-exist. The British Audit Commission (1989:3), for example, speaks of four levels: cost, resources, outputs, and outcomes. The U.S. Government Accounting Standard Board (Hatry et al. 1990), for its part, prefers a four-step model involving input, output, outcomes, and efficiency.[8] Some authors add to the 3 E's a fourth, that of equity, to account for the public service aspect of many public organization activities. Still others add excellence and enterprise so as to emphasize the need for public organizations' committing themselves to the philosophy of managerialism (see Rouse [1993:61] for references).

Recurrent references are made, as well, in these discussions of performance to accountability. For public organizations, accountability is a matter of the legal and moral imperative to inform the public of their activities. Boyne and Law (1991:179) describe the relation of performance to accountability in the following terms:

> As democratic institutions, it is essential that local authorities are accountable to local citizens for their performance. If service consumers or taxpayers are unhappy with their council's performance then, in principle, it is possible to seek improvement through the ballot box. Between elections, the public can press their claims in person, through pressure groups or through direct participation in the delivery of services. However, effective accountability in practice is impossible without accurate information on local authority performance.... The public cannot make valid judgment on council policies unless information is provided on the quantity, quality and cost of local services.

The British government, for instance, has enacted a variety of legislative measures to make local authorities more accountable, for example, requiring local authorities to publish annual reports, requiring them to publish specific information in the fields of housing and school provisions, requiring them to appoint a finance officer and a monitoring officer with statutory duties regarding the local authority's conduct, or changing the basis of local taxation from a property tax to a poll tax in order to create a more direct relationship between a local authority's financial performance and the financial burden placed on local taxpayers (Rogers 1994:2–3).

As information regarding past and present achievements, performance represents a critical element of accountability, the major issues being that of *which* information this involves for *whom*. *Which* information organizations are to provide about their performance depends entirely upon what organizational model one adopts, for example, whether the model is one that takes equity into account or not. The focus on performance can lead to an overemphasis on economic or easily quantifiable aspects of an activity and to accountability becoming biased in favor of these. Likewise, the interests of some groups may be given higher priority in performance assessments than the interests of others, or certain aspects of an organization's activities may be made more visible than others. One should bear in mind that the question of which information is to become the performance of an organization is a crucial and vital matter to the persons involved. To *whom* public organizations are accountable is likewise a matter of concern for organizational actors. Traditional views on accountability favor citizens and voters. In the current ideological climate, as Rouse (1993:74) observes, strong pressures have appeared in favor of defining accountability in terms of a narrow customer focus, detrimental to elected persons, professionals, interest groups, and citizens generally. Performance is indeed a matter with extensive implications for organizational politics.

Performance also has extensive implications for politics at large. Performance is described as a condition for democratic machinery's well functioning. It is also presented as a ground for political dispute as to how to define public organizations' activities, and to whom public organizations are accountable. Managerial surpluses, in this regard, stand in virtual opposition to democratic deficits—to reuse expressions employed by Painter et al. (1993:177)—and the assessment of performance becomes a locus where major political issues become concretized. This is what Ranson and Stewart (1994:222) express in emphasizing the need that performance reviews develop from the relative simplicities of performance measurement toward processes that enable political judgments to be made on what should count as good performance. Performance can in this view hardly be treated as a mere technical matter.

To sum up, there is thus much overlap between public and private performance literature. Like its private counterpart, public management literature depicts performance indifferently as a piece of accounting information, or as a manner of expressing results, closely allied with efficiency and effectiveness. It is associated with feedback about the past and preparation for the future, and is thus related to the manifestation of a will to have control. It is portrayed as something measured with comparison or competition in mind, with the modes of measurement varying in relation to context and intent. The performance notion is also presented as an imperative for the whole of an organization, in accordance with quite traditional mechanistic and systemic metaphors. The assumptions about the desirability, possibility, and potential for action that are present here refer to the accounting origin of the notion. The conceptual framework is the same: it is approximately the same notion that each domain of performance literature sets into motion. This may be largely due to the fact that performance, when it entered the public sector, rode on the wave of managerialism that itself is an explicit attempt to graft the private management concept onto public organizations.

One can observe significant differences, however, between how performance is used in the two sectors. First, private sector performance when presented in public sector literature tends to be (re-)read in the light of managerialism. This involves private sector performance being focused upon and being elevated to a kind of conceptual dignity for public performance literature to even refer to it, a dignity that goes far beyond what the case is in private sector literature. Second, in the public sector the notion of performance is cast in a time-specific and place-specific framework of political intent. It contributes to a specific conception of administration—an administrative fashion, one could say—to managerialism as we know it. Thirdly, and this is a corollary of the previous two points, in the public sector performance is given an explicit proselytizing dimension that it otherwise lacks. As Borges (1981) has pointed out, there is at least the fact of copying between the imitation and the original.

Other differences between the sectors in how the notion of performance is understood and in how performance relates to accountability are introduced. Whereas accountability only sporadically comes into view in private sector literature, most often reformulated as a demand that emanates from shareholders and mostly being implicit, public performance literature emphasizes repeatedly the role performance is to play in a renewed form of accountability within public organizations. In public management literature, performance is presented as a contribution to debates that may occur between various constituencies concerning the functioning of the organization (Kanter and Summer 1987). It is presented as an expression of the democratic principles that regulate the functioning of the public sector.

Still more differences may need to be taken into account in the future. As the interest in an appropriate theory of public management increases, one can imagine greater attention being directed in performance research at what Moe (1990:122) calls the political uncertainty and the political compromise of public organizations. Political uncertainty is of fundamental importance in distinguishing politics and economics. Whereas most political struggle concerns who will have the right, formal and informal, to make decisions for society, the task of designing political organizations is not simply the technical problem of finding efficient governance structures that link current power holders to their creations. The more fundamental task for political actors is to find and institute a governance structure that can protect public organizations from control by opponents. This leads to political compromise, to emphasizing that, whereas in an economic system an organization is generally designed by participants who want it to succeed, in the public sector organizations are designed in no small measures by participants who explicitly want them to fail (ibid., 125). Approaches to public sector performance in the future will need to take account of public sector organizations necessarily being involved in the controversial process of politics.

One can also suspect the need in the future to pay greater attention to what Hargrove and Glidewell (1990) have called the dimension of impossibility in public jobs. Think of justice, correction, rehabilitation, social work, education, culture, or health. For many public jobs, it seems impossible to achieve any of the manifest (and often generous) objectives of the mission ascribed to them. Add to this a context of uncertain tractability of clients, militant public conflicts, and strong economic constraints, and performing the job becomes a matter of coping with difficulties of balancing relative failures against relative success. Add also a monopolistic position, together with outputs that are particularly difficult to measure, a set of regulations that determines in detail the nature and level of activity as well as the geographical area or the clients it serves, and the legal interdiction of public service activities being discontinued or even downsized, and one ends up very far indeed from textbook versions of performance measurements. Dealing with impossible jobs may require, for example, that one separate more clearly the notions of achievement and success. One may also need to adjust the period of performance assessment to take account of historical advantages and drawbacks, or possibly of anticipations. Unless this is done, "impossible jobs" may well be deemed insufficient as performances and be condemned, whatever efforts one makes, simply because of their inadequacy, by their very nature, of measuring up to the dominant rhetoric of performance.

The performance of public organizations, as constructed in public management literature, may therefore very well undergo perceptible changes soon. One can suspect that these changes will emphasize the nonneutrality of performance appraisal technology, and that they will recognize performance being a construct. One can also suspect that such changes will be more sensitive than managerialism to the specificities of public organizations, in particular as regards their enacting democratic debate. If such is the case, I believe that these changes may well be indicative of the emergence of a new public accounting.

Object and Product of Measurements

Accounting textbooks, academic management papers, and public management literature involve the notion of performance in such notions as those of accountability, control, indicators, managerialism, measurement, results, as well as of achievement, communication, constituencies, economy, effectiveness, efficiency, information, organization theory, outputs, standards, strategy, success, and yardstick (and surely others, too). Cross-referencing, borrowing, and lending between these notions link them together and associate them with performance. Management accounting, for example, passes on to performance an explicit commitment to cybernetics and to accounting; in so doing it also passes on to it the assumptions such commitments entail. Performance, likewise, borrows from and lends legitimacy to managerialism. It is through such referencing, borrowing, and lending that accounts of performance can be meaningful and acquire a referential background.

Just as words acquire their meanings from the relationships they entertain with other words, it is through the relationships that performance has with other notions found in management literature that performance becomes a management notion. Performance is imbedded in the conceptual scheme of management. It is this scheme that determines what is made prominent or kept invisible, or what is uttered or what remains silent. Performance can hardly be studied in isolation from the notions that constitute its conceptual environment. (Not to forget here is the central role that specific institutions, such as the U.S. National Performance Review or the British Audit Commission, can play since these are constituted by, around, and for performance.)

One particular notion, intentionally left unattended to thus far, plays a cardinal role in this scheme: that of measurement. Together with the determinants and the behavioral implications of performance, performance measurement is one of the recurrent concerns of management texts on performance. Measurement, as a notion, pervades any text on performance. It is indeed the very condition allowing performance to exist.

This section focuses on the issue of performance measures. It first presents an inventory of them. It then discusses the impossibility of separating them from what they are intended to measure. Third, it depicts the arbitrariness in the choice of measures. It ends up then by concluding that performance is the collective creation of authors within the performance area.

Measures of Performance—An Inventory

Financial measures are those measures most frequently used in corporations to measure organizational performance. Financial measures are usually divided in two sorts: accounting-based and market-based ones. Accounting-based measures include, for example, sales, revenue, operative income, residual income, profit, cash flow, sales growth, growth in net assets, return on sales, return on investment, return on assets, return on equity, and earning per share. Market-based ones include percentage change in stock price (adjusted for splits and new issues), market-to-book value, stock market returns, and various other statistical ways of measuring the firm's performance on the stock market, sometimes balancing risk against return (as in Lubatkin, Merchant, and Srinivasan, 1993). Haveman (1992), for example, uses a regression model estimated on the basis of pooled cross-sectional and time-series data as follows:

$$Y_{t1} = \alpha Y_{t0} + \beta X_{t0} + \gamma \Delta X_{t0\text{-}t1} + \varepsilon$$

where Y_{t1} is the value of a firm's financial performance at the end of a period, Y_{t0} the value of this variable at the start of the period, X_{t0} is a vector of time-varying control variables measured at the start of the period (organizational characteristics, level of investment in eight different markets, and environmental forces) and $\Delta X_{t0\text{-}t1}$ is a vector of change between t0 and t1 in thrift investments in the eight markets.

In a sort of debate, supporters of each type of measure oppose each other (for a concise account of the arguments advanced in this debate, see McGuire et al. 1986). The debate largely centers around the praises of and criticisms directed at accounting and stock market information. Criticisms directed at accounting information are, among other things, that it is manipulable, that it uses irrelevant and outdated (historical) costs, and that it applies arbitrary principles of allocation of receipts, and arbitrary methods of valuation or depreciation. Criticisms directed at the stock exchange origin and the way of viewing market-based measures are, for example, that these give too much weight to the perspective of stockholders and that they unquestioningly assume the infallibility of the stock market.

That accounting-based and market-based measures are seen by some authors as being opposed to each other, does not hinder many other authors, however, from using a combination of both types of measures. Nayyar (1992, 1993), for example, measures performance by return on equity adjusted for industry and systematic risk, industry-adjusted market-to-book value of equity, and Jensen's alpha (i.e., a measure of operating performance based on a market model that compares the performance of a firm or a managed portfolio of stocks to that of firms in an unmanaged portfolio with similar market risk). Ketchen et al. (1993) select a measure in each of the categories that previous studies in the field have used to measure performance: net patient revenue (sales), return on equity (equity and investment), return on assets (assets), profit per discharge (margin and profit), and occupancy (overall performance). Thus, regardless of the uncertainties concerning the convergence of these two types of measures—Fryxell and Barton (1990:565) note that "at certain times and in certain contexts accounting-based and market-based indicators may converge on the same construct, but at other times they measure quite different performance constructs"—many authors regard the antagonism between accounting-based and market-based measures as not being so critical as to prevent their combining the two types.

Financial measures, moreover, are not the only measures of performance. Performance literature makes a strong case for using nonfinancial measures as well. Financial measures, Venkatraman and Ramanujam (1986:803) claim, correspond to a narrower conception of business performance, to a model that has been the dominant one in empirical strategy research and which assumes the dominance and legitimacy of financial goals. The authors suggest that, whereas financial performance constitutes a sort of inner circle of corporate performance, a broader and more adequate conceptualization would include an emphasis on operational (i.e., nonfinancial) performance. They consider it to be logical enough, along with financial measures, to deal with such measures as market share, new product introduction, product quality, marketing effectiveness, manufacturing value-added, and other measures of technological efficiency. This is a view that can even be broadened, the authors suggest, to a third circle, one in which the multiple and conflicting nature of organizational goals and the influence of multiple constituencies or stakeholders are superposed.

This third circle is what corporate social performance is about. Researchers there have developed a theory of corporate performance that encompasses the responsiveness of organizations toward *all* stakeholders, beyond those directly linked to the company; their theory also includes consideration of ethical, cultural, social, and environmental issues for attaining what they label a global assessment of corporate performance (Wood 1991; Clarkson 1995). This leads Graves and Waddock (1994:1038), for example, to assess a company's corporate social performances on the basis of: (*a*) relations the company maintains with the community, its employees, and the environment; (*b*) its products; (*c*) its treatment of women and minorities; and (*d*) its concluding of military contracts and its relations to nuclear power as well as to South Africa— a range of criteria with manifest political undertones.

Nonfinancial measures of corporate performance had their origins in the shortcomings of financial measures. Criticisms of the latter are numerous and resemble criticisms used in the debate opposing accounting-based and market-based measures. The criticisms also vary noticeably in strength from author to author. Venkatraman and Ramanujam (1986) are quite moderate in claiming that financial indicators are insufficient: they still state that they are unavoidable! Lothian (1987:3) is much more radical. For him, financial indicators are an irrevocably incomplete and ill-designed set of management tools that are strictly unidimensional in the view they permit of corporate activity. He emphasizes financial indicators being the result of the capital market's obsession with bottom line profit as being almost the sole indicator of corporate performance. Similarly, he emphasizes their being inherited from outdated conditions of mass production. This is indeed the same message that Johnson and Kaplan (1987) deliver when they stress that financial measures of corporate performance are not only exaggerated and unmotivated in today's economic environment, but also are a direct threat to an organization's survival. Hard criticisms are sometimes directed at financial performance measures.

There may be important differences, though, between how theoreticians and researchers, on the one hand, and practitioners, on the other, look at nonfinancial measures. Nonfinancial indicators have received strong support recently from influential researchers: for example,

Drucker's (1989) advice to business organizations to follow nonprofits in their comprehensive approach to the performance of their mission, and Kaplan and Norton's article on the balanced scorecard (1992). Notwithstanding, financial measures still dominate much of management literature. According to Eccle (1991:131), however, many companies have already undergone a revolutionary shift from treating financial measures as being the foundation for performance measurement to treating them as one among a broader set of measures, and placing all of them on an equal footing. Some of the signs of this revolution, according to Eccle, are the quality movement (with performance measures such as defect rates, response time, and delivery commitment), embryonic efforts to generate measures of customer satisfaction (e.g., customer retention rates, perceived value of goods and services), and competitive benchmarking. There are signs suggesting there to be a major discrepancy between how in theory and how in practice performance measurements take place. This, in turn, may portend dramatic changes soon in the literature on corporate performance measurement. Developing new performance measures and performance indicators is most likely to remain a major business of the performance industry.[9]

A similar interest in performance measurement runs through public management literature. Hundreds of performance indicators or more have been developed for each sector of activity and each type of public organization. These pertain to costs, inputs, outputs, and outcomes or, to use a different terminology, to economy, efficiency, and effectiveness. Efforts have been made, moreover, to account for equity, excellence, and also enterprise. The U.S. Government Accounting Standard Board, for example, has launched a broad project aimed at covering most of the federal activities (see Hatry et al. [1990] for an early overview and an extensive list of measures). Britain has likewise, after fifteen years of effort, managed to fill the entire public sector, including the National Health Service, with cascades of performance indicators. (Chapter 5 will provide a detailed discussion of performance indicators for public libraries).

Developing performance indicators and producing performance reports have indeed sometimes been made a legal imperative. The American Government Performance and Result Act, for example, requires that at least ten federal agencies develop measures of progress (Gore 1993). Likewise, it is now mandatory for British local governments to report their accomplishments regularly.

The rationale is to develop means of assessing whether programs and organizations are meeting their objectives (e.g., Gore 1993). It is also, as the Audit Commission indicates, to find surrogates for the discipline of the market (Boyne and Law 1991:183). The benefits of comparisons are frequently evoked, in this regard, just as are the possibilities that performance indicators provide in the matter of comparisons. A major motive is to look for measures that can act as surrogates for the private sector's profitability measures (Painter et al. 1993:175). The lack of profit is gravely resented in managerialist inspired public sector literature and public sector management. Performance indicators are presented as a remedy for this major impediment.

As Guthrie (1993:70) observes, however, the literature on public performance measurement has seriously underestimated some of the theoretical limitations, problems, and tensions that are associated with the mode of performance measurements it promotes. Guthrie points out that, whereas the model of performance measurement usually assumes that one can set clear objectives to which later performance comparisons can be compared, public sector organizations lack clear objectives, making the identification of outputs and the defining of the public interest problematical. He emphasizes, likewise, the difficulties encountered in equating monetary and nonmonetary costs and benefits, the variations in valuation and measurement within monetary units, the role played by subjective, normative, and value-laden assumptions—pertaining, for example, to the choice of discount rates, methods to allow for risk and uncertainty, and criteria for ranking—and recalls that the financial or economic form of many measurements tends to make other aspects of public services less visible, such as how public managers make users aware of the services available, the supply of services relative to demand, as well as predictability. (See Guthrie [1993] for references.) He concludes that the practice of performance measurement is quite far removed from textbook and official depiction of how performance indicators supposedly function; to judge from his arguments, it is not likely to get much closer.

For both sectors taken together, the private and the public, the accumulation of performance measures in performance literature clearly establishes performance as being something multidimensional requiring different indicators for its measurement. Dvir et al. (1993:157), for example, conceive performance of strategic business units in the electronics and computer industry in terms of four dimensions that combine financial, commercial, and technical aspects: (*a*) profitability level—how well the business unit meets its financial objectives and how well it is doing relative to similar business units; (*b*) generating orders—how well the business unit is doing in achieving sales objectives and creating future orders, what the current backlog is, and how orders will influence future cash requirements; (*c*) generating new opportunities—how successful the unit is in opening opportunities for new products and new markets, and whether the customers are satisfied with the quality of products and service and whether they will come back for further purchases; and (*d*) preparing the infrastructure for the future—whether the business unit possesses scientific and technological knowledge, and the equipment and facilities required for the development and production of future products.

The multitude of indicators, then, is a way of dealing with and voicing this multidimensionality. The multiplicity of indicators can be seen as a sign of disagreement as to what constitutes the notion of performance. It can be taken, as well, as a sign of agreement that performance is not reducible to a single dimension, and thus that it is a multidimensional construct. This multidimensionality of performance is acknowledged by U.K. accounting standards, which state that "it is not possible to distil the performance of a complex organisation into a single measure" (Financial Reporting Standards #3, paragraph 52). This multidimensionality is likewise expressed in the flora of adjectives one can find attached to performance: economic, financial, social, commercial, operational, and environmental (and probably soon ethical, aesthetic, and virtual). The multiplicity of indicators and the grammatical declension of the term both mirror and support each other. The multiplicity of indicators and adjectives also supports the idea discussed above, in connection with the presentation of the typology of Ford and Schellenberg (1982), that the performance of an organization is its ability to succeed whatever one may consider to be important. This provides for endless variations in how one can tell performance.

That performance is understood as being multidimensional does not prevent it, however, from usually being considered as a whole. Debates concerning performance measures do not really pit one measure against another. Rather, they align measures with one another, preparing them for any sort of combination that may be called for (which is just what senior executives do, at least according to Kaplan and Norton 1992). I would emphasize that when use of a measure is questioned, this is usually done with the claim that it does not measure performance well, seldom that it measures something other than performance. Somewhat paradoxically, although each measure is considered as unique, each is presented as pertaining to the same object, namely, the organization's performance. Along with consensus concerning the plurality of the notion, there is almost total agreement within management literature on performance that all measures concern the same unique and general feature of the organization. Performance is conceived as simultaneously being both multiple and unique.

The use of statistical methods able to handle multiple indicators of performance can aptly illustrate this simultaneous consideration by the measurement literature of organizational performance as being both a multidimensional and a comprehensive construct.[10] What multivariate methods allow is that one combine results attained by an organization along distinct dimensions. They enable global judgments to emerge in situations that, for analytical purposes, have been decomposed along independent dimensions. The strength of multivariate statistical methods is to simultaneously emphasize the multidimensionality and the unity of what is considered as an organization's performance.

Inseparability of the Measure and Its Object

An interesting though less emphasized aspect of discussions about the merits and drawbacks of the different ways of measuring performance that are available is that these discussions illustrate the impossibility of separating what is measured, namely, the organization's performance, from the measurement procedure employed, and the measures at hand.

Take, for example, Lubatkin and Shrieves' (1986) article in defense of market-based measures for assessing the performance of mergers and acquisitions. Their reasoning starts with the disagreement they observe between conclusions that have been reached in the fields of strategic management and of finance concerning the performance of mergers. Each field tends to measure performance in its own way. Whereas strategic management research tends to prefer traditional accounting measures—for example, such accounting-based indexes as those of return on assets and of sales growth—financial economics prefers market-based measures—for example, a measure developed from capital market theory assessing for general stock the "abnormal" effect of an event upon observed stock returns (appreciation plus dividends) given the general market effect. The point Lubatkin and Shrieves (1986:509) make is that "market-based performance measures can provide researchers of strategic management with a powerful test of corporate performance, though not the only test." Their conclusion is that if sufficient precautions are taken—Lubatkin and Shrieves (1986:509) underscore "the necessity for researchers to question the assumptions underlying the techniques of another discipline before borrowing them"—market-based measures can be used in strategic management.

A point Lubatkin and Shrieves allude to, though without developing it, is that the performance of a firm in connection with an event such as a merger is largely dependent upon which measurement technique is used to assess it. The authors discuss the drawbacks of different measures, for example, that each accounting-based measure captures only one dimension of performance, and that the importance of a measure may differ across strategic contexts; they also discuss the advantages of each type of measure. Stock prices, for example, are said not to be limited to a specific performance asset such as sales growth or profits, but rather to reflect all the relevant information aspects of performance, and to be reported objectively (ibid., 498–99). In this way, the authors indicate how the assumptions, modalities, and objectives of measurement influence any specific measure of an organization's performance. However, they fail to see the full implications of their observation.

Another conclusion I think one can draw from their article is that much of the results that measurement provides is contained in the features of the measurement procedure itself. Performance, in this regard, is *inside* of measurement, contained in the rules that govern it, rather than being *outside* of it. *Outside* would suggest here that performance and its measurements are separated from each other. The image then would be one of measuring a physical object: one approaches the table, or anything else, with a rule or a measuring tape to assess its length as an object, and one assumes that any rule or tape will provide adequate results for any object, provided the rule or the tape is accurate. Saying, in contrast, that performance is *inside* of measurement is to acknowledge that one cannot separate what is measured from what is measuring. This emphasizes measurement being the product of a measuring tool meeting a measured object, this meeting occurring under specific circumstances, and the result reflecting just as much the idiosyncrasies of the measuring device as the qualities of what is measured. It thus emphasizes performance being distinct from the organization's activity itself in that it tells of this activity, more precisely that the telling is dependent upon the measurement procedure selected and retained.

Most performance studies keep performance on the outside of measurement. McGuire et al. (1986), however, are among those who place it on the inside. Instead of following traditional logic that considers performance as a dependent variable, their study reverses the logic of argumentation and lets measurement of performance be the controlled variable so as to examine how different ways of measuring performance lead to different conclusions regarding a given managerial phenomenon. Their purpose is to assess the extent to which different measurement procedures induce different judgments regarding management tools and practices. As they put it: "A critical question…is whether firm performance would be appraised differently depending on the particular measure used" (McGuire et al. 1986:139).

Their answers to that question are not clear-cut, even if their answers *do* show that there are cases—particularly when one makes cross-industry comparisons—where "results may be an artifact of the accounting data used" (ibid., 150), which represent an important breach in the idea that performance is an objective feature of the organization's activity. McGuire et al.'s (1986) study suggests that performance may be a side-product of the measurement procedure.

Miller and Cardinal (1994:1662) suggest, in the same vein, in efforts to explain inconsistencies that can be observed between results of the last twenty years of empirical studies on strategic planning and firm performance, that one can attribute these very inconsistencies to methodological factors, in particular to measurement issues. Similarly, as Bell and Morey (1994) show, the identification of benchmarking partners is directly influenced by the choice of performance computing methods. Management literature on performance is, in this regard, far from unanimous in accepting the nonneutral character of measurement. Even if most studies consider measurement as neutral, a few have signaled that measurement is not simply a technique involving the attaching of a figure to a phenomenon and calling it a result. Performance has definitely been regarded by some as varying with *how* it is measured.

To me, the studies just referred to clearly indicate that what is said about a firm's performance cannot be separated from the procedure adopted for measuring performance. The measure and that which is measured have to be viewed together and close attention must be given to the features of the measurement technique used when one assesses what a study says of an organization's performance, so that one can ascertain how these features surface in what is measured. A reader cannot assess a measurement's result independently of the measurement technique used to produce it.

This inseparability of *what* is measured and *how* it is measured, in turn, raises the issue of the locus from which performance assessment can be made. Lubatkin and Shrieves (1986) have adopted the point of view of an external, noninvolved third party, a view that acknowledges the value of many sorts of measures. It would be sufficient, however, to repeat the reasoning above regarding the consequences of adopting a given point of view for the result an inquiry produces, to demonstrate the fragile arbitrariness of any particular point of view. It is not only the features of the measurement technique itself that readers should take into consideration, but also the features of the point of view the study adopts, their own point of view as readers, and so on, in an endless regression.

Discretion of Performance Measures

Performance literature does not usually enable one, however, to assess the assumptions, modalities, objectives, and point of view of performance measures. Most work here is extremely brief and abrupt in introducing measures. Authors often do not bother much with justifying the measures they make use of. The rhetoric employed is that of peremptory (though weak) assertions. Here are a few of many examples that can illustrate this point:

1. Gordon and Smith (1992:749) define performance as a long-term excess return to shareholders, as expressed by the formula:

$$P_i = R_i - [R_{f+} b_i (R_m - R_f)]$$

where P_i stands for performance of the firm i, R_i for return for the firm i, R_m for return of the market, R_f for risk-free rate of return, and b_i for the Beta of firm i. This is an interesting, indeed seducing, way of measuring performance. The motives for their choice, however, are not explicit in the text.

2. Lamont et al. (1994:158) do justify their choice: "industry-adjusted return on assets (ROA) was used as the performance indicator...because

it is robust to changes in firm size and allows comparisons with previous works" (providing at this point three references by other authors in support of their statement). One can easily agree with their claim regarding the robustness of return on assets, but one can nonetheless consider that since a similar claim could be attached to at least a dozen different indicators, it is hardly a sufficiently robust justification of their choice of return on assets.

3. Thomas et al. (1993:250) use three measures of performance: (1) occupancy, (2) profit per discharge, and (3) admissions. To motivate their choice, they indicate that some earlier reference had said that

> measures of performance outcomes for hospitals should reflect both efficiency indicators, such as productivity, and effectiveness, such as financial viability [here they mention a reference different from the earlier one].... efficiency measures, the authors pursue, such as the occupancy and admissions measures we used in this study, are important because competition for patients has been intensifying among hospitals [still another reference here]. Financial viability, measured here as profit, is crucial to survival in the dynamic health care environment [yet another reference here].

One can agree with the need to account for both efficiency and effectiveness. One can also agree that hospitals—some of them anyway— face intensified competition. It nevertheless seems quite a shortcut to claim that admission and occupancy (are not these two, by the way, related? Spontaneously, I would think they are) are measures of both efficiency and effectiveness. To be more precise, it appears to be a shortcut that assumes a situation of perfect competition. Such a point is highly questionable, especially for hospitals, but the authors do not raise the question.

4. To measure performance, Eilon (1992:337) prefers ratios, especially return on the capital employed (net profit per capital employed), profit margin (net profit per revenue) and asset turnover (revenue per capital employed), the first of these being obtained as the product of the latter two. Eilon acknowledges that the absolute values of many variables, such as profit, volume, revenue, costs, as well as many other key figures are obviously important; yet he claims that they are not enough, even when employed for comparisons of the performance of a given company at different time periods, or of different companies for the same period. He prefers ratios in that they express relationships between two variables, for example, between an output and an input, or between vari-

ous outputs (the product mix), or various inputs (the resource mix). His arguments are not totally convincing, however. Firstly, repeating his own reasoning, one could say that absolute values, which most often are a sum or a difference of two or more absolute values, express just as well as ratios do the relationship between two variables. Secondly, to understand how a ratio evolves, one has to understand how each of the absolute values that constitute this ratio has evolved, which means that attending to ratios in any case involves attending to absolute values. What at first seemed to be an adequate justification of one type of measure as being better than another soon becomes a matter of taste and a preference for multiplication or division before addition or subtraction, which has little to do with objective advantage or genuine superiority.

These are examples of the frail state of justifications, the pseudo-grounds that are given, and the weak claims by which management authors present those performance indicators they have selected for computing performance.

Authors can invoke a necessity, of course, "dictated" by either the nature of the issue, the characteristics of the organization(s) concerned, or the availability of data. Kalleberg and Leicht (1991:145), for instance, write: "Our measure of success [read 'performance'] was based on a company's gross earnings, *the only quantitative indicator of success available in the data set*" (emphasis added).[11]

The most frequent mode of justification is to refer to earlier works—as can be seen by two of the examples above, Thomas et al. (1993) and Lamont et al. (1994)—a common thing in academic works. References suggest that the measure in question has stood the test of time, they place the work within a tradition, and they suggest, accordingly, the idea of an accumulation of knowledge. Still, a reference only displaces the issue from one of choosing between measures to one of choosing between traditions. Far from being a technical argumentation going outside the discourse of performance, it is a self-referring justification, caught within that discourse, where the past justifies the present and the present enhances, for the occasion involved, the status of the past. The practice of referring to earlier works, thus, hardly diminishes the discretionary character of the choice of indicators.

Choices of indicators float in a kind of opaque arbitrariness. Silent as authors are regarding their motives, one can only surmise what underlies their choices. Authors provide remarkably little account of the theoretical, political, social, and rhetorical aspects of their choices, however important and significant these may be for what they claim is an organization's performance. The only aspects they genuinely account for are those pertaining to technical aspects of measurement (e.g., gathering of data, or computing method), which, in my eyes, clearly indicates a strong tendency to address measurement primarily as a technical issue. In their accounts, most authors simply ignore modes of measuring that differ from their own. At best, they contextualize their choice(s) within what they give as the purpose of their paper. There is an impressive distance, in this regard, between, on the one hand, the care they usually give to the theoretical positioning of the issue, detailing the research process, and specifying of the nature of the results, and, on the other hand, the abrupt incertitude they create concerning the choice of a measure.[12]

A gaping hole in the scientific surface of management studies is opened by the way in which management authors motivate their choice of performance measures. What happens is that each author produces, through the measurement procedure employed, one's own definition of performance: a new definition for each measure. This definition emerges from the language practice each author initiates when indicating how performance is to be measured. To paraphrase Latour (1986:273), it is *in practice*, and *through their practice*, for each study they design, that authors of literature on performance measurement define what is to be understood as an organization's performance. Each study produces its own ad-hoc definition for the purpose at hand.

Conclusion: Self-Referring Measurements

Management literature on performance provides us, then, with numerous answers as to what the three division managers featured in the previous chapter can mean when they speak of performance. Performance literature prompts a massive, elaborate, and diversified vision of the notion of performance that constructs the notion both as an action and as a result. It depicts performance as a comprehensive package of descriptions (performance is this, performance is that), norms (what others do, what you should do), methodologies and technologies (analytical frameworks, statistical methods, performance indicators, measurement procedures, management information systems, expert systems), and principles of narration and of interpretation (what to say, how to say it, and how to read it). The notion of performance is infused with the positive qualities of a sophisticated technique that is indispensable to modern organizations.

I have identified various ambiguities, incongruities, and contradictions, however, in how management literature approaches performance that cast serious doubts on the logical soundness of such a vision. It is uncertain, for example, what management literature on performance means by "an organization's performance": It is indeed an incongruity in a literature otherwise so consciously committed to clarity. It is surprising too that so little note has been taken of the documented effect of measuring techniques upon phenomena that are measured whereas careful attention is usually directed at eliminating whatever noise might disturb a study.

The inseparability of the object from its measurement, in particular, points to a major contradiction within managerial discourse. Contrary to what most of management literature on performance implicitly assumes, this inseparability clearly indicates that an organization's performance can hardly be considered as a feature of the organization but that it must be viewed instead as a feature of the measurement technique selected. The inseparability of the object from its measurement is, in this respect, a strong indication that what is *decisive* for what is considered to be an organization's performance is not simply the state of the organization but just as much the characteristics of measurement. Still, only few management texts fully acknowledge that performance is a measurement construct that strictly depends upon these characteristics.

By implicitly adopting what could be labeled a naturalistic approach (in reference to natural sciences), most management literature texts have approached performance as an organizational feature that is open to measurement. Exemplifying such an approach are numerous discussions of the accuracy, reliability, or objectivity of some specific performance measures. Most performance texts thus neglect or at best underestimate the impact of their measurement techniques upon what they think themselves to be measuring. This impact, however, is completely decisive: instead of being some organizational trait waiting for measurement, performance is something that depends upon the criteria used for its measurement. Performance is caught within measurement rather than freely circulating around it, so dramatically caught that it is nothing more and nothing less than what texts on performance claim it is on the basis of the

measurements they use. Whereas most texts within performance literature approach performance as something external to managerial discourse,
then, the fissures in performance literature opened by the contradictions
in the measurement literature conceptions of performance discussed above
clearly indicate that it is, instead, the product of this discourse.

There is a perfect coincidence between what is measured as being an
organization's performance and what is said to be the organization's performance. What literature on performance measurement does, in this regard, when it produces hundreds of performance measures and combines
these in the most innovative ways, is to produce just as many different
expressions of what the performance of an organization is. Performance
statements, in this regard, are akin to performatives, as defined by Austin (1962), that is, to utterances that perform the action they describe (as
opposed to constative utterances, which are statements that describe a
state of affairs): they turn what they say is a performance into performance.[13] Performance literature, on the whole, appears to be a self-refer-
ential discourse that defines by its mere existence what it says it has as
an object of study.

To stay within management literature can, under such circumstances,
provide access to only those aspects of performance captured within the
circularity of this self-referentiality (the chapter has listed several of them:
the focusing of performance on results, the use of performance for control purposes, its being featured as an all-encompassing imperative for
the organization, or—in the public sector—its maintaining a narrow relationship with managerialism). To gain access to other aspects, I suggest
that one leave the context of management literature and look for how the
notion is embodied in other contexts.

The aim of the following two chapters is to study how the notion of
performance is enlivened in the universe of sports. That sports have been
chosen is because they give performance a position that is particularly
central and visible. Also, as a major metaphorical reference for organizations, sports today have a perceptible impact upon ways of looking at
things and people within organizations, not the least as regards performance; as used in organizations, performance stems at least in part from
sports. Delving into sports is delving into the historical and philosophical background of the notion of performance. It is thus also adopting a
position from which one can possibly acquire new insights as to the use
of the notion in the context of organizations.

Notes

1. In *Simulacre et simulations* (Paris: Galilée). "All Western faith and good faith became engaged in this wager on representation: that a sign could be exchanged for meaning and that something could guarantee this exchange—God of course." In *Simulacra and Simulation,* translated by Sheila Faria Glaser (Ann Arbor, Mich.: University Press), page 5.

2. This metaphor of success is indeed a second-level metaphor. Second-level metaphors, Alvesson (1993:118) explains, are metaphors structuring the understanding of the metaphors used to view a phenomenon. If, for example, the organization is seen as a culture, and the culture is seen as a holy cow, then organization/culture is the first-level metaphor, whereas culture/holy cow is the second level. What Ford and Schellenberg (1982) do is that they use two different first-level metaphors to speak of organizations—the organization as a tool and the organization as a resource-organizing device—but use for both of these the same second-level metaphor to define performance—the metaphor of success—saying that performance is the ability to be successful, either at being a tool or at securing resources.

3. That is, as seen "from the inside"; one will have recognized here the description given by Latour (1986:271), and later by Czarniawska-Joerges, of a performative definition, as opposed to an ostensive one:

   > Ostensive definitions assume that social processes are basically identical with physical objects, that they have a limited number of determined properties which can be discovered and described "from outside", and then demonstrated to an audience.... Performative definitions, on the other hand, are creatures of language and thus always created "on the inside", by people using the language. (Czarniawska-Joerges 1993:8)

4. Control is, for Anthony et al. (1989:6), the process by which a variable or a set of variables is directed at realizing a goal. It is basically a dynamic loop that passes through observation, evaluation, modification, and communication, such as, for example, a thermostat connected to a furnace.

5. From the book's back cover:

   > Roger Moores is a consultant with over 25 years' experience in employee relations. He is an Associate Adviser to The Industrial Society—The Industrial Society is the UK's largest independent advisory and training organisation promoting ethics and excellence at work and influencing for change and opportunity.

6. This is a nonsystematic, nonexhaustive, arbitrarily, anonymously organized, and deliberately short list referring to examples from the last four years of the *Academy of Management Journal and Review; Accounting, Organization and Society; Administrative Science Quarterly; Advances in International Accounting; Harvard Business Review; Journal of Management; Journal of Management Studies; Long Range Planning; Management Science; Omega; Organization Science; Organization Studies; Revue française de gestion; Scandinavian Journal of Management;* and *Strategic Management Journal.*

7. For additional references see reviews by Boyd 1991; Pearce et al. 1987; Miller and Cardinal 1994. For earlier references see Ventrakaman and Ramanujam 1986.

8. To be noted here is that the Government Accounting Standard Board (Hatry et al. 1990) speaks of Service Efforts and Accomplishment (SEA) rather than of performance. For a discussion of performance by the same authors see: J. S. Wholey and H. P. Hatry, "The Case for Performance Monitoring," *Public Administration Review* 52, no. 6 (September/October 1992): 604–10. For a comment upon the GASB project see P. D. Epstein, "Get Ready: The Time for Performance Measurement is Finally Coming!" *Public Administration Review* 52, no. 5 (September/October 1992): 513–19.

9. The present inventory is based upon the opposition of accounting-based and market-based measures, and of financial and nonfinancial measures. Ventrakaman and Ramanujam (1986) build a strong case for another classificatory scheme, one that combines (a) the distinction between a primary data source (i.e., data collected directly from the target organization) and a secondary data source (i.e., data collected from sources external to the target organization) with (b) the distinction between an objective mode of performance assessment, that is, based on some established system such as internal accounting, or systematic tracking by external agencies, and perceptual ones, that is, judgments made by executives. (e.g., Covin et al. 1994; Roth and Ricks 1994; Tan and Litschert 1994 provide recent examples of the use of perceptual measures.) It is to be noted that Ventrakaman and Ramanujam insist that perceptual judgments are as valid as anything else in evaluating a company's performance.

10. See, for example, Calori and Sarnin 1991; Diakoulaki et al. 1992; Fernandez-Castro and Smith 1994; Koch and Cebula 1994; Molinero and Ezzamel 1991; Schefczyk 1993.

11. These authors re-emphasize in their conclusion that their data have several obvious and important limitations and that they would have preferred to have more objective information on profits, market share, and other indicators of business success.

12. This opaqueness might well, to a certain extent, be a matter of writing. Nayyar, for example, published two studies on service firms in the *Academy of Management Journal*, one in 1992 and another in 1993 (Nayyar 1992, 1993), that use exactly the same measures, among them return on equity. The 1992 paper says that return on equity was chosen "*because* return on investment and return on assets present difficulties where investment and assets levels are almost nonexistent, as they are, for example, in consulting, insurance and banking," which is a very acceptable motive. This motivation has disappeared in the 1993 paper, however. The latter states: "The *need* for a common measure of performance appropriate to a cross-sectional sample *dictated* the choice of ROE as an accounting-based measure of firm performance." For some reason, the reasoned choice of 1992 had become an imperative need in 1993.

13. Lyotard (1979:21 n. 30), indeed, observes that performative and performance are, in this regard, not completely foreign to each other. He points out that Austin's performative is the optimal performance in that it achieves perfectly what it sets out to do. The reasoning presented here reverses the latter proposition, and suggests instead that performance statements be regarded as performatives in the sense that performance is exactly and only what performance statements say it is.

3

A Modern Story:
Performance in Professional Sports

Introduction: Dorando Pietri's Falls

The finish of the 1908 Olympics Marathon race must rank as one of the most dramatic of sports history. Dorando Pietri was first to reach the White City Stadium. He entered the stadium opposite the straight line where the Royal Box and the finishing line were, with some 250 meters left to cover. But he was literally numbed with fatigue. Upon reaching the track, he went in the wrong direction. He fell for the first time after some twenty meters. Officials helped him to rise from lying on his back. His legs no longer obeyed him: he could not stretch them when they were bent, nor bend them when they were stretched. Staggering ahead, he fell another three times in the curve. Each time, officials helped him rise to his feet. As he fell for the fifth time, less than thirty meters from the finish line, the man then second in the race, Hayes, entered the stadium. In a thundering tumult, some officials rushed to help the crawling Pietri to stand up again. He rose once again and fell across the finish line. He fainted as soon as he had passed it. After protests by the American team, Pietri was disqualified for having been helped. In consequence, John J. Hayes, seventeen years old, was proclaimed official winner of the 1908 Olympic Marathon.

Dorando Pietri immediately became a hero, though. Prompted by Sir Arthur Conan Doyle, Queen Alexandra offered him a gold cup that was an exact replica of that awarded to Hayes. Soon, Dorando Pietri went to the United States to become a professional long distance runner. A rematch was staged at Madison Square Garden on 25 November 1908. Pietri defeated Hayes by eighty meters. The conditions of the race were incredible in today's eyes: 260 laps on an indoor track, in front of a half-crazed crowd. Within a couple of months, race promoters organized several other marathon duels on the same pattern. Dorando Pietri participated, with shifting success, in more than half of them. His and his fellow champion's pugnacity created a mass attraction for the marathon. Enormous national and individual pride were invested in the races. Through their repeated appearance in these fateful contests, these runners, and more particularly Dorando Pietri, became epic heroes of modern times.

One cannot deny that Dorando Pietri was a great marathon runner. He had won the Paris and the Turin marathon in 1906. Yet one cannot deny that without his falls he would not be remembered any more today than Thomas Longboat or Henri St. Yves, two other champions of the time. Dorando Pietri's falls were very spectacular. Could the madness of self-indulged suffering have been expressed in a stronger way? Could one imagine a more intense account of his thirst for the finish line, for accomplishment, and for victory? Could any film director equal the dramatic qualities of Dorando's swaying toward the line with Hayes sprinting less than fifty meters behind him? Definitely not. The finish of the 1908 Olympics Marathon was a paramount drama.

The dramatic character of Pietri's run would not have reached us, though, had not his arrival been accurately registered on still as well as moving pictures. Pietri not only fell in front of the eyes of the spectators, among them international personalities and the royal family, but he also fell in front of camera lenses. Media hungrily captured his agony. Jack Andrew, the official who, with a boater on his head and a megaphone in his hand, received Dorando in his arm when the latter fell, tried to argue his innocence, for example, by referring to "animated photographs." (Andrew's claims were of little effect and Pietri's disqualification stood anyway.)

The camera could also reproduce at will the course of the event it had recorded for the archives. It could provide its audience with an opulent richness of details. Dorando Pietri's fragile silhouette, in white T-shirt and large dark shorts, with his hands clenching a handkerchief, was to be shown to millions of spectators and newspaper readers around the world. The dramatic character of the scene could be brought to the public under conditions of readability that were at least as good as for those who had followed it live. The recording of his falls led to the birth of the legend of Dorando Pietri's performance.

Pietri's own bearing contributed decisively to this legend. He created his own persona intensively by participating in a large number of competitions and by repeatedly exhibiting his ability to run to the extreme. He fell from exhaustion again, for example, in a duel with Thomas Longboat on 15 December 1908. (Actually, he also drew upon himself then the accusation of intentionally turning his participation in marathons into a show.)

There was another feature that contributed to dramatizing Dorando Pietri's finish: for the 1908 London Olympics, the length of the race had been increased by 335 meters as compared to the previous Olympics. The motive was to allow appropriate viewing from the Royal Box and still enable the start to be from Windsor Castle. This fanciful and even capricious choice was to have an unexpected effect on the race's outcome and a man's fate.

Still another major contribution to the turning of Dorando's performance into a legend was provided by the composer Irving Berlin. Berlin wrote a song with the title "Dorando," and the song became a hit. Whether by ignorance or artistic whim, Berlin confused the athlete's first name and his surname, with the result that many people came to believe that Dorando was Pietri's family name. Thanks to Irving Berlin, Dorando Pietri became a celebrated hero musically. His feat was turned into a sung story. He had been enlarged to a *dramatis personna*. Ironically enough, though, this musical fame dispossessed him of his civil identity. Pietri entered the legend as Dorando. There he joined Pheidippides, the Athenian hemerodromoi, a running message bearer who, as legend says, died while announcing the Athenian victory of Marathon in the year 490 B.C.

The falls of Dorando Pietri are illustrative of the ambiguities of modern sports performances, with competition prompting the outer limits of achievement, self-inflicted suffering, heroism bordering on nonsense, publicly defined success challenging legalist success, full-fledged national pride, and hypertrophied media coverage of the event producing images of athletes more real than the athletes themselves. An epic hero for some, Pietri was a dangerous-to-himself fool for others. His falls blurred the notions of success and failure. The success of the esteem the public and the royal Loge granted him contrasted with his disqualification by the official authorities. Pietri won, then he lost. Then he won again, this time, in part outside the track, as a screen and song star.

Pietri's fate followed indeterminate oscillations between success and failure, an illustration of the relative nature of the notion of successful achievement. His finish is at the same time dramatically readable and robustly ambiguous. To be constituted as a performance, his finish had to be recorded so that its dramatic qualities could be dispatched in a collective revival of the scene (a revival of which this text, by the way, is a part)—a scene, for that matter, where Dorando the legend, representing romance, stands in ironical confrontation to Pietri the individual, representing tragedy.[1]

Pietri's falls belong to sports history. The notion of performance they so dramatically embodied, however, stands as one of the central notions of modern sports, precisely the form of sports that organizations are enthralled by. As compared with earlier forms of physical exercise, modern elite sports appear focused upon and organized around a systematic quest for performance. As this chapter will show, the two notions, that of modern sports and that of performance, surface as companion notions that are closely interrelated and interconnected. They are born and have grown together, and each is the architect of the other. Performance is the mark of modern sports and, conversely, modern sports has produced the contemporary vision of performance.

Pietri's falls also exemplify the narrative dimension of sports and of performance. His falls and the rest of his extraordinary career are paramount examples of how it is through narration that achievements are constructed as performances. It is only under conditions of being placed in a story that his physically falling of exhaustion becomes a performance. His legend, more generally, is an exemplary illustration of the complex relationship that exists between doing and accounting for what is done.

Bringing together this modernistic and this narrative dimension of sports performance is the purpose of this chapter. Section one contrasts modern sports with earlier forms of sports activities and describes how modern sports has come to be what it is. Section two depicts the relationship of professional sports to ideas of modernity, suggesting that sports is one of the narratives produced by modernity. Section three builds on this idea of sports being a narrative and features sports performances as stories, discussing, in particular, the interpretation of these tales and the impact they have on the behaviors they account for. The next chapter will examine parallels between performance in sports and in organizations. The present chapter focuses on sports with the aim of depicting the origin of the performance notion.

From Ancient to Modern Sports

Not all competitors in athletic events have been interested in something called performance. In the thousands of years of physical exercise, the notion of performance has a history of its own. Yet its history in sports does not go much further back than a couple of centuries.

Ancient Sports

Numerous references are made in modern sports, and in the modern Olympic Games in particular, to Greek tradition. These references tend to suggest that sports in ancient Greece were a direct ancestor of modern sports. Such a claim, however, is in serious need of clarification.

To begin with, one should observe that ancient Greek sports is not one but three: mythological with Homer, it had become Olympic with Pindar, before turning into a state ideology during the fifth century (Jeu 1987:76). In some ways, Homeric sports did portend modern sports. For example, lanes were drawn at random, winners were rewarded, and supporters were attracted to it. However, in that mythological age, sports was an activity impregnated with religiosity. It was associated with the initiation ceremonies of passage into adulthood or into the world of the dead. Sports was a solemn consecration of the athlete (Jeu 1987:77). Five centuries later, Pindar depicts in "The First Olympics" a sports that is still much imbued with poetics and heroism. He celebrates the archetypal value of the gesture of the athlete, its totemic meaning. Sports is for him a device to honor the aristocratic social order by organizing a circulation of the theme of the *ariston*—the most able, or the best—between the order in the stadium and the tyrannical order (Jeu 1987:86). Soon, sports was to be harnessed by state views on education and on the military. A race in arms, for example, was introduced at the fifty-sixth Olympic Games, in 520 B.C. In 424 B.C., Alcibiades demanded the command of an expedition to Sicily on the basis of his having had three chariots among the first four at the eighty-ninth Olympiad. Rival cities agreed on a truce to their military disputes and participated in the same sports contests. The institution of sports had lost its sacred aura and had become subjugated to state ideology. What had once been a source of emotion, and been perceived as a value in itself, had become a purposeful activity considered as a means to an end. The body of the athlete was still a symbol of ideal proportions, and sports was still regarded as a way of maintaining the soul, but it had become increasingly secular (Jeu 1987:102).

Throughout its history, though, ancient Greek sports differed significantly from modern sports in that the Greeks laid great importance on victory—the winner of the Olympics became a mythological hero—but showed only little interest in measuring athletes' results. No statistical records seem to have been kept of the competitors' performances. This can hardly be explained by the differences in the lengths of stadiums or in the weight of the discus. Standardization could have easily been achieved and the Greeks had access to adequate ways of measuring both distance and weight. One should instead look for an explanation of this lack of interest in performance measurement in how the Greeks envisioned human beings. As Guttmann (1977:49) says:

> Pythagoras, Archimedes, Euclid, and others made great contributions to mathematics, especially to geometry, but Greek civilization was not obsessed with the need to quantify. For them, man was still the measure of all things, not the object of endless measurements. To wear the victor's leafy crown, to be the best of those who had on that cloudless day contested for glory and fame at Olympia or Corinth— that was sufficient.

Human beings were the measure of all things. They were not, as today, the object of strategies of measurement. There was thus no need for the ancient Greeks to keep track of earlier performances. Competition was a confrontation between humans who were present at a given place at a given time. It concerned exclusively those who were present that day. Guttmann (ibid.) again:

> Comparability beyond the circle of athletes gathered together for the event was never sought and quantification of the result was unnecessary. The closest approach to our modern sense of quantification was in the numeration of achievements. Just as Herakles performed ten labors, Milo of Croton was famed for five victories at Olympia, six at the Pythian games, ten at the Isthmian games, and nine at Nemea.

The numeration of victories is a far cry from the obsession of our time for measuring every single aspect of competition.

Ignoring measurement, the Greeks thus ignored the notion of record. Again, this can be related to the metaphysical position of theirs. As Ulmann (1965:336) states: "Greek gymnastics was inseparable from a conception of the body which was itself conditioned by a metaphysics of finiteness" (my translation). This was a metaphysical position that contrasts with that of modern sports in the sense that: "Sports of the Moderns is animated by a philosophy more or less diffuse and coherent, a theory of progress. One goes forward. One gathers knowledge, disciplines and material, and conquers new fields; one is involved in an endless move" (Ulmann, 1965:336, my translation). When comparing metaphysics of finiteness against metaphysics of progress, the difference is a significant one. This is why, despite the references of the modern Olympics, for example, to ancient Greece, ancient Greek sports cannot without serious limitations be regarded as an ancestor of modern sports.

Sports in the Middle Ages

Under the Roman influence, sports became totally secular, reflective more of a snobbish than of a religious or a philosophical attitude. Abandoning most traditional athletic disciplines, they focused on events involving fights. They also introduced animals and allowed slaves to participate. The last Olympiad, which took place in 393, was only met by indifference.[2]

The fall of the Roman empire entailed the quasi-total disappearance, at least in Western Europe, of organized sports-like activities. Although some form of regular physical contests did survive, for example, in Ireland, this was on a limited scale only. The history of organized sports-like activities that led to modern sports can be said to have first resumed with tournaments and ball games in the Middle Ages.

Tournaments were at their peak during the twelfth and thirteenth centuries. These were exercises for aristocrats. The participating knights, who were divided into two teams, met each other in a series of assaults during which they tried to acquire spoils (horses and harnesses) and take prisoners they could hold for ransom. Tournaments were substitutes for real wars. They were for that matter as brutal as real wars, often with casualties as a result, which is exceptional and unacceptable by modern sports standards. The institution of duel, however, was to survive until the twentieth century.[3]

In some ways, tournaments announced the advent of modern sports. The fighting was limited, for example, in space and in time. It was also a much appreciated spectacle, which medieval literature, similar in this respect to modern media, commented on abundantly, as Vargas (1992:72) has noted. It is there, however, that the similarities end. Bouet (1968:245) emphasizes, for example, the nearly complete lack of rules to regulate the fights, except for the general principles of courage, honor, and virtue that governed knighthood at large, at least until the twelfth century. One could also mention the practice of stripping and ransoming the defeated participants that were inherent features of tournaments.[4] It is unlikely that tournaments would be called sports today.

The ball game of *soule* or *choule* [French] was a precursor too of modern sports. It consisted in the, for us, well-known idea of carrying a ball from one place to another, in that case between two villages or from one end of a street to another. It was not governed by any rules, was not ruled by any referee and it could be rather violent at times. The game could not end in a draw and went on until some team won. It was a game dominated by the search, on the basis of competition, for a winner and a loser (Bouet 1968:256).

Bouet (1968:261) has summarized the relationship of sports in the Middle Ages to modern sports as follows: "The Middle ages contained all the material that which would become sports…, though in a way that was crude and unpolished, and even sometimes completely foreign to the structure taken on in modern sports by the themes of performance and competition" (my translation). Thus, even if similarities can easily be found between medieval and modern sports, tournaments and medieval ball games can only be regarded as remote ancestors of sports as we know them today. Their sources of inspiration, as well as their formal features, were too different from those of modern sports. The notion of performance was simply not in use.

The Emergence of Modern Sports

It is in Great Britain, toward the beginning of eighteenth century that the early signs of a modern form of sports can be found. The first title of champion was attributed to a boxer named Figg in 1720 and the first running competitions that aimed at establishing records date from about the same time. Two early records were, for example, that in 1740 of 17.3 kilometers being walked within an hour and that in 1787 of an English mile being run in four minutes and thirty seconds. This was also the time of the creation of the first clubs: the Jockey Club in 1750 and the Saint Andrews golf club in 1754.[5]

During the nineteenth century, the process of the institutionalization of sports accelerated. The first rowing race between Oxford and Cambridge took place in 1829. Football, rugby, golf, and cricket competitions were soon to be born. Most sports federations were created, accordingly, between about 1860 and 1900: the Football Association in 1863, the Amateur Athletic Club in 1866, the Amateur Metropolitan of Swimming Association in 1869, the Rugby Football Association in 1871, the Bicyclists' Union in 1878, the National Skating Association in 1879, the Metropolitan Rowing Association in 1879, the Amateur Boxing Association in 1884, the Hockey Association in 1886, the Lawn Tennis Association in 1895, and the Amateur Fencing Association in 1898. Thanks to the organizing role played by these federations, rules became harmonized and results started to be collected systematically.

Britain was far ahead of other European nations in institutionalizing sports. It was in Britain, for example, around 1840, that sports first became a full part of formal school education and thus entered every educated boy's curriculum. (Basketball and volleyball were nevertheless to be born in the United States of America, in 1892 and 1895, respectively, to meet the need for indoor sports on winter evenings.) Inspired as much by contemporary English sports as by classic Greek ideals, Georges de Saint Pierre and Pierre de Coubertin undertook to extend to all nations invitations to the Olympic Games that previously had taken place in Greece for Greek citizens only in 1859, 1870, and 1875. The first international Olympics took place in 1896, and with them was created one of the major loci for the quest of performances.

By the First World War, modern sports was born. Professional athletes were no longer so few in number. Sports had become rigorously institutionalized. As a result, competitions were increasingly codified and standardized. Meetings were held on a regular basis. Results were increasingly publicized. Sports had also become extremely popular. Large stadiums were built in all Western countries to host large sports events and large audiences. A specialized sports press was born. Movies, radio, and television were soon to follow. These new media immediately settled on prolonging, echoing, and retaining in archives the deeds of athletes. New sports disciplines appeared with the invention of the automobile and of the airplanes, which opened new arenas to the ideas of competition, victory, and records.[6]

Modern Sports as a Product and a Vector of Modernity

As the above chronology shows, modern sports are contemporary to industrial civilization. They are of the same age as industrial factories, the urbanization process, and the development of modern means of transportation and of communication. They thus have the same age as scientific experience, the concern for precise measurement, and the idea of positive truth. They also have the same age as the idea of controlling time, the idea of the market, and the ideology of liberalism.

Along with social and religious changes, technological progress has had a decisive impact on the development of modern sports (Sage 1990:87). The first interest in athletic records, for example, was almost exactly coincidental with the invention of the chronometer in 1731 (Brohm 1992:120). More generally, as Betts (1981:273) claims, technological developments proved extremely significant for the birth of modern sports:

> The impact of invention had a decisive influence on the rise of sports in the latter half of the century. By 1900 sports had attained an unprecedented prominence in the daily lives of millions of Americans, and this remarkable development had been achieved in great part through the steamboat, the railroad, the telegraph, the penny press, the electric light, the streetcar, the camera, the bicycle, the automobile, and the mass production of sporting goods.

This idea of a joint development of sports and of industrial society has been developed further by authors of Marxist and neo-Marxist inspiration, who suggest the existence of a parallel between the features of modern sports and of industrialism. To them, the specialization of the sports athlete corresponds to that of the worker, the accumulation of records to the accumulation of goods, the mass character of sports spectacles to that of industrial products, the strategies of control of the body of the athlete to that of the control of the body of the worker, both universes being permeated by a common obsession for time and production measurement. Accordingly, these authors claim that sports activities are narrowly conditioned by the state of development of the forces of production, and that in this regard sports, with its belief in a scientific organization of labor and its pragmatic confidence in human progress, is a typical activity of industrial societies.[7] As seducing as this analysis may be, it calls for nuances.

In fact, as Guttmann (1977:57) shows, one cannot really establish, as the (neo-) Marxists do, any one-to-one correspondence between the state of development of industrial forces and that of sports. Similarly one can hardly, he says, quoting Lüschen (1967:130), establish any correspondence of Weberian inspiration between, on the one hand, the success of some particular sports discipline, and, on the other hand, the Protestant ethic and its emphasis on achievement. Sports is both too diversified and too unified to fit into any of these determinisms.

This is the reason for Guttmann (1977 :85) claiming that: "The emergence of modern sports represents neither the triumph of capitalism nor the rise of Protestantism but rather the slow development of an empirical, experimental, mathematical *Weltanschauung*." To this he adds the following: "England's early leadership has less to do with the Protestant ethic and the spirit of capitalism than with the intellectual revolution symbolized by the names of Isaac Newton and John Locke and institutionalized in the Royal Society, founded during the Restoration, in 1662, for the advancement of science" (ibid.).

This *Weltanschauung* is that of modernity. Modernity is, for Habermas (1981/1985), a project. Specific to that "project of modernity," as formulated in the eighteenth century by the philosophers of the Enlightenment, is that it involved an effort to develop objective science, universal morality and law, and autonomous art according to a logic of its own; the philosophers of the Enlightenment wanted to utilize this accumulation of specialized culture for a rational organization of everyday social life; science in particular was expected to facilitate not only the control of natural forces, but also an understanding of the world and of the self, moral progress, the justice of institutions, and even the happiness of human beings (1981/1985:8).[8] These are ideas that, according to Giddens (1990:16), resulted in the separation of time and space (through time measurement techniques that were no longer bound to geographical determinants), the disembedding of social systems (lifting social relations out of local contexts of interaction and restructuring them across indefinite spans of time-space), and the reflexive ordering and reordering of social relations in the light of continual inputs of knowledge that affected the actions of individuals and of groups (altering practice through knowledge and altering knowledge through practice: an idea expressed and developèd earlier by Foucault 1966, 1975). This is a set of ideas concerning knowledge and society that, according to Lyotard (1979), can be regarded as the production of meta-narratives such as emancipation, accumulation, history, or science and the constitution of these meta-narratives into as many projects, all sustained by instrumental knowledge and by a corresponding technoscience.

Sports can be regarded as one of the narratives that modernity has produced. Late nineteenth-century sports became part of a modernist cultural project that promoted a civilizing amateurism and a healthy body as positive social forces; it involved a politics of the body, promoting its systematic normalization and its rationalization (Gruneau 1993).

Sports entails controlling natural forces through law and universal morality. Sports also claims the right to be governed according to its own rules. It affirms, likewise, its dedication to the improvement of self-understanding and of moral standards. Sports accommodates the modern ideas of accumulation (of records), of emancipation (from gravity or from natural kinetics), of indisputable knowledge (the sanctioned performance is, in this regard, equivalent to positivist scientific knowledge), or of discipline and classification (discipline of the body and discipline as an institution, rankings) (Foucault 1975). It also accommodates the separation of time and space (all contests belong to a given place but no result does), of the disembedding of social practices (rules of sports events are universal), of performativity being a justificational mode (Lyotard 1979:69) (the winner is by definition the best), or of an ever-increasing speed of life (a feature of modernity identified by Virilio 1977).

A feature of modernity that is expressed with particular salience in sports is that of progress. In sports, and particularly in such sports as track and field events, records are the manifestation of progress. A record is a surpassing; it is a form of progress. By definition, records are the highest performances ever; as such they symbolize the front line of human progress, humanity's *ariston*. Moreover, in a dynamic perspective, each new record signals an increase in the efficiency of the human race: *citius, altius, fortius*—faster, higher, stronger. What fascinates in records is the quantum that each adds to its predecessor (Gelhen as quoted in Brohm 1992:159), so that records stand as the marks of human progression toward the better: a progression that is sealed in series of records and championship titles and that entails in all competitions the idea of conquest.

As exemplified by Swedish gymnastics, the projects of sports and modernity enter into mutually supportive relationships with each other. Whereas gymnastics was modeled in accordance with the modern values of health, cleanliness, fitness, and rationality, it was also one of the means by which Swedes were led into the new Swedish nationality that was invented and constructed for them in the name of modernity (after Frykman 1993).

Sports maintains multiform relationships with modernity. On the one hand, sports is a product of modernity in the sense that the categories of its development—individuality, rationality, competition, measurement—are those that constitute modern intelligibility. On the other hand, modern sports is a vector of modernity in the sense that it constitutes a locus in which modern categories of intelligibility can be embodied, enacted, and thus advertised and spread. The same web of assumptions, mutually supportive notions, contradictions, necessary conditions, and equivalence run through both of them.

Reading Sports Performance

The idea of sports being one of the narratives of modernity prompts the idea of reading sports. Indeed, as Harris and Hills (1993) have pointed out, sports can appropriately be considered as having a story-like structure, one organized around the resolution of two basic uncertainties: "Who will win?" and "How?". This is particularly true of television, where visual dramatization has been turned into a basic feature of sports programs (Alexander 1991:52).

Regarding the question of "who will win," we know, just as in the case of old-fashioned detective stories in which the detective gathers all the protagonists in a single room before pointing out the murderer, that the winner is among the participating athletes. As characters, athletes are very active. Their relentless activity is indeed what supports the audience's attention. It is through their activity that athletes express their moral, dispositional, and emotional qualities. Athletes mostly show; they hardly ever speak, except during interviews. Yet interviews are separated from the sports event itself. Interviews take place either before or after a sports event, or during an interruption of it. Interviews do not belong to the event but to its margins. As exemplified by the falls of Dorando Pietri, sports is a visual story and athletes are characters enclosed in what they can show through their acting.

"When will the winner be known" is not a problematic issue, on the other hand. Aside from occasional exceptions, the time of this disclosure can be set in advance. Anyone can read in television timetables at what time, at the latest, the name of the world cup winner will be known. Sports stories are framed within a strictly predetermined span of time, and closure comes in time.

"How?" is the other main question that inhabits sports stories. "How" is displayed openly for everyone to see. A particular trait of sports is that no hidden purposes or off-field factors are allowed to blur what happens. Readers of sports events are entitled to demand that they be provided with all the necessary information. Sports stories have to be transparent. It is also a particular trait of sports stories that sports events follow a very detailed set of rules and a strict progression. Sports events are full of suspense and surprises, but only a few types of unexpected incidents are allowed. Rules literally constitute sports events and sports disciplines.

Under these premises, sports stories are easily read and are extremely intelligible. They are all the more readable and intelligible in that sports rules are systematically taught in school and that one is repeatedly reminded of them by sports commentaries. No wonder then if one also takes into account the great scenic efficiency and the tense dramatic character of many sports events, so that sports stories are among the most preferred stories of our time.

Performance Stories

Performance is a central element in sports stories. Both "Who will win" and "how will the winner win" are matters of performance. "Who will win" corresponds to the achievement sense of the term, whereas "how will the winner win" is the behavioral one. The two central questions in sports stories are also the two main senses in which the term performance is used. Performance is thus not only a central element of modern sports in that the systematic quest for performance has historically become the distinctive character of professional modern sports, but performance also turns out, in its polysemy, to capture the most central interrogations one can find in sports stories. Closely related to winning, as an act as well as a result, performance represents a pervasive element of sports stories.

At the same time, performances are stories in their own right. Facing a mass of events, performance accounts select and order some of these in terms of the results achieved. Performance accounts turn the profusion of individual events that constitute the organization's life into something consistent: an achievement. This achievement signals the passage from a state A to a state B. Whether this passage refers to necessity and causality (first A and because of that B) or whether it leaves much to hazard and chance (first A and then B, although no one can say why), A and B are made, through narration, the spatio-temporal bounds of a chronological progression (first A and later B).

Performance is the tale of this progression. It is the story of the achievement that the passage from state A to state B represents. Through a selection and an ordering of events, performance stories link, in a meaningful manner, situation A to the later situation B. It is this textualizing of events in a chronological manner that makes performance a story.

Regarding individual events, it is when these are made a part of this story—organized and framed within its narrative scheme of integration—that they acquire meaning. The meaning of events results from the story to which they belong. It may even be the case that events have not yet been identified as such when the story is constructed; the performance story, then, not only provides events with meaning, it also produces them.

The meaning given to specific events comes from the place these have in the chain of events, from the opening to the final result, which together constitute the story. Depending upon how this story unfolds, events can appear as having either contributed to, hindered, or diverted the final result. They have thus been made a part of the tale. They have been turned into episodes of a story: a tale that orders events and makes them intelligible. Through constructing linearity, performance narration is an enterprise of producing meaning.

Contextualization, that is to say, the placing of a particular event in a chain of events, is decisive to this production of meaning. Depending upon which story is under construction, a particular event (e.g., a pass) can be contextualized: (a) as a single action (e.g., a pass that results in a counterattack), (b) as the whole match (e.g., the counterattack that resulted in two points being scored), (c) in terms of the individual history of the player (e.g., an incredible miss for a player of X's class), or (d) in terms of the history of the club (e.g., another example of the calamitous misfortune of Club Y). For every story that is chosen, the event is given a different meaning. There are as many performances, therefore, as there are stories that can ascribe meaning to the event.

A performance emerges, in consequence, not only as a story, but also as one story out of a series of many possible stories. A performance is always one, therefore, out of many possible performances. Accordingly, it is first in relationship to other stories (other tales related to the same event, or unrelated tales) that a performance story is able to acquire its meaning.

Stories of performance borrow much meaning from sports stories and lend the latter much meaning too. Performance stories get into sports stories to become part of the events of these. A missed pass (the smaller story), for example, can be seen as another example of the decline of X as a player (the larger story). Sports stories, conversely, act as an interpretative framework for performance stories. For example, it is because basketball is popular in the United States that Magic Johnson's announcement of his being HIV-positive, of his leaving the basketball scene, and later of his coming back are significant events.

Likewise, performance stories make more complex the dramatic features of sports stories by contributing to the meaning of loss and victory. Considering that one could say of past performances what Umminger (as quoted in Brohm 1992:188) says of records, namely, that they take part in all competitions as ghost participants and are therefore omnipresent, then in these terms, performance stories take sports stories beyond the simpler schemes of immediate success and failure (not unlike what the metaphysics of the *ariston* did for ancient sports). Performance attaches to victory, for example, a connotation of progress. It also doubles the suspense of who will win through the suspense of how large the victory or loss will be. It likewise brings to light individual characters who might remain anonymous in a simpler win or loose story but who can become extremely visible in a story that systematically computes what everyone does so as to compare that with what all others in a similar position have done: this contributes decisively to sports stories' looking inhabited.

There are intense exchanges between sports stories and sports performance stories. Each provides the other with elements that are essential to their becoming meaningful. Sports stories act as a background to performance stories, and, conversely, performance stories contribute to turning sports into good stories. In the exchanges that take place between the two lies the creation of meaning.

A Matter of Interpretation

As a story, performance represents a set of signs—a textual chain—that an athlete or an organization presents to a reader. If, as reception theory says, the meaning of a text emerges from the meeting between the text and a reader (Newton 1990:130), then the meaning of this textual chain will emerge from its meeting with an audience. Performance will have to be read to exist and it will be what comes out of its meeting with its readers.

Reception theory defines a work by its effect. It focuses on the dialectics of effect and reception. In this way, the aesthetics of reception reinstates the recipient of a work of art in his or her own right as the bearer of aesthetic culture. Reception theory also focuses on the formation and restructuration of canons. It poses the problem of dialogic understanding over a distance in time. Opposing the traditional aesthetics of the work of art and its function of representation, it defines, in short, aesthetic experience in terms of a productive, receptive, and communicative activity (Jauss 1990).

Performance, under such conditions, is co-produced by the performer and the audience. The audience is not simply a passive receiver of performance; it is also a co-producer of performance. Let us look at the football player who just scored a goal: he raises his arms to the sky in a claim for attribution, he hugs his fellow competitors and finally he waves his hand to the audience; some even kneel in front of their public in a prayer-like manner while the crowd stands applauding. So do the gymnast and the ice skater. This can be compared to the presentation of annual reports in a large company. There one finds the same gestures of offertory. Performance is not a property of the athlete or of a managerial team. On the contrary, as soon as their deeds have been recorded and turned into performances, these are, so to speak, offered to the audience, not under the sign of a generalized altruism among athletes or managers, but rather as an acknowledgment that the performance engages the performer as well as the audience, and that even if a performance is ascribed to an athlete or to an organization, the latter are not the sole owners of it. Athletes and CEOs know that it is in the audience that the performance will live. It is there that it will become mythical and adulated or that it will be neglected or virtually erased: the audience will decide! Great performances occur in a communion between the performer and the audience.

Since a performance is something that is recorded and that can therefore last in collective memory, it can be relevant to apply Jauss' theory of the reception of a literary work to performances. For Jauss, the reception and the influence of a literary work can be seen as a dialogue between the text and its succession of audiences, one that takes place at both an aesthetic and a historical level. Jauss (1982:20) writes:

> The relationship of literature and reader has aesthetic as well as historical implications. The aesthetic implication lies in the fact that the first reception of a work by the reader includes a test of its aesthetic value in comparison with works already read. The obvious historical implication of this is that the understanding of the first reader will be sustained and enriched in a chain of reception from generation to generation; in this way the historical significance of a work will be decided and its aesthetic value made evident. In this process of the history of reception..., the reappropriation of past works occurs simultaneously with the perpetual mediation of past and present art and of traditional evaluation and current literary attempts.

What Jauss claims is that texts should be considered with regard to the evolution of the reading the general public does with them. As this reading evolves, a historical tradition of critical interpretation and evaluation emerges that determines the significance, the value, and much of the content of the text. Replicating Jauss' reasoning in the case of performance, one could say that the meaning and the value of a performance emerge from the chain of readings that occur when, through story telling, the story is repeated over and over, and that various audiences successively acquaint themselves with the story of the deed.

In this chain of reading the meaning of a performance derives from its relationships to other performances, especially performance belonging to the same genre, in an endless game of differences. As Roberts (1992) pointed out, it is through being replayed over and over that sports actions are made and remade and placed within the world. A performance is not single: it belongs to an interperformancy as a text is part of an intertextuality.

Champions and records are historical milestones in this interperformancy. Certain performances are even more than this. They become symbols of turning points. This was the case, for example, on the day in 1954 when Bannister took the record for the British mile, under 4 minutes, just as it was on the day in January 1992 when Microsoft's market value surpassed that of General Motors.[9] Such performances become historical steps for an athlete, an organization, a sports discipline, or an industry. They become historical references upon which new traditions can be built. They are symbolic acts of founding. Great performances belong to the realm of those symbols that are present in the common memory of the audience. Great performances also stage aesthetic canons; they delimit and define the aesthetic aspects of performance. They constitute what Jauss in his literary theory calls "horizons of expectations," that is to say, the expectations in terms of which a reader will receive new and coming works (Newton 1990:132).

The competence of the audience is a key element in the reception of performance. Making sense out of a performance requires of the audience that it has adequate protocols of reading (Scholes 1989). A performance is directed at informed readers. It belongs first and foremost to those who can appreciate its shades of greatness. It belongs to the audience that possesses sufficient knowledge, pre-understanding, and sensitivity to identify the greatness of the feat and place it in a historical context. It is within this knowledgeable audience—an audience that it helps to organize—that a deed can acquire signification as a performance. In some cases, this may mean that only peers—in the sense of people with similar experience and knowledge—can actually make a judgment. This, of course, limits the understanding of the performance to the context of a specific audience. Those for whom performance is significant and who acknowledge a performance as such are those who share a community of knowledge, and who, in organizations, share the same view of what matters for the organization and the same criteria of performance. As Fish (1980:171) states, an audience with comparable interpretative strategies could be said to constitute an interpretative community. A performance can scarcely cross the frontiers of this community. Conversely, different audiences will attach different values to the same deed, which binds the value of a performance to the specific social context in which the reading occurs.

With each audience producing its own readings, performances are open to endless variations of interpretation. They are, in this regard, open works (Eco 1962/1965). It is only in their appearance that they are straightforward signifiers. Their being expressed in figures—going as far in detail as to the hundredth of a second—is illusive in this regard.

Performances accommodate ambiguous multitudes of meanings. They are works in movement. Just as with pieces of contemporary music, they open to their audience, despite their being materially achieved, a virtually endless repertoire of combinations of elements, each of these combinations enlivening the work in a particular and definitive way. It is through this variety of form that performances exist.

Even though performances are duly recorded and stored, performances are thus also elements of an extremely unstable dynamic series. Champions, records, and stars from the stock exchange replace each other in a rapid and seemingly endless roundabout. The dominant positions that last as long as Bob Beamon's fantastic leap or the dominance of IBM are few. "Great" performances rapidly take over from one another. Time may indicate, for example, how certain past performances resulted from inordinate speculation that bordered on criminality, such as when in the early 1990s the Swedish banking sector and East German sports, two once highly performant sectors, almost simultaneously lost much of the credentials they had acquired in the 1980s through the grounds for their success becoming better known. It may well be too that techniques will evolve, that new protagonists will arise and old ones disappear, that new managerial innovations will become fashionable, and that such changes will bring about dramatic modifications in sports rankings or in corporate scales of excellence. The steel industry, for example, is a potent example of how the industrial glories of one period can become the social nightmares of another. Patterns of reading are ceaselessly being transformed. The stature that performance is granted evolves accordingly. Performance, when it emerges, is thus not only socially but also temporally bounded.

This, in turn, raises the issue of how significant various historical series are in terms of performance. Historical series stumble over both the difficulty of interpretation of an old text and the lack of commensurability of phenomena separated in time. We can surely discuss and compare Jesse Owens and Carl Lewis, or discuss and compare the Roaring Twenties and the dynamic eighties. It is less certain, however, that we can take such a discussion further than what Eco has labeled, for sports, a chattering (1969/1985:172). It seems difficult to dismember performance from its temporality.

Similarly, the precariousness of performance raises the issue of how to account for modifications of performance across time. Since performances themselves are precarious, assessing them in a definite and time-less manner seems impossible. Still, there seems to be a demand for certitude and definitiveness at the heart of performance literature. These two demands appear irreconcilable.[10]

Performance Driven Behaviors

Performance stories are not only involved in endless reinterpretations of past achievements. Performances are also parts of the expectations that both performers and the audience place in an event. Achievements are what the audience come to see, and performers know that the story of their achievements is what make them liable for rewards. In this manner, performance stories, even as yet unwritten, have a decisive impact upon the activity they recount. The mere awareness that an event will be narrated in terms of performance and that a significant status is going to be attached to it by, for example, media customers or top level management, aligns behaviors with the features of the performance story thereby produced. Anticipation lets behaviors become performance driven.

This impact of performance upon behaviors by means of a process of anticipation can be made explicit by comparing a reading made by a connoisseur of a sports event with a reading made by a spectator who focuses on performance. As Bourdieu (1984:184) declares:

> The "connoisseur" has schemes of perception and appreciation which enable him to see what the layman cannot see, to perceive a necessity where the outsider sees only violence and confusion, and so to find in the promptness of a movement, in the unforeseeable inevitability of a successful combination or the near-miraculous orchestration of a team strategy, a pleasure no less intense and learned than the pleasure a music-lover derives from a particularly successful rendering of a favorite work. (Translation Richard Nice in Mukerji and Schudson 1991:364 [see Bourdieu 1984])

The decoding that the connoisseur makes of an event—this is true of a specialist in any activity—requires the mastering of sophisticated technical knowledge, knowledge that often assumes a practicing of the sports discipline in question. From this knowledge, the connoisseur derives a specific pleasure that is something of a privilege. While absorbed in the intrinsic characteristics of the event, not the least its beauty, the connoisseur is in a position to derive from the event an intense emotion that has deep roots in her or his person.

The performance-focused spectator sees something quite different. He—let us assume it is a he—places less importance on the beauty of carrying things out and favors instead the outcome of the contest. Whereas the connoisseur enjoys the manner in which the story unfolds, and thus approaches performance in terms of a process, the performance-focused reader is merely interested in the event's result. The tension observed earlier between these two conceptions of the term performance is at work again (just as it is between connoisseur-managers who focus on how things are done and performance-focused managers who concentrate on outcomes). The performance-focused reader's attention is less on the instant or time interval when the action takes place than on its outcome. The performance-focused spectator focuses on the bottom line and the suspense attached to it. This involves a flattening of the sports story. Accordingly, the performance-focused spectator has a lesser need of technical knowledge in order to follow the game. For him, a general acquaintance with the rules and an ability to identify the key figures of the event are sufficient. He does not need to bother himself with technical finesses and can even afford being blind to them. His eyes are less on the athletes than on the clock or the scoreboard. The score, which for the sports connoisseur is a more-or-less fair reward for excellence, is for the performance-focused sports reader the immediate sign of excellence.

Correspondingly, the performance-focused reader has to accept the procedures through which performance is constructed—among these the metrological procedures and the decisions of the referee—to a much larger extent than the connoisseur, whose reading of the event is more personal and therefore less dependent on the official results. When one moves from the connoisseur to the performance-focused viewer, interest in the spectacle is displaced from that of practice to that of a result seen as part of a series of results.

Since connoisseurs and performance-focused readers differ in how they direct their attention at what they view, they also influence, in ways that differ, what they will be presented with in the future. Any specific focus, indeed, is likely to influence how performers view their own activity, in particular through conditioning what they are to regard as important (and therefore worth doing) and what is not. This is especially the case if spectators are those who, in one way or another, control the performers' access to financing, fame, career, or other rewards. Few athletes today can afford to ignore the volume of their television audience being critical in determining how much money they can make from their sports. Similarly, few public organizations today can disregard the reading that the appointed politicians, their constituencies, and citizens at large make of their activity. In both cases, one can safely assume that performers will calculatingly modulate their behavior so as to please their audience, enabling them to gain the acknowledgment that their future activities depend on.

This is particularly true of the focus on performance. By inducing a specific mode of reading of an event, a focus on performance will influence what future events of the same kind will be like. One can therefore predict, for example, that a decrease in the share of connoisseurs in the audience will increase the frequency of spectacular strikes and of thrilling effects aimed at sustaining the dramatic tension of the story. Similarly, one can predict that as the fine art of doing things becomes less of an end in itself and results acquire greater significance, less attention will be paid to the former while behaviors that improve the result will be increasingly emphasized.

This is why it is important to follow how and by whom performance criteria are set. Today's dominant views on performance are likely to become a norm for tomorrow's activity. This is particularly important in organizations where different constituencies can maintain differing views on how to define performance. This explains the struggle that can take place—for example between the stock market, customers, and the local community—regarding who should define what performance is. The competence of those in charge of reading performance is a critical aspect in performance stories. In practice, the competence of the readers not only determines, as was shown above, what sort of reading is to be made of what is achieved today, but it also determines, as just indicated, which directions the activity is likely to take in the future.

The future impact on tomorrow's activity of today's criteria of performance adds particular dynamics to the performance notion. Reading performance is not only dynamic in the sense that a performance produced at a certain moment can be read in different manners at later dates. It is also dynamic in the sense that a reading made by the spectator at a certain moment, as soon as it is endorsed by the performers, shapes the future of the activity concerned. Anticipations turn today's readers not only into co-producers of today's performance but also into co-architects of tomorrow's.

Conclusion

The present chapter has been concerned with two main ideas: first, that performance is a cardinal element in modern sports, and second, that performances are narrative productions.

As the Dorando Pietri case exemplified, performances are dramatic stories dealing with competition, efforts, speed, achievements, control, and even institutionalized justice. In a more general sense, performance stories are stories of the rational control of human and natural forces, and stories of both progress and accumulation. They evoke ideas of measurement, of rules, of discipline, of self-enforced morality, of modulated rewards, of hierarchy, of identification, and of classification, all of these being notions described by Foucault (1975) as being specific to the modern way of thinking.

Performances are stories of modernity, of being full-fledged members of the modernity club. Just as in the case of sports, they are intricately rooted in modernist thinking. (They were, for that matter, born under the technical, social, and epistemological conditions of modern industrial societies.) Performance stories contain rationales of causality. They recount behaviors efficiently, making reference to chains of goals and means: to rationales of plans that precede activities, activities that have to conform to plans, and assessments of how plans have been followed. As such, performance stories evoke efficient science, positive knowledge, and effective technology.

One could object with Baudrillard (1986:25), however, that contemporary interest in performance stories has gone too far and has become the precursory sign of a new form of fanaticism, that of an evidence without end. Baudrillard seems to think that we all tend to become performance-focused spectators, and he finds much support for this in the recent history of modern sports. "I did it" is for him a sign of the pure but empty form of challenge addressed to oneself that performance represents. Performance would have succeeded in replacing the Promethean ecstasies of competition, of effort, and of success. The New York marathon is for Baudrillard the international symbol of this fetishism of performance, of this delirium of empty victories, of the exaltation of feat deprived of consequences: "I have run the New York marathon: I did it! I have climbed the Anapurna: I did it!" (Baudrillard 1986:25; my translation, "I did it" being originally in English in both cases). These are signs of a degree of uselessness that, for Baudrillard, inhabits all executions of a program and all deeds aimed at proving that one is able to achieve what one has promised.

When reduced to accounts of outcomes, performance stories indeed crown the triumph of a morality of the fait accompli. The winner is by definition the best; what is efficient is by definition to be preferred. The why, the how, the where, the who, and the in which way tend all to be subjugated to the what. Performance-focused spectators advocate a form of pragmatism in which the goodness and validity of an act are entailed by their representing achievement. The corresponding moral position is clear and unambiguous: it a teleological position acknowledging the supremacy of results. Connoisseurs have a different approach. They are more respectful of intentions, more observant of respect for deontological rules, and more tolerant of failure. The adoption of diverging ethical standpoints is implicit in the dichotomy of considering performance as results versus considering it as a process.

The next chapter will show that organizations, fascinated as they are by sports, are filled, both in their imagination and in their behaviors, with references to sports. Organizational performance stories resemble their sports counterparts in many respects. Yet organizations are not really athletes, and the world of organizations is not really the world of sports. This means that moving from the one context to the other cannot be done without important questions being raised regarding what is it one means in speaking of organizational performance.

Notes

1. References used in this account: Bengtsson (1979:107); Martin et al. (1977:827); Nilsson and Wigg (1982:14).
2. The passage on Roman sports is based on Bouet (1968:238) and Kihlberg (1983:20).
3. The passage on tournaments is based on Delort (1972:180) and on Duby and Mandrou (1968:73).
4. As witnessed by the remarkable life of William Marshal, the best knight in the world, tournaments could prove to be extremely efficient ways of getting both rich and politically influential (Duby 1984).
5. Jeu (1987:118) draws attention, by the way, to the fact that the term club came about through metonymic transformation, stemming from the instrument used in golf. Golf players will most probably appreciate the consecration by vocabulary of the generic character of their discipline.
6. This historical presentation is based upon Betts (1981), Brohm (1992) and Sandblad (1985).

7. See Brohm (1992) for a benevolent review of such theories.
8. As Habermas (1981/1985:3) observes, debates about the notion of modernity can be traced back to the late fifth century, when the term modernity was used to distinguish the present, which had become officially Christian, from the Roman and pagan past ideas.
9. *Business Week* (24 February 1992): 32–39.
10. There is a solution I could imagine, though, aimed at solving this irreconciliability: an index associated with performance. The idea is to peg performance onto the double horizon of acting and of writing. The index would tell one when the performance statement had been enunciated and what period of time historically it concerned. This would indicate to the reader how to orient himself or herself toward the contradictions introduced by the element of time. One could imagine that this index also be extended so as to depict the type of competition involved through information being provided concerning the terms of competition (e.g., the characteristics of the protagonists, the meteorological tools employed, the local condition of the contest) and the chain of reading involved (who read what how, when, why, and with which reaction). Such a series of indexes could, for example, be called the pedigree of a performance. The issue, however, is whether such a pedigree, which definitely signals the contextuality of a performance, would fit with performance discourse generally and its propensity for concise, numerical, and cumulative information.

4

The Signature of Modern *Agon*:
Performance in Sports and in Organizations

*There is one and one only social responsibility
of business—to use its resources and engage in
activities designed to increase its profits so
long as it stays within the rules of the game,
which is to say, engages in open and free
competition without deception or fraud.*

—Milton Friedman[1]

Sports, in our societies, tends to be everywhere. Newspapers, television, radio, and informal chats ensure daily its comprehensive coverage. Similarly, advertisements, publications of many sorts, and fashion are active in spreading its themes to the fields of hygiene, health, food, work, social relationships—including love—and still more. You—the reader—for example, may well practice sports yourself. If you do not, some close acquaintance of yours may do so. You are likely, in any case, to soon be met or overtaken by one of the runners who have turned every town and countryside into an arena for their efforts. Polymorphous in its manifestation, sports have successfully penetrated the most diverse spaces of our modernity. Its motifs are now to be found among all social classes, among all age groups (the younger ones are happily still shielded, but for how long?) and across all countries. They have become a sort of universal locus, a meta-linguistic world language. Today, they are a global referential model.

In this context of the frenetic omnipresence of sports, it is no surprise that economic organizations are invaded by the imagery of sports. Sports are a highly popular vehicle for conceiving of corporate image, personnel policy, and organizational strategy. Sports today are one of contemporary organizations' major sources of inspiration.

Organizations are mesmerized by how modern sports embody the notion of performance. Modern sports make performance particularly visible. They produce legions of high performers and top performances, and bring them into the brilliant glimmer of media light. Modern sports also make performance particularly readable. The relationships between performance and, for example, competition, measurement, and hierarchy of achievement are nowhere as intelligible as in sports. This readability of sports performance only adds to the interest of organizations in sports. Sports are not only a social activity that produces performances, they are also an activity that makes it easier to understand the nature of performance.

My aim in the present chapter is to elucidate, on the one hand, the fascination that sports exert upon organizations, and, on the other hand, the visibility and readability of performance in sports, specifying what performance stories are about. The first section describes the fascination of organizations for modern sports and discusses some of the motifs for it. This section takes up, in particular, the idea that sports are a major referential model for contemporary organizations. Building upon this idea, the second section presents a study of parallels between the notion of performance in sports and in organizations. How performance relates to competition, comparison, measurement, commensurability, hierarchy of achievements, and justice is discussed, both in the context of sports and in that of organizations.

Quite a precise picture of the specificity of performance stories emerges from the details of these relationships. The notion of *modern agon* is introduced to capture this specificity. *Agon* is a term used in ancient Greece to depict an active quest for excellence and the struggle to gain honor through competitive achievements in contest situations where individuals placed their self-esteem, moral character, and, at times, their very lives at stake. This quest for excellence was a model of achieving that was organized around the ideal of *ariston*. It involved becoming the best by preparation and training to excel over all others, testing in the course of competition this best against one's equal, beating the best of one's peers in contests, and being the best by receiving the acknowledgment that one is first among equals. In schematic terms, three main ideas underlie agon: first, an intense spirit of rivalry and competition; second, an emphasis on individualism; and third, an extreme emphasis on the pursuit of fame, glory, and honor, all of them imbedded in the mythological, religious, and political spirit that was that of ancient sport (Loy and Hesketh 1984).

Nearer for us, Huizinga (1938/1966) considers agon, in his theory of the *homo ludens*, to be one of the ideas to which one can attach the basic activities underlying the development of culture and civilization, for example:

> From the life of childhood right up to the highest achievements of civilization one of the strongest incentives to perfection, both individual and social, is the desire to be praised and honoured for one's excellence. In praising another each praises himself. We want to be honoured for our virtues. We want the satisfaction of having done something well. Doing something well means doing it better than others. In order to excel one must prove one's excellence; in order to merit recognition, merit must be made manifest. Competition serves to give proof of superiority. (ibid., 63)

Beyond its historical specificities, agon is a recurrent motif in human history. The claim of the present chapter is that performance is the distinctive mark of modern agon. Modern agon has inherited most of ancient agon's features, for example, the systematic and rational preparation to struggle, the competition, the desire for hierarchies, the quest for excellence, the celebration of the ariston, and the moral elevation of victory. It is secularized and imbedded, though, not in ancient traditions, but in the contemporary division of labor (professionalism), the pervasiveness of monetary priorities, and the omnipresence of the media. Moreover, it is organized much more around records, science (measurements), and time series than its ancient counterpart; it is much more institutionalized, too. Modern agon is built upon the contemporary connotations of notions of fights, rivalry, competition, excellence, and superiority.

The chapter features performance as the signature of modern agon: as that which makes it possible to distinguish modern agon from other forms of agon belonging to other historical contexts. Viewed the other way round, modern agon emerges as the central theme of performance stories.

The Fascination of Organizations for Sports

According to Ehrenberg (1991:95)—who speaks of France—interest in organizations for sports can be traced back to the mid 1970s, a time when the generic image of sports evolved from being stale to being chic. One should observe, however, that Huizinga had already noted more than fifty years ago that "there is now a sporting side to almost every triumph of commerce or technology: the highest turnover, the biggest tonnage, the fastest crossing, the greatest altitude, etc." and that "some of the great business concerns deliberately instil the play-spirit into their workers so as to step up production" (1938/1966:200), announcing therewith, some decades in advance, the contemporary success of the sports metaphor in enterprises and in public organizations.

Assume, however, that Ehrenberg is right and that use of the sports metaphor in organizations is twenty years old. This is the adult age, some will say. It is the age of first appraisals, others will think, among them the author.

Organizations the Sports Way

Today's organizations make many references to the universe of sports. Even organizations that do not, strictly speaking, have sports-related business activities do so. Sports are often used as a theme in advertisement and in job announcement columns. They are also a popular object of sponsoring operations. Sports celebrities are regularly hired for in-store promotions, and for other operations of many kinds intended to establish positive business relationships with customers. Some companies recruit famous players so as to acquire a share of their fame, while others organize sports events, such as mountain climbing, for their employees. Organizations explicitly place themselves in situations of apprenticeship toward the universe of sports, such as when successful trainers are hired to pass on to managers their experience in motivation techniques,[2] when ex-coaches become strategy consultants,[3] or when renowned athletes are solicited to participate in conferences to reveal there the secrets of their successful careers.[4]

One should note that such references to sport can be found in all types of organizations. Following the lead of privately run companies, public organizations and local communities have also gone into sports recently. As a result, one can encounter in a transatlantic boat race the somewhat surrealistic spectacle of one region competing board to board with a brand of sausages or a credit card.

It has become current to speak of organizations using phrases and concepts borrowed directly from the universe of sports. One can hear organizational actors, for example, using sports terms to depict their activity, such as a consultant advising companies to "establish a training program as quickly as possible (if you do not already have one going)";[5] or a stockbroker describing as "training" the reading he does of the daily newspaper every morning before arriving at work;[6] or, again, a marketing manager expressing why she is positive about a television advertisement campaign by saying that "the personnel in a store sometimes feel proud when they see their product shown on TV. They feel they are in the top league";[7] or a municipal director of finance comparing a tendering process to "a race."[8]

Journalists, likewise, frequently supplement their discourse with references derived from the sports arena, such as when an influential stock exchange journalist describes the lengthy bargaining that took place between the Swedish state and private banks in the aftermath of the Swedish financial crisis of 1992 as a match; giving a point for each good strike, he evaluates the preliminary results of bargaining as corresponding to a score of 3 to 1 at half time and qualifies in this way the parties' skills in defending their positions.[9]

Writers within management too refer to sports to present their ideas. Rosabeth Moss Kanter (1989), for example, chooses "Mastering the Challenges of Strategy, Management and Careers in the 1990s" as the subtitle of her book, using the theme of the "corporate Olympics" as one of her major red threads of thought. To her "the global economy in which American business now operates is like a corporate Olympics—a series of games played all over the world with international as well as domestic competitors" (ibid., 18). Chapter 2 is called "Getting in Shape for the Contest: The Response," chapter 8: "Swimming in Newstream: Mastering Innovation Dilemmas," and chapter 11: "From Climbing to Hopping: The Contingent Job and the Post-Entrepreneurial Career," Further she speaks of the "business athlete" (ibid., 361) to describe the transformation of U.S. enterprises or of "home team and home-field advantage" (ibid., 372), in describing the advantage American companies have with such a large home market as theirs. Whatever message the book conveys, the sports metaphor is a part of it. Similarly, one can use American football and rugby in comparing American and English innovation,[10] or make use of football to describe the process of investment calculation.[11]

Writings about sports and about organizations have become increasingly similar in their approach. This is illustrated by the introduction to the book *Red Gold-Peak Performance Techniques of the Russian and*

East-German Olympic Victors. The book was written by the former "motivational psychologist for the USSR Olympic team," Grigori Raiport (1990). Raiport's book intends to reveal, from the inside, the principles of the psychological preparation of East German and Soviet athletes. In its inspiration, the book strongly reminds one of William G. Ouchi's (1981) best-seller, *Theory Z*, and the latter's depiction of the principles of Japanese management. Both books, Raiport's and Ouchi's, each written in its field, aim at unveiling for an American audience the secret keys to success of the United States' most successful competitor. The interpenetration of their influences does not end there. The preface to Raiport's book is written by Spencer Johnson, co-author of *The One Minute Manager* (Blanchard and Johnson 1982), a management best-seller. There is little surprise that the resemblance between the universe of sports and that of organizations is precisely what his preface deals with:

> Interest in peak performance has in recent years moved from the athletic fields to the workplace—especially as it relates to the key positions of manager and CEO.
>
> Peak-performance techniques, once the secret province of some professional and Olympic coaches and top Soviet athletes, increasingly are being explored in articles, books, and on television.
>
> From one-minute managers to celebrated pumpers of iron, from the Olympic playing fields, where gold medals are awarded, to the boardrooms of America's largest corporations, where another kind of gold is the reward, the passion for peak performance has become a national priority.
>
> Why? Because America, once the undisputed dominant force in international athletics and business, is now placing an increasingly distant second or worse. (Johnson in Raiport 1990:xi)

The message is clear: directors in boardrooms and athletes on sports fields alike have to dive into competition, focus on peak performance, learn from one's competitors, and, regard the search for performance as a "national priority." That one is dealing with sports or with an organization is immaterial in this regard.

What all these examples illustrate is the same set of ideas, namely, that what is valid on the track is valid on the shop floor or in the office, that one can legitimately deal with organizations as if they were some sort of athletes, and that sports can be regarded as a sort of model of behavior to which organizations and their members can aspire.

One should note that it is not only organizations that borrow from sports, but the reverse is true as well, that sports borrow intensively from economic organizations. Athletes become business people, sports clubs become enterprises, and sports authorities become increasingly bureaucratized (Andersson 1989). Sports have become a commodity (Sage 1990:104; Duncan and Brummett 1987:174; Duncan and Brummett 1989:199). Vocabulary, ideas, and concepts come to be used as often in the one context as in the other. Ways of seeing things circulate freely between them. Organizations and sports have become each other's references. The former's themes become the latter's and vice versa . They imitate each other. We are witnessing the universes of sports and economic organizations merging and their ways of seeing, thinking, and speaking becoming increasingly exchangeable and cognate.

The military and the churches have long served as a privileged metaphorical reference for private as well as public organizations, mostly because of their much admired ability to organize and structure activities, balance individual against collective commitments, accomplish their goals, and achieve a durable longevity (Boyer and Equilibrey 1990:55). What we are currently witnessing is the installation of sports as one of the leading metaphors in organizations. Sport is now taking a place partly alongside and partly in place of these traditional metaphors in providing points of reference and orientation for organizations. This has already gone quite far. References to sports are not necessarily understood any longer as metaphorical, the metaphor seeming more and more frequently to be taken in a literal manner, as if it were "for real" that organizations are athletes on the track or on the field, which is a form of banalization and naturalization of the metaphor.

As this occurs, organizations and their members are increasingly pressured to view themselves as athletes and to behave accordingly. Think of the chief police inspector in the film *Falling Down* who practices his boxing moves while lecturing a subordinate he deems not sufficiently possessed of a fighting spirit.[12] Think, likewise, of the former chairman of the board of the Volvo group, Pehr G. Gyllenhammar, agitating for equal opportunity by praising horse riding as "one of the few sports where women and men, and girls and boys, have equal chances," adding "let sport show the way to a society of equality of the sexes."[13] In both cases, these are executives who explicitly make a detour through sports to express how they wish their subordinates and their organizations to behave. More generally, as Jackall (1988:53) observes, sports references are used to commit employees to the official reality as if it were the only one.

Employees are invited to take care of their bodies at the corporate gym center or at a local fitness center (at discounted fares). Some companies and administrations have created the possibility for personnel of training regularly during paid working hours. Some even take their employees off on wilderness experiences or to bungee-jumping sessions. Smoking is of course widely discouraged. Participating in a new mode of modeling the body of organizational members (Bialot 1987:58), sports take part in the corporate search for an ever more efficient use of corporal and corporate resources.

It is felt that ideally the formal organization and the bodies on the job should be as slim and performant as the bodies of athletes in training . The same concern for fitness animates both corporate goals and people engaged in training work. The search for body excellence glides back and forth in perfect style between the office and the training bench. The ideal qualities of the organization and its members are modeled on those of the athlete.

What is involved here is that organizations try to get their members, with the open assent of public health and industrial hygiene authorities, to endorse a sports-like view of themselves, that they try to have their employees adopt a self-image of have-to-be athletes. A remodeling of their very persons, and a manipulation of their desires and of their representation of themselves is aimed at, a representation that is expected to align itself with the canons of sports. In the process, sports categories such as competition, fighting spirit, fair play, winning combinations of individual and collective talents, self-induced suffering or sacrifice and performance, of course, are ascribed to what is assumed to be the imagined efficient worker of the 1990s. Use of the sports metaphor, as Boland (1996) observed, makes it perfectly legitimate to employ the causal analysis of agency in discussing and attributing merits and rewards to organizations and their actors.

To summarize, contemporary organizations are not only eager to hear tales from the track and are prompt at using them for their own needs, but are also on their way to endorsing much of the imaginary elements of sports. This endorsement is a matter of fascination, a fascination built on the assumption that what is valid for sports is also valid for organizations. Fascinated by sports, organizations aspire to transform their members into top performing athletes by infusing them with the themes, values, attitudes, and ways of thinking of the elite in sports.

Motifs of the Fascination of Organizations for Sports

"Yet why are organizations so interested in sports ?" one could ask. The fascination of organizations for sports is indeed in itself fascinating. To meet this fascination, here are a few cursory propositions concerning why organizations do find sports so alluring. These propositions deal with the success of sports in mass media, with the aesthetic strength of sports, and with the capacity of sports to provide a model of efficacy. Other aspects of sports could well be taken up, for example, the flaunted masculinity of sports. However, the aim is not to present a comprehensive analysis of this fascination. Rather, it is to be indexical and to indicate which sorts of mechanisms are at work when organizations let themselves be invaded by the imagery of sports.

Modern sports enjoy considerable audience and media success. As a consequence of this, the different categories of sports are now intelligible to most people. One can consider today that the rules governing, for example, off-side in football and false start in track are a sort of universal knowledge. In this sense, sport has become a universal language, and this universality has not passed unnoticed to organizations with international activities. Sports and the internationalization of economic exchange, both global phenomena, could not avoid meeting. What makes sport particularly interesting for organizations in this context is that it has achieved a worldwide spread, while managing to respect various local features. The origin of sports endeavors in a local community is still a major feature of modern sports, partly because the practice of certain sports is bound to specific geographic areas (e.g., cricket, baseball, or rugby), partly because some nations have well-established traditions of their own within a sports discipline (compare, for example, Brazilian and German football), and partly because the geographic origin of athletes or teams is over-signified and is repeatedly emphasized. Sports have shown a remarkable capacity for articulating both globalness and localness. This could not have been ignored by organizations faced with the challenge of simultaneously accommodating cosmopolitanism and multiculturalism.

Sports is also endowed with a multifaceted aesthetic strength (Lowe 1977), and that too makes it attractive to organizations. Through its elements of drama and tragedy, it is close to theater. Its symbolic and aesthetic uses of movement remind one of dance or mime. Its proclivity toward extreme situations recalls the world of the circus. Its capacity of playing with color and form reminds one of the art of painting, and its tridimensional staging of the body reminds one of statuary. It has the epic breath of literature and it stages movement as cinema does. With the possible exception of music, the aesthetics of sports gets in on all forms of Western art. Sports, moreover, have a remarkable capacity of appealing to a wide range of aesthetic tastes. An imaginary gallery, for example, could display romanticism dealing with defeat, futurism with movement, (hyper)realism with banality in close shots, expressionism with effort, pop art with supporters, and minimalism with the perfect gesture of the winning throw, the latter taking up again in this way Greek tradition of art patterns. Furthermore, the aesthetics of sports is one of immediate visualization fitting press and television techniques particularly well, and television has succeeded in imposing its own conventions, for example, its rigid time segmentation, on all the sports events that it mediates (Duncan and Brummett 1987:175). These are all sufficient motifs for an organization to try to appropriate for itself the aesthetic qualities of sports just as it has tried to appropriate for itself the symbolic qualities of culture (see Petersson 1988). The pureness of competition, the beauty of a gesture, and the happiness of a champion are potent means by which an organization can attempt to acquire an extended legitimacy in the eyes of its members, who are caught up in the dullness of the daily routines of their purposeful actions.

Still, the most important single reason for the seduction of organizations that sports enjoys is surely its capacity to stand as a model of efficacy. This occurs through the narrowing of the universe of sports to that of champions. Nonwinning protagonists hardly matter: "We are the champions, No time for losers" as the musical group Queen sings.[14] Champions are indeed heralds of the idea of efficacy; they embody it; they are its physical representation. Their bodies and their moves tend to be taken as normative models of efficient use of the body (Brohm 1992:342). Their victories, which are the sign of their being champions, are also signs of their superior ability to attain goals they set. Champions are by definition those of all participants who are best at attaining these goals. Since participants are assumed to be equal, champions are therefore, *by definition*, those most efficient in their sports discipline. No wonder then that organizations wish to observe, follow, hire, interrogate, and listen to them: organizations are eager to appropriate for themselves the qualities these heroes supposedly possess. Organizations wish to achieve this coveted state of efficacy that champions have attained. Their fascination with sports is a quest, and champions represent the paradigm of the philosophical stone that is the object of this quest.

A communicative capacity, an aesthetic potential and an ability to stand for perfect efficacy are only a few of the motifs that make sports so alluring for organizations. They are elements in the broader dynamics that have led organizations to compare their products and leaders to champions, to hire sports people and to try to get their members to view themselves as athletes, and to speak of themselves using sports vocabulary, references, values, norms, or mental representations.

The examples above illustrate how sport has become a part of the language that organizations use to describe and construct themselves. To say that a leader or a product is a market champion is a very specific way of qualifying what one is speaking of. Likewise, to say that a department is a team, having a sports team in mind as a model, is a very specific way of indicating how this team is to view itself and to act. This specificity is surely partly that of the organization itself. Yet, it also refers in part to how sports have traditionally defined a champion or a team. To understand these two words or notions, one has to go back to their original context, that of sports, and trace their evolution back there, unfolding the content they possess. This is equally true of the notion of performance, the success of which in recent years in an organizational context cannot be totally isolated from the supremacy it has acquired in sports during the present century.

The Signature of Modern *Agon*

Let us now, in exploring performance stories in sports and organizational contexts, bring together the centrality of performance in modern sports, as featured in the previous chapter, and the fascination modern sports exerts on organizations, as depicted above.

How performance stories are constructed in various contexts will be contrasted. The aim here is not, as with a mere comparison, to assess whether sports performance is more of something A and less of something B than organizational performance is. Its purpose is, instead, to explore the meanings attached to performance, to unfold which notions are set into motion by a discourse on performance, and to reveal how these notions relate to each other and constitute the conceptual web that surrounds the notion of performance.

The discussion is conceived as follows. Taking advantage of the readability of the notion in sports, sports performance is given the function of a red thread. Interesting points are first identified and examined in a sports context, and immediately after that, in an organizational context, the sports context serving as a background to discussion of the organizational context. Sports performance is used, in other words, as a heuristic detour to the study of organizational performance. This design, incidentally, enables one to appraise point-for-point how the notion varies or remains the same when one moves from one context to another, and to gain insight into the degree of contextuality of the notion.

The approach employed in this chapter can be viewed as a hybrid of traditional qualitative comparisons (e.g., Ragin 1987), on the one hand, and methods used in cultural studies (e.g., Denzin 1992), on the other. From qualitative comparisons, the ideas have been taken of using material from at least two different contexts, of the making of comparisons being a potent way of interpreting and making sense, and of its being necessary to be sensitive to the idiosyncrasies of all the elements compared. From cultural studies, the ideas have been taken of studying both what is taken for granted and the problematic webs of significance and meaning that human beings produce and act on when doing things together, and thus of studying how subjects are constructed by stories that are told, in particular stories, produced by and within popular culture (Denzin 1992:73–91).

Competition

Observers of sports agree on one point: that in modern times, ever-increasing importance has been assigned to competition (e.g., Michener 1976:420; Bouet 1968:37), competition having become the mainspring of modern sports (e.g., Patriksson 1982:15; Engström 1989:83; Ehrenberg 1991; Brohm 1992:141). Modern sports has increasingly been focused on competition.

The idea of sports competition has been so successful that it has been promulgated as being a specific form of interhuman relationship (Bouet 1968:45). Today, it is not only in sports that this form of relationship has been established as a norm. Rather, in as diverse fields as education, consumption, and organizational life, competition has been adopted as a desirable way of behaving, indeed as a model of human interaction (Ehrenberg 1991).

A sports performance can only occur in a competitive context, not because competition is some overpowering incentive to effort and therefore to performance, but because competition is where results are measured. Competition is where officials are, and thus where a result can be acknowledged. One has to enter competition, or stage one's own competition, if one is to establish a performance. Accordingly, painstaking efforts are made in sports to isolate the sports arena from external contingencies, to foresee all possible developments, to prevent any bypassing of existing regulations, and on the whole to provide a maximum guarantee of equal opportunity of success to all participants. Sports competition, as a result, is impeccable. It is as close as one can come to ideal competition, and it is because sports competition is so impeccable that the notion of performance appears as so consummate in sports.

The crux of the matter is that competition between organizations is far from being that perfect.[15] It is only in the rarefied world of pure competition that no individual participant is able to influence how competition unfolds, that all participants pursue exactly the same goal, that all have access to the same technology, that all are informed without cost of the position of every other competitor, and that on all occasions all participants compete against all.[16] In the mundane world of business, organizational actors enact their environment, develop agendas of their own, build and encounter privileged access to technology, actively give shape to information and search for it (while dreaming of information that is impossible to acquire). The rivals whom they meet are a heterogeneous and shifting population of competitors, some of them involved in more than one arena at a given time and others not even consciously competing in the arena in question. Not to mention public organizations in which the idea of competition is perceived as being anything from redemption of the sector, to managerial fashion, to a form of political (in)correctness.

One can be tempted, therefore, to make competition between organizations resemble competition between athletes. This is what Konkurrensverket, the Swedish Competition Authority,[17] does in the business world. In one of its brochures on the new Swedish legislation on competition one can read, for example:

There will be no record if she has overstepped the board.

Obviously not.

The world of sport is carefully regulated. Action is taken against any overstepping of the rules. If there is to be any point to competing, the same rules must apply to all. Competition is to be under equal conditions for all. This is what spectators pay to watch.

The same idea is the basis for the new Swedish law on competition which has applied since July 1, 1993 and will apply in the coming EES agreement.

There are thus strong reasons for the business and the public sector to take a critical look at old agreements and old ways of doing things. It can cost more than is gained to overstep the rules.

What it can cost is record high!

(Konkurrensverket 1993a:9; translation Robert Goldsmith)

(The text is on the right-hand page, facing a picture on the left of a women athlete landing in the jumping pit. The picture is taken from the front, as a close shot, black and white, reproduced full page).

In such a text, sports is turned from a freely adopted source of mimetic inspiration for some into something imposed on all. Sports is presented here as a compulsory metaphor—organizations have to view themselves as sports competitors do—promises being made of record fines to recalcitrants. Sports are thus imposed upon the viewer as a normative referential model, being elevated, in the process, to the dignity of a principle of law or to that of a philosophical principle upon which legislators and judges base the law they create. The legitimacy of sports is enlarged in proportion to this. Implicitly, the principle *ignorantia legis neminem excusat*—ignorance of the law excuses nobody—is expanded to encompass sports.

What is striking is that it is not sports in all their richness, but sports in a reduced and idealized form, that are celebrated in this way. Konkurrensverket's text reduces sports to sports for the elite, and sports for the elite to the establishing of records. The role of rules is reduced to being the basis for punishment, the fact that they are constitutive elements of all sports disciplines being ignored. It is not only because she will step over the line that her jump will not be a record; it will also not be a record if she jumps too short, if she is simply training, if she has taken prohibited substances, if the wind is too strong, if no official attends to her jump, if it is her fourth try that day, if she has not passed the biological tests of femininity, or if she is not a member of the Swedish federation of athletics. Sport is a comprehensive institution, but the text above ignores that point. It ignores much of what—from the schedule of meets, matches, and competitions to the training techniques employed, not to mention the individual or financial interests involved—has a direct impact on how and when records are set. Konkurrensverket's text does not allude at all to the complexity of sport. As in many other cases of organizational reference to sports, it is an idealized form of sports that is referred to. It is a reference that ignores audience violence, doping, elitism, and corruption. Obviously, this is because the reference to sport functions better when sport has been weeded out of its local contingencies, detached from the particularities of each discipline and separated from its negative features. The reference to sport is an issue of image. It matters that the image is a good one.

Notwithstanding the simplism of the image of sports employed, the text presents sports as a model of competition and a model of performance for organizations. It displays a caricature of sports, yet it demands that organizations view themselves in keeping with it and, what is more, that they behave accordingly. Readers are assumed to spontaneously tune themselves in on the very specific view that the authority in question entertains of sports. They are likewise assumed by the same authority to spontaneously accept a reforming of their conceptions of organizational competition in this way. How this is to happen is not taken up, even though "record-high" penalties are pending for those who do not comply with this injunction.

Aligning organizational competition and sports competition, as Konkurrensverket suggests, however, is not the most common way of dealing with the problems caused by the imperfection of competition between organizations. Most scholars interested in organizational performance prefer instead to address the issue by focusing on listed companies (see reviews by Boyd 1991; Datta et al. 1991; Pearce et al. 1987). Various factors contribute to this choice. For one thing, the economic importance of listed companies is significant. Significant too is the adequacy of publicly available financial information, both to the traditional interest of performance studies for financial indicators (Venkatraman and Ramanujam 1986), and to the use of quantitative methodologies. In addition to these social and technical arguments, moreover, listed companies seem particularly suitable to serve as samples for performance studies because their results are determined in an arena that can be regarded as the best proxy of pure competition available. Their results can therefore be considered as "hard" or "objective" information compared with what self-evaluation, for example, can produce. Conversely, the latter type of information can at best represent "reasonable substitutes" for the former, to use Covin's (1991:448) way of putting it.

Through their preference for listed companies, scholars validate the idea that perfect, or at least nearly perfect, conditions of competition are necessary for a discourse on performance. The features of the competitive conditions under which a result is achieved appear, therefore, to have a decisive impact on the possibility of speaking of performance. Conditions of competition have to be flawless if one is to be in a position to speak of performance in a manner that makes sense.

In terms of formal mathematical logic, competition represents a necessary though not sufficient condition for performance. As a result, advocacy of use of the notion of performance in an organizational context tends to imply the advocacy of better and more intensive conditions of competition. The two discourses involving advocacy overlap and mutually support each other. We have seen above how this is true of modern sports, equally focused as they are on competition and on performance. Let me now present three examples from an organizational context.

- The Swedish Authority for Competition, so desirous of inducing all organizations to view themselves as athletes, is just as intensively eager to point out: (1) that Swedish kindergartens can be made more (cost) efficient through an intensification of competition; (2) that municipalities should be more active in introducing competition in the sectors where they thus far have had a monopoly; (3) that kindergartens should be organized as result centers; and (4) that kindergartens should make greater efforts, as all municipal services should, to account for their (cost) performance (Konkurrensverket 1993b:7).[18]
- Similarly, much of the reforms aimed at making the British public sector more efficient involved both reinforcing competition (e.g., compulsory competitive tendering) and introducing performance reviews (e.g., value-for-money audits) (Politt 1993:50).
- Likewise, in the United States the National Performance Review Commission, presided over by Vice President Gore, suggested in September 1993 making government work better and cost less through introducing market dynamics and thus competition into the administration, the Democratic Congress passing in July 1993 the Government Performance and Results Act requiring that at least ten federal agencies launch three-year pilot projects to develop annual performance plans (Gore 1993).

In each of the three countries, Sweden, Britain, and the United States, the same voices and the same arguments can be heard advocating performance and competition. In a self-sustaining loop, competition is advocated so as to improve performance, while performance is taken as a sign of well-functioning competition. The two discourses become so intermingled that they melt into one.

To preserve their theoretical coherence, organizational performance studies, in summary, have to be carried out in well-functioning, competitive environments. Being rather close *in practice* to good—read pure—conditions of competition is a necessity for anyone who wants to speak of performance. Thus, propagating the idea of performance tends to mean advocating better conditions of competition, and vice versa.

Comparisons

One of the functions of competition is to permit a comparison of participants. The other way around, comparisons can be regarded as abstract substitutes for competitions. Admittedly, comparisons do not allow immediate and mutual adjustments in the behavior of the competitors to be made. Likewise, comparisons are less dynamic than competition is in immediately sanctioning wrong moves. Similarly, they can hardly equal competition's dramatic character. Yet comparisons also possess some advantages over competition. Comparisons are free from many material contingencies that pertain to competition: for example, one can stage comparisons across different periods of time or across national borders that no one can cross. Moreover, in contrast to competition, the list of participants in comparisons knows virtually no limit.

In an organizational context, where competition, as already indicated, is usually under far from perfect conditions, comparison is a common way of dealing with performance. Various forms of comparison may be involved. One can compare organizations with organizations or parts of organizations with parts of organizations. One can compare organizations with themselves over time. One can also compare organizations with standards. Frequently, one compares achievements to pre-set objectives or goals.

It is not just any sort of organizations that are compared. Comparisons usually involve samples of organizations, organizations being selected on the basis of their activity, their size, the country in which they are located (e.g., Hitchens and O'Farell 1988), or any other set of discriminating features (for examples of reviews, see Boyd, 1991; Datta et al. 1991). Such a segmentation reminds one of the segmentation made in sport, based upon sex, age or weight. The rationale behind sampling is to limit differences between the organizations that are compared so that one is able to study how just one, two, or three specific features of the organizations are related to performance, a classic version of causal analysis.

If differences cannot be avoided, however, or are to be kept, one might just as well integrate them into the comparison. This can be done, for example, by first mapping the particular profile of each organization with point ratings and, secondly, computing performance with the help of a weighted average of the results the organization shows for each of these points (e.g., Abernethy and Stoelwinder 1991; Covin et al. 1994).

Metaphorically speaking, one can say that comparisons between organizations are ways of recreating *in vitro* competitive situations that resemble the *in vivo* situations of sports competitions. What is important then is to create good conditions of comparisons, if possible to create as good conditions as those of sports competitions. The conditions of comparison are, in this respect, determinant for how relevant it will be to speak of performance.

Commensurability

Sports competition rests on the possibility of agents (individuals, clubs, nations, and organizations or political systems as well) opposing each other on the homogeneous basis of their accomplishment of identical tasks (from Brohm 1992:146). Competition thus supposes some form of homogeneity between contestants. Still, competition is not war. Rather, it presumes that the contestants can be framed within similar assumptions, for example, regarding rules and goals. It assumes that contestants share certain values. This can be achieved through a contract passed between the contestants, or through comparison. What matters is that one manages to align agents who can be assumed to have something in common. Competition assumes similarity as much as opposition. Bouet (1968:52) says that competition associates positive sociality—cooperation toward a common activity—with negative sociality—struggle. Competitions and comparisons are systems of opposition, though opposition that is framed within the principle of similarity. Competition requires as much likeness and collaboration as it does differences and oppositions.

Commensurability has to be regarded then as one of the basic principles of competition and of comparison. Anything will do to stage a
competition or a comparison, as long as some feature is common to two
or more agents. Sports competition is usually organized around features
of speed, height, or strength, while organizational comparisons deal instead with financial, commercial, or social features; yet, in each case,
there can be as many different competitions or comparisons as one wishes.
Commensurability is a matter of choice, and for each choice made a new
competition or comparison can be staged. For each choice, to be sure,
the nature of the competition or of the comparisons will be different, and
so will the performance.

Accordingly, commensurability emerges as one of the starting points
for the construction of performance. If commensurability conditions the
nature of competition, it conditions by that very fact the nature of performance as well. Performance depends upon more than the mere intrinsic qualities of the contestants. The choice of the features in terms of
which a competition is staged or a comparison is made surfaces as a
dramatic determinant, as more determinant than the participants' capacities themselves. Intrinsic qualities of the competitors matter, but only
insofar as the terms of the competition or comparison allow them to.
Performances are settled long before competitors are invited to display
their skills. Above all else, performances are determined by the choice of
the features in terms of which the competition or comparison is to be
articulated. Winners and losers are fingered by the competition's design
before they are nominated on the basis of their skills. One becomes a
winner first in the eyes of the competition's or comparison's designer.
The choice of strength before speed, or of economy before citizen participation, is critical to the process of who will be proclaimed best.

Performance assumes commensurability. Therefore, before it can be
regarded as an attribute of the competitor, performance must be regarded
as an attribute of the commensurability that underlies the competition or
the comparison in which it is to be produced. Accordingly, performance
is as much produced by the system of shared features that commensurability assumes as by the system of opposition that competition assumes.

Measurement

Commensurability expresses the idea that two agents have a feature in
common that can be measured. Yet, until measurement is carried out,

commensurability is merely virtual: it is a potential only. Commensurability is a potential that has to be activated by measurement. Measurement is what gives expression to the between-agents similitude that commensurability assumes. Measurement is also what gives expression to the differences between these agents. In this respect, measurement is what gives expression to the game of differences and similitudes that is to be found in competition and comparisons.

More generally, measurement is what enables passage from an act or a situation into a sign, such as a rating or a number. In mathematical terms, measurement is a projection in meaning that an n-dimension vector expresses through a p-dimension vector, with p being inferior to n. In literary terms, measurement is an operation of translation. It expresses something through the intermediary of something else. A series of actions, for example, is expressed by a figure—in ice skating, for example—or a situation is represented by a code—for example, a rating of a credit institute.

As indicated by both metaphors above, the mathematical and the literary one, measuring also involves losing information. Some information will be lost in projections as well as in translations. A score is never as rich as a match that ended with a score. Yet measuring is not simply loss. It also permits expression to occur. For performance, being measured means the beginning of its existence. Through providing performance with signs, thanks to which it can be told, measurement provides performance with a means of existence. The actualization of the potential contained in commensurability is also the actualization of the potential of an action which is to be regarded as a performance. It is only when it can be told that a performance can start to be one.

However, the means of existence that measurement provides performance with are quite limited. First, they are limited to what a figure or a rating can say. Regardless of how popular figures can be in our societies, their expressive capacities are quite restricted. Figures provide precision, reliability, or objectivity; they permit multiple computations; and they are easy to translate from one language into another, along with other qualities. Still, in many cases they are much less telling than images, sounds, verbal descriptions, and reconstructions. Put in banal terms, as a means of expression, figures can be rather good and they can also be rather poor, depending upon what is to be said. Measurement provides performance then with a means of expression and thus of existence, but these means are bound to the limited expressive capacities that figures have as rhetorical devices.

Second, the means of expression that measurement provides performance with are limited by the capacities of the metrological techniques employed. This argument is less relevant in sports, however, where a discipline exists only if an adequate metrology exists—who could imagine a sports discipline in which results would be impossible to measure?—than in an organizational context in which activities exist that are particularly resistant to measurement. The more sophisticated and adequate metrology techniques are, the richer the means available are for the expression of performance. (Chapter 5 will discuss at some length how measurement imprints its technical, social, and narrative marks upon what organizational performance is said to be.)

Measurement, which follows directly from the idea of commensurability in that it makes its virtual potential active, is thus an important step in the establishing of performance stories. It is what stops the clock, gets the acting or the situation to come to a standstill, and, through a translation or projection, endows performance with signs that make its expression possible. At the same time, measurement is what imprisons performance within the over-rigid framework of a rhetoric of figures and confines it within the limited capacities of the metrology available, as if it would immediately take back much of the life it has just granted performance, thus emphasizing the result dimension of performance to the detriment of the process one.

Hierarchy of Achievements

In most areas of social life, hierarchy has been identified, denounced, and subjected to continual criticism. Political life, labor relationships, parent-child relationships, fashion, and patterns of cultural consumption are only a few of the many examples one can name in which the idea of hierarchy has been, if not eradicated, at least seriously challenged in its legitimacy, and therefore partly discarded as old-fashioned—not the least by the revolts of the 1960s and the radical criticisms of the 1970s. Yet not in sport. The questioning of the idea of hierarchy that has characterized the evolution of Western democracies during the last two hundred years does not seem to have reached it. Sports, Asplund says (1989:139), have remained attached to a traditional view of the world in which, on the one hand, everyone has a place of one's own and, on the other hand, each place is occupied by someone (even though, at the same time, every sport competition is a delightful challenge to the order previous to the contest and is therefore a permanent questioning of this order [Asplund 1987:30]; sports hierarchies are always temporary). In sports, hierarchy is as legitimate as it is in the most perfect Darwinist model, where the fittest is at the top and the masses are below. Sports stands, with the military with which it shares the use of such symbols as anthems, flags, and medals, as one of the most prominent vectors of hierarchic thinking in our societies.

One can wonder how interesting for organizations this recurrent presence of hierarchy in sports is. I cannot imagine the viability of the hierarchy found in sports being something that has passed unnoticed to those who make use of the sports metaphor in organizations: scores, rankings, and championships *are* modern sports. I believe sports are a convenient way of reintroducing hierarchy into the corporation. It is a way of voicing hierarchy in a new manner, a way for organizations to take hierarchy back from the social disgrace into which it has fallen, and of presenting it, dressed in some Emperor's New Clothes, to the corporate public of the 1990s so as to establish a new form of meritocracy. Addressing this question in more detail would require a research project of its own that cannot be carried out or presented here. An assumption could be that when referring to sport, organizations are casting loving sidelong glances to a subculture in which the idea of hierarchy is as unchallenged as it possibly may be toward the end of the twentieth century. If this was to hold, it would be an interesting way of reformulating the interest of contemporary organizations in modern sports.

At any rate, the hierarchy that sport produces is that of performance. Once measured, the results of the participants in a competition can be compared to one another and ordered. Through looking at results in comparative terms, those of performance, a distinction between participants can be created. Performance discerns high and low performers. This is not fortuitous. Performance aims at making differences. Performance is a discriminating device. In sports, this discriminating device is ordinal, attributing a rank to every competitor. It is cardinal as well, attributing a measure to each feat. As such, it represents a very sophisticated discriminating process that takes place in sports, so sophisticated that it might indeed be difficult to find its match in an organizational context. In contrast to sports, where the ends and the criteria of success are given, the results of organizational action are decidedly ambiguous.

Organizational outputs are usually diverse and mingle with each other in ways that make it difficult to tell one from another. Think of companies looking simultaneously for short-term financial results and long-term commercial achievements. Think, likewise, of kindergartens (taking care of children, educating them, promoting playfulness) or the correctional system (punishing crime and preparing for the social rehabilitation of the inmates), which serve divergent goals simultaneously and produce complex patterns of results. Think, again, of organizations in which various constituencies hold different ideological standpoints that result in diverging views on what the organization's mission is, with the result that the criteria for performance differ (Kanter and Summer 1987). Placing outputs or organizations in hierarchical order in such cases is not only difficult, but also unavoidably left to personal choices.

As mentioned earlier in the discussion on commensurability, any comparison is only one of many. Thus, results of any organizational ranking are only one of many that are possible. A comparison is based on a definition of which accomplishments count and which do not. All that fails to meet the criteria of performance, and all that fails to be registered by the measurement techniques, falls into oblivion. This can be true of bravery and of elegance, and it can be true of meanness as well. Therefore, any rank order is discretionary, depending upon the choice of return on investment to return on sales, or to growth of profit rate. While agreement regarding the criteria exists in sports, the determination of criteria in organizational contexts is open to organizational politics.

The arbitrary character of performance hierarchies has a different status in sports, though, than in an organizational context. This is why a political reading of the use of the sports metaphor in organizational settings is really needed. Sports can absorb arbitrariness thanks to their game dimension. One who accepts participating in or watching a sports contest implicitly accepts that behaviors be judged by particular rules during a given period of time and that the results of these behaviors be endowed with the character given them by these rules. The game dimension buffers sports from criticisms one could potentially direct at them in the name of arbitrariness.

Such is not the case in organizational contexts, however. Organizations, for their part, do not deal with some well-identified game parentheses in our lives, but with our very existence. What regulates organizational behavior and performance has a direct impact on our lives. Closing down a hospital, developing new products, modifying the routes of a local bus company or investing in a new plant are performance-motivated decisions that directly affect our lives and do so in a decisive manner. These are decisions of consequence for where and how people can live. This is why, since what can be regarded as the performance of an organization can be of major significance for our daily lives, it is important to not consider performance as an objective and indisputable feature of an organization. The social consequences of how performance is defined make it crucial to emphasize its dimension of social construction and to debunk its arbitrariness. This is indeed the main reason why I believe a critical questioning of the mechanisms and assumptions behind discourses on organizational performance is important and is worthy of attention.

Independent of their arbitrariness, however, performance hierarchies are potent expressions of an agent's identity. Performance enters into the ontology of the agents involved and becomes a constitutive element in their social identity. This is an individualist identity, even for a team which is then the individual. A performance is always the performance of someone. Singling out individuals is a counterpart to ranking them. Figures that stand for performance are always matched by the name of the performing agent. Names and figures are advertised in parallel. Medals celebrating a performance are ceremoniously placed around the athletes' neck in an acknowledgment by the community of the symbolic osmosis of the performer and the performance. The raising of the flag and the playing of the anthem underline the national origin of the athlete. Performance identifies the performer and vice versa. It is a means of recognition and a means of constituting the individual. It is a part of the self of the athlete or the organization. Performance contributes to the logic of individual identity that, whether in fashion or politics, crosses contemporary Western societies (Lipovietski 1987).

As exemplified by champions—heralds of the idea of efficacy—performance provides an identity organized around the ideas of efficiency and effectiveness, one that is spun around the ability to pursue and achieve goals. It is a disciplined identity, too, the discipline nesting itself into the athlete's subjectivity. It is a discipline of the self as well as a self-discipline, and it is a discipline that imprints itself in her or his body through drills, exercises, regular movement, increasing loads, increased repetitions, toughened tasks, and pyramidal training plans. As a goal and an effect of this discipline, it is an identity of normalization that is enforced, an identity removed from social and psychological irregularities, which thus produces useful and docile bodies and subjects. It is a linguistic discipline, too, one that prescribes adequate and prohibits nonadequate terminology for characterizing athletes. As a result, it is an identity of subjects—in the double sense of one's being subjected to external control as well as being (self-) reflected upon—of an economy of endless performance enhancements in which one can always regret not having done better (Heikkala 1993).

It is also an identity by numbers. Athletes are their own ranking and companies are their own results. Numbers enable performance to enjoy, as a means of identification, an extreme intelligibility. Numbers stand for objectivity. They are easily advertised and easily communicated. They can be commented on at length and allow endless comparisons to be made. Thanks to its quantification, performance is able to provide intelligibility in a world that otherwise remains complex and resistant to the production of meaning.

This is indeed a point of interest to performance assessment in organizations with complex and ambiguous activities. In contrast to what many others might say, I would claim that the complexity of an activity is no hindrance to performance evaluation. On the contrary, it is because an activity is complex that looking at it in terms of performance is interesting. Complexity and lack of immediate intelligibility are just what prompt an interest in performance accounts. Performance thrives on difficulty; what is obvious can hardly be dealt with in terms of performance, since obviousness undoes complexity and provides in itself for intelligibility.

The identity referred to above is also one acquired in a competitive situation. It is thus an expression of value, a new form of value. It is not value determined by work input, or trade value, or the value of usefulness, or moral value. Rather, it is a value in competition, a value that is attached to individual competitiveness, one that is a source of prestige and is independent of dynastic, clan, geographical, or class membership or belongingness. Performance indicates in a concentrated and focused manner how good or bad a given agent is in relationship to the other contestants. Performance provides a comparative and contrastable identity. It values that which can lead to victory, such as combativeness, risk

taking, capacity of enduring suffering, and also respect of rules, thor-
ough preparation, and well-formulated strategy. It is a value of excellence—but only after excellence has been reduced to victory (Autrement
1987).

At the same time, it is a precarious identity. Hierarchies are likely to
be modified at any moment. Performance belongs to an unstable world.
New champions and new star companies continually replace old ones on
both the sports and the stock market Parnassus. Few performances can
stand the test of time. Counter-performance and failure lurk at every
moment. Oblivion rapidly replaces fame. The identity granted by performance is temporary.

Once given birth to by measurement, performance is organized in hierarchies. These provide an expression of social relationships that have
been formed under the sign of competition and they provide contestants
with elements allowing them to construct their identity as contestants.
Though bound to the arbitrariness of the terms of the competition and the
possibility of measurement, performance can serve then as a measure of
the value of the performance of the participants, a form of value that is
different from traditional economic values such as exchange value and
value for use. Performance is a yardstick of success at fight, a gauge of
excellence, and more generally a measure of efficient goal achievement.
When it has been ordered in hierarchies, performance is ready to be read.

Justice

Still another notion that has close relationships with the notion of performance is that of justice. To be interesting, a sports competition has to
occur under satisfactory conditions of justice. An unfair competition (or,
for that matter, a competition with too great a difference between participants) has very limited appeal. Sports rules provide for participants to
meet, therefore, on terms as equal as possible. This does not mean that
all participants will be given identical conditions—handicaps can be introduced at times—but all will be provided with as similar a chance as
possible of winning. To be sure, one can find in the sport approach to
justice a form of institutionalized hypocrisy, since this concern for fairness
is oriented to rewarding the very differences found between participants;
similarly, as Guttmann did (1977:15), one can point out that from a historical point of view many restrictions have barred less fortunate people,

ethnic minorities, and women from participating in sports. Still, justice is regarded as a basic tenet of modern sports: everyone is to be placed at the start with a possibility to win and the differences that emerge are to emerge during the contest only, neither before nor after. At least this is the image that the world of sports has been successful in maintaining.

The apparatus for maintaining justice in sports is impressive. Rules attempt to cover all possible situations, officials are posted along the whole track, metrology techniques are as detailed as possible, and so on. The use of stimulating substances and other technical means likely to bias the terms of competition are, of course, systematically ruled out. All of this is to maintain the idea that the one who wins is a winner under the sign of fairness, and that he or she can be celebrated accordingly. Similarly, it is to maintain the signification of sports performance.

A major issue then is whether conditions of justice can be satisfied in competition in an organizational context. Think, for example, of the differences between an organization such as the Swedish post and its competitor City Mail. Drastic historical differences and legal obligations oppose two organizations that radically bend the terms of competition. Think, in the same manner, of the differences between organizations involved in textile or industrial assembling that operate in countries with radically different social laws and wage levels. In such a case, it is not simply managerial competencies that are in competition but also the respective countries' societal systems at large. In such cases, who will win the competition is mainly determined by conditions outside the reach of organizational influence so that much of the competition is settled before it even starts.[19]

Still other differences between sports and organizations relevant for this issue can be indicated. Williamson (1985), for example, insistently points out the implications of asset specificities for organizational performances. One can also mention the importance of being a first mover and the signification of size (Chandler 1990). One can discuss differences in access to the capital market and to the labor market as well. Is it reasonable then to speak of a competition between Hasselblad and Nikon? Organizations *are* different; actually, they work intensively at achieving and maintaining these differences.

Legislation tries to level these differences. Nevertheless, the regulation of company competition does far less to provide for equality between participants than sports regulations do. Legal regulations here stop at prohibiting unfair competition; they do not aim at restoring fairness. Thus, even if one can argue casuistically that athletes too are different, and may be as different as organizations are, fairness happens to actually be much more at odds in competition between organizations than in sports competition. Many more elements external to the arena are permitted to play a role in organizational than in sports contexts.

Here again, one can understand why so many performance studies deal with listed companies. (For that matter, one can observe that stock markets resemble sports in that the concern for fairness has been delegated to control bureaucracies that have the triple mission of defining the rules of the competition, keeping watch over their enforcement and punishing trespassers, and that the credibility of such bureaucracies depends upon their ability to fulfill these three roles.) One understands why so many performance studies make use of comparisons. Comparisons might be even better than real competitions at providing for fairness. They can account for the differences, for example, that one can find between organizations. It all depends upon how well they are designed.

To summarize, justice—or at least fairness—is a requirement if a discourse on performance is to be serious. This is a question not only of credibility, but of a performance claim having meaning or not. In many ways, sports have been successful in standing for an image of fairness— justified or not—required for one to legitimately speak of performance. The situation for organizations seems to be more critical. If these too are to speak of performance, and be taken seriously, they will have to find ways of showing that fairness is satisfactorily enforced.

Conclusion: Modern Agon Stories

The previous chapter featured performances as stories. What the present chapter shows is that these stories, in sports just as in organizations, are about the existence of competition, one as pure as possible, one in which justice is provided to the competitors. Performance tales tell of competitions aimed at permitting comparisons, or comparisons that are abstract competitions. They recount the production of hierarchies based on merit or abilities, allowing participants to be distinguished from each other, and either to be punished or rewarded. Performance tales are stories of hierarchies, precarious ones for that matter. The hierarchies are based upon the assumption that some form of commensurability exists between participants. This commensurability is activated through the procedure of measurement. Measurements represent key elements in these stories. They largely condition, by their technical and rhetorical features, how a performance will be expressed. Figures are prominent signs in performance stories in that they stand for the specificity of the narrative intelligibility of the stories.

Performance stories, more precisely, are about a particular form of agon brought forth in our time: modern agon. Modern agon is a universe of fair competition in which detailed regulations see to it that fairness is achieved and maintained. Within contests, actors are supposed to be involved in purposeful actions in the sense of following predetermined cascades of goals that are more or less delayed in time and more or less general in their formulation. Success is supposed to be a function of adequate planning, monitoring, and control.

In modern agon, competitions are staged to prompt excellent achievements, the motive of this excellence being efficacy. Efficacy is an all-encompassing imperative. Accordingly, modern agon is a matter of efficient behavior, that is to say, behavior that maximizes the ratio of output to input, with there being only limited roles, for example, for ethical or aesthetic aspects of these behaviors (except to the extent these can be redefined in terms of efficacy).

Somehow, moreover, modern agon encompasses the idea that it is not enough for people to be efficient, that they must also account for this efficacy to others. Modern agon achievements are not supposed to remain private matters, but should be displayed publicly. The means of communication are central in determining what is regarded as an achievement and what is not. This is where performance stories become vectors of accountability.

Modern agon's achievements also have to be assessed in terms of scientific procedures, read adequate measurements. Measurements have to be exact so that progress can be assessed with precision. Modern agon is dedicated to progress. A commitment to progress is required of all participants, who should be aiming at achievements as well as improvements. Dedication is also required of participants. Lay-abouts and free-riders are strongly discouraged. This supposes protocols of exclusions, even if the existence of these is usually kept quite discreet. Under such circumstances, top performers are embodiments of this excellence. They provide performance stories with a physical resonance.

Performance stories, on the other hand, decisively contribute to building up their identity.

Performances are modern agonetic stories. As stories, their focus on the achievements of some performers tend to turn them into moral tales about the politics of success, or into a parabola on how human progress can be ascertained through competition, provided that fairness is respected.

Saying that performances are stories does not mean that they are fictions. The veracity of stories is secured at many points so as to sustain the claim that what the stories tell does correspond to something that has really happened. In this sense, performance stories are representative efforts, where representation is to be understood as the making present in a tangible and readable manner of something that is absent. Yet, it is when made part of a story that performances become meaningful.

Claiming, in this regard, that performances are stories says that performances are products of writing and of reading, that they are textual products, or, in other words, narrative constructions. Performances are tales that are collectively scripted within the organization and are read, as stories, by a range of audiences. They are tales in the highly traditional sense of being articulated assemblings of words and figures aimed at telling in a written form a chain of events.

A corollary to this idea is that performances have no reality outside their textual manifestation. Performance is what the stories that recount it says it is. Saying that performances are stories is just another way of saying that a performance is not some intrinsic and indisputable quality of a performer but rather is something recounted about an action that this performer has accomplished. Along with accounting, about which Nelson (1993:208) said that the defining horizon of its practice is narration, or advertising, which is now regularly studied in semiotics terms (e.g., Umiker-Sebeok 1987), performances belong to the discursive practices one can find within organizations.

Performances are not just any sort of story, and it is to the exploration, analysis, and discussion of the particular type of story they represent that this work is dedicated. Bolstered by the insight gained into the study of performance in sports and in organizations, one can focus now on how specific organizations construct the story of their performances. The next chapter deals with the developing of a performance indicator set in a public library. The chapter after that studies how public libraries narrate their performances in their activity reports.

Notes

1. M. Friedman, *Capitalism and Freedom* (Chicago: University of Chicago Press), 1962.
2. E.g., when *Harvard Business Review* published an interview with Bill Walsh, "To Build a Winning Team—An Interview with Head Coach Bill Walsh," *Harvard Business Review* (January-February 1993): 110–20; and a reply by R. W. Keidel, "The Problem with Football," *Harvard Business Review* (May-June 1993): 175–76; or when Jean-Claude Perrin, coach of the French national team of pole vaulting and adviser to the winning Davis cup team, was hired by 3M-France to train sales managers, *Libération* (29 June 1993): 15.
3. E.g., Bengt Baron, 1980 Olympic champion in 100 meters backstroke, was hired by McKinsey before he became an executive at Swedish Coca-Cola; "Första steget mot toppjobb" [First Steps Toward a Top-Job], *Dagens Nyheter,* Del C (27 December 1993): 1.
4. Gunde Swan, for example, participated in the capacity of being a "multiple world and Olympic champion" in the conference *Vinnande Ledarskap—Winning Leadership*, organized by the European Foundation for Quality Management, 8–9 February 1994, Folkets Hus, Stockholm.
5. Tore Sjödin, "Mästare drabbas inte av muskelvärk" [Champions Seldom Suffer Muscular Pain], *QA Magazine* 2/93/årgång 3, p. 27; my translation.
6. Torbjörn Peterson in "Mäklare i hetluften igen" [Broker Again in Hot Air], *Dagens Nyheter,* Del C, sida 2, (5 augusti 1993).
7. Pia Skagermark in "Stort genomslag med enkla budskap" [Good Penetration with an Easy Message], *Dagens Nyheter*, Del C (24 August 1993): 8, my translation, emphasis added.
8. Original in English. In Bengt Jacobsson, *Kraftsamlingem—Politik och Företagande i parallella processer* [Coalition of Forces—Politics and Entrepreneurship in Parallel Processes] (Lund: Doxa Ekonomi), 1987.
9. Per Afrell, "Bankerna friskare men faran inte över" [Banks are Healthier, but the Risk is not Over], *Dagens Nyheter*, Del A (29 Augusti 1993): 16.
10. P. A. Clark, *Anglo-American Innovation* (Berlin: De Gruyter, 1987), 186–91.
11. D. Jansson, *Spelet kring investeringskalkyler* [The Game of Investment Calculations] (Stockholm: Norstedts, 1992), 158–60.
12. *Falling Down,* directed by Joel Schumacher, produced by Warner Bros. and Le Studio Canal, 1992.
13. "Gyllenhammar kvinnokamp" [Gyllenhammar's Women's Cause], *Dagens Nyheter*, Del A (2 September 1993): 4, translation Robert Goldsmith. P.G. Gyllenhammar is, by the way, an illustrative example of the interpenetration of the world of business and that of sport. An influential industrialist, Gyllenhammar was also president of the Swedish Equestrian Federation, a founder of the Gothenburg Scandinavium Horse Show, and one of the organizers of the first World Equestrian Games held in Stockholm in 1990.
14. Queen, "We are the Champions," song written by F. Mercury, recorded on the LP record *News of the World,* produced by Queen in 1977, distributed by Pathe Marconi/EMI Records.
15. One can note that the French language has two different terms for *competition* (English): *compétition* (French), which applies to sports, and *concurrence* (French), which applies to organizations (e.g., Ehrenberg 1991).

16. From a description of pure competition by Raymond Barre (1975:579).
17. Konkurrensverket is a Swedish state agency with the mission of promoting competition between organizations, public as well as private. It participates in the drafting of legislation, informs about competition regulations, and occasionally brings about legal actions (Konkurrensverket 1993a).
18. See Per-Arne Sundbom, "Gör Daghemmen till företag" [Turn Kindergartens into Companies], *Dagens Nyheter* (16 August 1993): A4; and Lars Farago, "Privata Daghem dyrare" [Private Kindergartens More Expensive], *Dagens Nyheter* (3 September 1993): A4, for a contradictory debate about the report in question.
19. As argued by A. Zaeringher in Jacques Richard (1989:13).

5

Activity by Numbers: Performance Indicators

When you have found a means of measurement
you have a ground for controversy,
and so it is a means of progress.

—Alfred Marshall[1]

Measurement being performance's most decisive means of existence makes it all the more necessary to pay particular attention to performance indicators. Indicators have to do with the textualization of an organization's activity, that is, the enclosing of activity within the framework of an actual text, where *text* is to be understood in the traditional (and narrow) sense of sequences of letters and figures aimed at being meaningful. Together with the next chapter, which is devoted to performance accounts, this chapter endeavors to cast light upon how an organization's activity, read as an activity, is expressed in a series of statements, which, taken together, are to be regarded as the organization's performance.

Both the chapter on performance literature and the two chapters on sports and organizations have pointed to the key role measurement plays in the performance discourse. The compulsive collection of scores, times, lengths, weights, or points, and the obsessive quest for records and champions that can be observed in sports reflects the abundant production of performance measures and the all-encompassing concern for monitoring organizations' performance, which performance literature displays. Measurement and its technology are considered here to generally be a major component in the construction of performance.

This chapter elaborates on this idea of the centrality of measurement in the discourse on performance and emphasizes how important the conditions under which performance indicators are imagined, created, and

119

brought into use are for the text of an organization's performance. The chapter is organized around a study of how a performance indicator set was developed in a public library. The chapter recounts the case of the creation of a set of performance indicators. It traces this from the first manifestations of interest in performance indicators to the creation of a performance measurement set for use as a managerial tool. In the case studied, the developing of a performance indicator set is described as a hesitating and uncertain ad-hoc assembly of various bits and pieces. Performance indicators, far from imposing themselves on their users on the basis of some unavoidable and unquestionable necessity, are described as having been developed through a process, partly contingent and partly discretionary, involving a complex of individual intentions, questions concerning social acceptance, technical feasibility and political correctness, narrative qualities, and random influences.

The aim here is to approach the construction of performance stories through considering the construction of performance indicators. The case describes how the account given of an organization's performance came about through intricate interactions of social, technical, and narrative considerations. The chapter explores the pragmatics of writing performance stories.

Studying the creation of performance indicators in a public library is a way of capturing the discourse of performance at one of the points where this discourse is emerging. Since the case depicts efforts aimed at developing what is intended as a new and different way of presenting a library's activity, it is an illustration of how considering an organization in terms of performance involves developing a specific way of considering that activity. The case provides, in this regard, an example of how the performance discourse, when reduced to performance indicators, shows the intertwining of a concern for organizational change aimed at efficiency and effectiveness, with a concern for control and accountability. The case, likewise, illustrates how speaking of performance, even without explicit reference to sports, involves searching for commensurability so as to be able to produce fair comparisons upon which to construct justifiable hierarchies of achievements. The case illustrates too how in practice, in managerialism at work, are combined the basic components of the discourse.

The chapter unfolds as follows. The first section presents the topic of performance measurement in public libraries, the specific library case, the case itself, and a discussion of the developing process. The second section discusses then the role that performance indicators play in the narration of an organization's performance.

Crafting a Set of Performance Indicators

The case describes the crafting of a set of performance indicators by particular persons in a particular organization. The focus is on the motives for and the reasoning behind these indicators being chosen. The intrinsic qualities of the indicators and their drawbacks are of lesser interest in this context and will not be considered. My aim is definitely not to establish whether what Robertsson, Norman, and the rest of the staff of the Storköping Public Library did should be considered as good or as bad managerial practice, but rather to provide an example of how an organization's performance can be constructed.

The presentation of the case opens with a prologue introducing the topics of performance measurement in public libraries generally, characteristics of the Storköping Public Library, and the statistics that were available in the library at the start of the case. Then comes a description of the case itself and of the process by which indicators were developed, and thereafter a few reflections concerning this process.

Prologue

Performance measurement in public libraries. Interest in a formal system for performance evaluation in a public library was no odd phenomenon in the late 1980s. An interest such as that at the Storköping Public Library was a genuine expression of the reconceptualization in management terms that the library world made at around this time of its traditional interest in measurement.

Library literature had accumulated a myriad of papers on the topics of performance evaluation, performance-, activity- or output measurement (see, e.g., the thousands of references that can be retrieved on these keywords from the database Library and Information Science Abstract—LISA). Hundreds of performance indicators in addition to the traditional one of circulation per inhabitant had been discussed, indicators such as exposure of the individual to documents of recorded human experience (Hamburg 1974), total contact time per potential user (Kantor 1976), user satisfaction (D'Elia and Walsh 1985), circulation per acquisition ratio (Levine 1980), and many more.[2]

Activity measurement is not simply a recent concern in the library world. In the early 1940s, for example, an investigation carried out at the Stockholm Public Library (Stockholms Folkbibliotek) aimed "to study the work load of the various library departments during the day, to provide a quantified estimation of the relative share each had of the various library tasks, and to estimate the extent to which the librarians execute clerical work" (Folke Löfgren in Ahlstedt 1952:65; my translation).

Measurements of library activities were placed at this time under the heading of library organization or of library rationalization. Using the two expressions nearly as synonyms, the Göteborg city librarian, Sigurd Möhlenbrock, for example, wrote *Rationalizing by Studying Work* (1953), *Library Organization* (1956), and *Two Studies on Organizations* (1959).

In 1960, a special committee of Swedish librarians published *Organization and Methods of Work in Public Libraries,* which, in its own words, had as its purpose "to create guidelines of general validity for an efficient and effective organization of libraries of various sizes and structures" (Organisation och arbetsmetoder vid kommunala bibliotek 1960:185; my translation).

Providing a broad review of what were regarded as modern techniques of librarianship, the latter study, which came to be known as the *1960 Rationalization Study* represented at the time the state of the art in Swedish library administration. Of particular interest for the present study is the fact that, even if the study stressed mostly the importance of time and motion measurement studies, it also pointed to the need for a library being able to account for both its performance and what this cost (ibid., 182).

The *1960 Rationalization Study* consecrated and systematized a decade of efforts at library activities quantification. It created a major stir in Sweden, and in Denmark as well, where a similar study was produced in 1964. The original study was discussed in numerous articles, and was also basically replicated 10 years later (Biblioteksarbete 1972). It established the legitimacy of systematic activity measurement and gave a decisive impulse to the topics of library statistics,[3] library budget,[4] and the rationalization of library organization.[5]

For a long period of time, however, measurement was to interest only a handful of people. This continued until at least around 1980, when it

became increasingly common to discuss a library in terms of productivity,[6] efficacy,[7] quality,[8] management by objectives,[9] control,[10] organizational change,[11] and service companies.[12] Managerialism had made its
entry into the library world, and with this an interest in performance
measurement[13] found its way into an increasing number of Swedish public libraries,[14] at least at the level of intent.[15] Accordingly, in 1989, when
the case study starts the idea of creating performance measurement for
the Storköping Public Library could definitively be regarded as lying
well within its time.

   Presentation of the Storköping Public Library. In Sweden, public libraries are municipal organizations. They are financed almost exclusively by tax money. Each of the 284 Swedish municipalities has a public
library service. The head of a library's operations, the city librarian, is
responsible to the representatives of the municipality who sit in the library committee (or its equivalent), as well as in the municipal council
and the municipal executive committee.

   The Storköping Public Library is both a municipal library system and
a county library. The municipal library system serves the municipality of
Storköping. It is run from a main library, ten library branches, a department for recorded media, a book bus, three hospital libraries, and a department for outreach librarianship in kindergartens, workplaces, and
old age care centers. The county activity is one of support to the smaller
municipal libraries of the county. The support consists mainly in providing expert help in librarianship techniques (including library management) and providing the libraries with specialized media.

   As in any large modern public library, activities at Storköping Public
Library are varied and multifaceted. Loans to the public in 1991 com-
prised 1.8 million items (mostly books, but also records, cassettes, compact discs, sheet music and scores, video films, recorded language courses,
newspapers, magazines, and microfilmed documents for genealogical
researches). The various library units received 1.4 million visits of its
clients altogether. Staff at the information desks answered some 600,000
reference questions. Several hundred hours of storytelling and puppet
theater shows were staged for children. Numerous actions for the promotion of books and of reading were staged at preschools, schools, correctional institutions, workplaces, day care centers and old age care centers.
The library also offers, and did then too, on a regular basis, cultural
programs such as exhibitions and meetings with writers.

Running expenses for 1991 amounted to 60 million Swedish crowns (a little more than 6 million ECU). Their distribution was as follows: staff 63 percent, purchase of material 12 percent, buildings and rented space 12 percent, and other expenses 13 percent. Some 250 people, representing 190 full-time equivalents worked at the Storköping Public Library. Additions amounted to 55,000 items stocks being over 1 million.

All book lending is free of charge but fines are levied for overdue books.

Availability of activity statistics previous to the case. Numerous statistics on Storköping Public Library's activity were collected at the start of the period studied. The 1988 Annual Report, for example, displayed figures concerning:

- opening hours for each branch of the municipal library system
- stocks by type of material (books for adults, books for children, subscription to newspaper and other periodicals, audio material)
- acquisitions and sorting outs
- circulation by type of material (fiction media for adults, nonfiction media for adults, media for children)
- circulation by type of borrower (adult and children)
- cultural programs by type of activity (theater, music, authors' evenings, exhibitions)
- distribution of borrowers by loan frequency, age, and sex
- distribution of visitors in terms of borrowers and nonborrowers, branch by branch
- number of questions asked at the information desk.

This was little more than what Statistics Sweden (Statistiska Central Byrån) requires from all Swedish public libraries, and it represents a reasonable amount of information regarding the library's activity. However, this information was hardly used with a management perspective in mind. As presented in the annual reports, the figures did not allow one to appreciate what was actually done in the library. Very little was said about the context of operations. Even figures generally considered as important, such as stock, visits, or circulation, were usually presented without comment, whereas other figures such as the numbers of people benefiting from the home delivery of books (Boken kommer) were quoted and commented upon year after year. Revealingly, when interviewed about evaluation of the library's performance, the person who was chief librarian at the time said that one does not have adequate indicators in the library world. Changes were on their way, though, in the form of a more management inspired way of looking at this statistical material.

Developing Performance Indicators for the Storköping Public Library

The case is based on a range of written documents (e.g., internal notes, planning reports, press articles), interviews (about twelve of them, between thirty minutes and three hours each, some of them contemporary to the case and various others carried out later), participation in meetings or local conferences (about six of them), and firsthand experience of the library as a patron. A chronological order is followed.

In every study of this kind, one has to choose a beginning and an end. The arrival of Norman in the office of chief librarian of the Storköping Public Library, in August 1989, appeared a particularly adequate time to start the case; his arrival initiated a series of major changes in the library, and his entry into the city librarian office was at a time when several of the managerial staff had begun to express very concrete concerns for better ways of accounting for the library's performance. Bringing the case to an end proved to be more difficult than setting a time to start, however. I chose to close the case two and a half years after it began, that is to say, in the last months of 1991. This date corresponds to the end of the phase of the performance indicators' lives when these could be seen as being in gestation (even if one could easily claim—and I would indeed agree—that such managerial tools as performance indicators are permanently in gestation) and the beginning of their existence as managerial tools. The case remains focused in this way upon the *developing* of performance indicators.

Before turning to the presentation of the case, let me introduce the two main characters, Norman and Robertsson. Norman is the chief librarian of the Storköping Public Library. He came from a job as municipal cultural department head, and has a background as associate professor of literary science. He is not a librarian by training. Robertsson is a young librarian who was already at the Storköping Public Library when Norman arrived, and who has a particular interest in computers and in user surveys.

In attempting to describe for me his impressions of the Storköping public library as he began his appointment as city librarian in the middle of 1989, Norman used the metaphor "the castle of the Sleeping Beauty." It had been an exemplary public library in the past, but during the last two decades the evolution had progressively come to a stop, and on his arrival he found that people were more interested in the glorious past than in the future. This was illustrated well, he said, by the annual reports his predecessor presented, which, though extremely rich in factual and quantitative information, did not provide any coherent assessment of the performance of the given year nor any indications of what was to come. Norman felt uncomfortable about this. Ambitious and energetic, he championed the cause of placing himself and the Storköping Public Library on the map of Swedish cultural institutions. In the attempt to do this, he immediately initiated a broad program of discussions, studies, and reorganizations which he placed under the generic theme of organizational change. I believe that, in contrast to his predecessor, he viewed himself as a manager. He was to run the Storköping Public Library accordingly.

In order to assess the current state of the organization, soon after he entered office, he required every department of the library system to prepare a list of their present activities (with particular mention of their weaknesses) and of the changes they could imagine introducing in the coming three years. He gathered the answers in an eighty-page document that he introduced as the first attempt at comprehensive planning for the Storköping Public Library activities. It is in this document that he mentioned performance indicators for the first time. The document provides no detailed information on what is meant by indicators, except that the library's managerial staff is expected to work at "follow-up and evaluation, that is developing and implementing performance indicators and methods." At best, by a careful reading, one can find some indications in it that the developing of indicators had something to do with planning, change, and decentralization.

About half a year later, Norman mentioned performance indicators again, this time in a document which, under the explicit influence of manuals from the American Library Association (McClure et al. 1987; Van House et al. 1987), presented how one could discuss the goal of the Storköping Public Library in terms of a portfolio of roles. Taking up in parts the roles discussed in the manuals, but mainly the Swedish tradition of librarianship, Norman proposed to discuss the following roles: an up-to-date library, the community's archives, a library for younger people, a library for the pleasure of reading, a center for research and self-studies, an information center, and an outreach library. As in the manuals of the American Library Association, the document discussed each role in a few lines and suggested a short list of performance indicators to assess how well the library performed the role in question. Altogether, the document proposed about fifty different indicators. Ranging from traditional ones (such as loans and opening hours) to less common, homemade ones (such as support for book reading, indicators of quality, and indicators of catalogues), this list displayed a low grade of technical feasibility: indicators were many, several of them looked more like target statements than performance indicators, and only a few matched available statistical material. Still, the document clearly showed that Norman had started to give some substance to his idea of developing performance indicators. In six months, the development of performance indicators had advanced from a vague idea to something worthy of attention as such. It had become a genuine topic, open for further discussion.

A few months later, in August 1990, I met Norman for my first interview. At this time he had been city librarian for a year. At the start of the interview, I did not know of the two documents described above, but from what he told me I understood rapidly enough that he had paid close attention to evaluation issues and to performance indicators. Questioned about the evaluation of the library's activity, he read through and commented on the document based upon the manuals from the American Library Association, speaking mostly of which portfolio of roles the library in Storköping should have. As I questioned him further on evaluation, he described the following four indicators: number of hours worked per hour the library was open, number of loans per full-time equivalent staff member, number of visits per full-time equivalent staff member, and an unspecified indicator of stock turnover. The first indicator, he said, would help to show how much staff was required for each hour the library was open. In the second indicator, number of loans per full-time equivalent staff member—which was already used by the *1960 Rationalization Study*, as he pointed out—he saw as a good measure since "people are there to take out books," but only if used together with several other measures, his insisting upon "several" so as to prevent any focus of mine upon circulation. He believed the third indicator, number of visits per full-time equivalent staff member, provided an adequate expression of visits, also a product of the library. He was less precise about what the fourth indicator should be, except that it was to indicate rotation of the book stock. When questioned on the shortcomings of these indicators, he mentioned that since none of these took into account the use of rooms or the proactive social activities of libraries, these aspects had to be addressed later.

Though only a sketch, I think this set had already left behind most of the drawbacks that had marred the previous list he had established. In addition, this set indicated that Norman had developed a comprehensive view of what he meant by developing performance indicators for the Storköping Public Library. His ideal was to arrive at "a few measures," "simple ratios that express much." He told, for example, though almost in a self-derisory manner, how he could imagine having at his disposal "a single ratio that would give us some kind of total temperature of our performance," such as "in companies where one has simple indicators to see how things are going." He regretted that "in the library world, we lack indicators of this sort and that makes it difficult for us to see if we are good or bad." Such a comment is revealing of the origin and nature of Norman's desires and intentions in developing performance measures. Adopting the logic of modern agon, the Storköping Public Library had to find effective ways of telling (the world) how excellent it is at achieving its mission, the derisory style he employed being a way of indicating that the library would probably not be able to do as well as a private company, but that one should excuse a novice for having a weakness of this sort. To him, indicators could play a central role in the implementation of changes at the Storköping Public Library by contributing to the possibilities for ascertaining how different the library branches were from one another. He wanted the indicators to link the library's performance with its resources as well.

From what he said, as compared with what he had written earlier, I can now see how he had started to address performance indicators as a subject in itself. I can now see in his words how he had attached specific categories of analysis to these indicators, such as what each was saying and not saying, how they fitted together, and what functions they were to fulfill in the organization. To me, this is a sign that performance indicators were no longer a mere topic of interest but had become something of broader importance. Provided with a dynamic of their own, they had become a real issue.

In the months that followed, this issue was to receive an impetus that turned the idea of developing performance indicators into something much more formalized: a project of its own. Several factors contributed to this evolution.

Largely unaware of Norman's interest in the topic, Robertsson, a subordinate of the latter, had published a paper in the professional press in which he recapped the traditional criticism of the no less traditional loans-per-inhabitant indicator, restating, for example, that this indicator does not account for the diversity of the activities of libraries. Robertsson advocated there the development of library-made accounting procedures and warned the Swedish library world of the risk of having outsiders forcing libraries to use performance measures that were not developed by librarians themselves and that would not necessarily do justice to the libraries' activities, in particular to their richness. As he put it: "We are moving into a time when we are going to be obliged to account for our performance in a new way, a more performance oriented way. Let us stay ahead of this trend and form and present ourselves the methods which can be tools for quality improvements as well as ways of gaining support and means for our activity". To him, new ways of accounting for the library's activities were necessary tools for the bettering of public libraries and for their securing adequate resources.[16]

At the same time, the Storköping county librarian, another subordinate of Norman's, became increasingly drawn towards ways of comparing the results of the different municipal library systems of the county. This growing interest, among the Storköping public library managerial staff, in new ways of assessing and describing the library activity was found to be related to the fact that this was a time when the degradation of the economic situation of libraries began to become more perceivable. In most municipal library systems, including that of Storköping, book borrowing figures had been decreasing for six years in a row, and this trend worried many, both inside and outside the library world. Parallel to this, cuts in municipal budgets had started to become a reality in many municipalities. This resulted in some municipalities speaking, for the first time ever, of drastically reducing the size of their library systems, for example by closing down branches or moving their main libraries into smaller premises. There were many indications that public libraries were heading for harder times. This tended to increase the Swedish library world's interest in performance indicators.

Norman had additional motives for developing performance indicators. He had started to investigate the possibility of decentralizing the activity of the Storköping Public Library according to a client-contractor model. This model, from the late 1980s on, had become increasingly popular among Swedish municipalities.[17] The basic idea behind it is to distinguish in a municipal service between a client (or purchaser) function and a contractor (or provider) one, so that these two functions, traditionally considered together, became separated and better defined—isolated as the rhetoric said. On paper, the model improves an organization's efficacy by decentralizing the organization and replacing traditional administration by market-inspired mechanisms. Competition among service providers is one of its recurrent themes and the market one of its master metaphors.[18]

The model can be applied at two levels: either to the whole municipality or to a municipal service only, allowing one in this case to speak of an internal client-contractor model of organization. Norman chose the latter version of the model, and presented this organizational model as an alternative to a possible contracting of the library to a private company and as a way of clarifying the sharing of responsibility between politicians and civil servants.

By suggesting that such a model be implemented at the Storköping public library, Norman wanted the relationships between the chief librarian (that is to say, himself) and the heads of the different branches of the library to be regulated by contracts. These contracts, which were to be negotiated between the respective branch and the city librarian, were to specify, on the one side, minimal levels of performance for the branches and, on the other side, the corresponding funding level. To be able to be implemented and to later function, such a model required that one be able to express the performance of the library branches in indisputable terms. Adequate performance indicators—Norman spoke of "indicators of results"—become in this regard a must, and these were, as an imperative, to "combine performance and resource."

Developing performance indicators had thus become sufficiently interesting for Norman to appoint Robertsson to carry out the practical work of finding which combination of indicators would best be adapted to the various purposes he assigned performance indicators. As we saw it, other members of the staff were interested as well. As Robertsson observed, "Norman's ideas about performance indicators were not intro-

duced into a vacuum, but matched the climate of ideas of the time."
(Quite contrary, by the way, to what most people involved with indicators thought at the time, positive attitudes toward measurement probably largely outnumbered negative ones.) A working group was created to support Robertsson in his task.

As I was to belong to this group, it might be appropriate to describe the terms of my participation in the developing process. I was invited by Norman to participate in the working group on an informal no-pay, no-commitment to results basis. In this capacity, I met Robertsson on several occasions. He described for me how he was working and I provided him with comments and library literature on the topic, including a paper of mine (see Corvellec 1991). He later confessed that he hardly read the papers I gave him. In the capacity of a working group member, I also met the other members of the group and participated in the meetings they held. At first, my attitude was that of participating in these various things with, to the best of my knowledge, a genuine involvement. As time went by, however, I became more and more reserved, and even became reluctant to share my views with other members of the group, with Norman and Robertsson in particular. During the last and decisive meeting of the working group I remained completely silent. I had progressively come to gain insight into the potential value of the material I was gathering as a case and I opted for a less involved attitude. As I see it now, I had only general comments, based on the literature I had to come up with, to make anyway. When the group ceased its activities, I continued, nevertheless, to meet Robertsson regularly, mostly to follow what had happened with the indicators. When I finally wrote an account of the case, two years later, I carried out a few complementary interviews and asked him and Norman to read through my account of the process. In the meanwhile, the developing of indicators had obviously dropped out of their current concerns: they read my account more out of politeness than of interest and made very few comments. (Most of these I have taken into account, and I have signaled in the present text the points where our views diverge.) Incidentally, a few months later, Norman told me why he had invited me to participate in the working group: to use me against eventual opponents (though he did not mention which). I do not know if he did, but I learned that lies by omission might well be part of the game.

The existence of the working group was made public during a meeting of the chief librarians of the county in October 1990. Discussing, among other forms of turbulence, a recent example of municipal library privatization and the generally unfavorable evolution of the economic conditions of libraries, Norman announced that within a year the Storköping Public Library was to develop a set of "practical measures" that would enable it to account in a concise manner for the activity of the library. A recurrent phrase was "simple measures that say much" and, as attached themes again, change and planning. Norman left it open how these indicators were to look, except for dismissing the idea that there could be a unique indicator. He presented the audience, however, the set he had introduced me to a few months earlier as a starting point for the project (as a reminder: number of hours worked per hour the library was open, number of loans per full-time equivalent staff member, number of visits per full-time equivalent staff member, and an indicator of stock turnover). On that occasion, he added that such indicators could contribute to improving the quality of the dialogue between civil servants and the political representative, a point that could not be uninteresting for an audience of chief librarians, and which directly reminds one of what he said when introducing the client-contractor model.

Significant to the process was that someone—in this case inside the library—had been made formally responsible for carrying out the task by a publicly announced deadline. From that point onwards, the development of performance indicators had become what could be called a project.[19] In less than a year, developing performance indicators had evolved from a vague idea, what I have called a topic, to an issue, that is to say, something worthy of particular attention, and finally to a project of its own. No practical results had as yet been achieved, but important conditions for a successful outcome had been brought together. A formalization of responsibility had been made, several categories of analysis had been identified (e.g., technical feasibility and political usefulness), specific time resources had been granted, interested people had been grouped, and the obligation of presenting results assigned to a deadline had been introduced.

It was significant that Norman's interest in a client-contractor model had added a new and important motive for developing performance indicators. Performance indicators were no longer interesting simply as a support to planning. They had become interesting too for the decentralization of the library's activities. The schedule of their development had become vaguely attached to the schedule for developing the client-contractor model. They had indirectly become related to such concepts as contract and market. Of course, they still had special relationships with "planning," with "implementing change," and with "developing various roles for the library," but in a manner that newcomers had modified. The linking of performance indicators to the client-contractor project had meant an important rearrangement of the conceptual network into which performance indicators had become integrated. This rearrangement was to have a nonnegligible influence on how the rest of the process evolved.

Robertsson had no previous experience with such work. Once in charge of the project, he gathered available statistics and tried to see how he could combine them. He read a few papers on performance evaluation in public libraries, but without finding what he had in mind: something simple to use that encompassed the entire performance of the library.

Norman, on his part, wrote an internal note on indicators. The note used a typology of the library's activities based on resources defined as staff, premises, and collections, instead of roles as earlier, and he suggested how each post of this typology could be expressed by indicators. The note indicated as well that indicators should: (*a*) cover the entirety of library activity, not simply some particular aspect of it; (*b*) relate existing resources—defined as staff, stocks, and space—to the activity; (*c*) permit comparisons across time and across units; and (*d*) permit continuous measurement. These criteria were probably a good synthesis of Norman's ideas at the time. Together, these criteria draw quite a precise portrait of how indicators were to look, however, without declaring what they should be. There were about fifteen indicators that were mentioned— all of them able to be put into practice immediately on the basis of available statistics—but these were merely examples. Norman proposed, for instance, that use of the premises be assessed with the help of surface per visitor, premises cost per visit, premises cost per opening hours, and an index of distance. It is unclear what impact this note had on Robertsson. Two years later, for example, he could hardly remember the existence of a note of that kind. Possibly, the note contributed to his being convinced of the necessity of the set so as to enable comparisons of units one with another to be made.

At about the same time, the working group on the client-contractor model took its first steps; Norman worked further on the library's roles, but without mentioning indicators; more and more organizational innovations were introduced in Swedish municipalities—including the opening of the first privately run municipal library; and the Democratic Republic of Germany disappeared as an independent state.

After six months of work on the project, Robertsson called for a meeting of the working group on indicators in May 1991. The purpose of the meeting was to summarize what had already be done and to set concrete guidelines for the future. In the preparatory material, Robertsson reminded recipients of the importance that the library develop indicators of its own during a period in which it had to defend its resources and consider that other forces might be tempted to impose on it the use of inadequate measures. He also advocated the idea that one should not measure anything unless one had the capacity to implement change, which is an interesting reversal of how these two arguments of change and measure are usually combined. His proposal presented a list of a dozen indicators: ratio of hours worked to hours open, ratio of staff available to number of visitors, average number of visitors at a given time, surface area available per visitor, cost of library space per visitor, number of books on the shelves, loans per visitor, percentage of borrowers among the visitors, total loans, number of reference inquires answered, ratio of readers registered to the total population, and frequency of visits of registered readers. This list of indicators was accompanied by data on them for various library branches—"snapshots" of the branches—which could easily be compared with each other.

To Robertsson, this list was a sketch, an early prototype that he wished to see discussed. Yet the meeting hardly dealt with the technical features of his sketch. Instead, the discussion concerned more general aspects of the project: the need for indicators to link activity with resources, interest in being able to compare the results of different units and assess their differences, and the role performance indicators play in a client-contractor model. The meeting also gave Norman the opportunity to state again that indicators should enable one to assess how the various units fulfilled the general mission of the library—being open, enabling visits to take place, lending books. To me, it seemed that no one except Norman and Robertsson was sufficiently acquainted with the technical aspects of the project to be able to engage in a discussion of the technical aspects of the indicator set.

One point of crucial interest was touched upon during the meeting, though: that comparing units with one another might not necessarily show how well these units fulfilled the goals that were specific to them. The issue was rapidly passed over in the discussion. However, the discussion had pointed at something important: the limited compatibility of the ideas of working according to local profiles, local roles, and local goals in the different units of the library system, on the one hand, with the idea of comparing all these units on a few standard measures, on the other. For a moment, the discussion indeed foretold what was to happen toward the end of the project: its splitting into two parts with a subproject aimed at developing standard performance indicators for the implementation of a client-contractor model, on the one hand, and a subproject aiming at providing each unit of the municipal library system with tailor-made means of evaluating the achievements of its self-determined goals thanks to specific profile performance indicators, on the other.

For Robertsson, who still had to turn this proposal into something operational, and this in less than six months, the meeting proved to be of very little help, except that it had signaled the acceptance of the main features of the project by the managerial staff of the library. In terms of social acceptance, this meeting was an important stage in the process.

Robertsson discarded his own proposition less than two months later. In his own words, he came to the view that his proposal "did not hold water," partly because it generated too much data for the user to be able to get a general view and thus lacked operativeness, and partly because it generated figures that lied at "different levels." After consulting with Norman, Robertsson settled on a maximum of six indicators. What he did here was to weigh one indicator against another, to look for the most evocative ones, to check which of them were affected in a similar way by a given change, and to find ones that were not correlated. He also had sporadic contact with people working on the client-contractor model so as to stay informed of how they approached the quantification of the library's activity.

Robertsson continued his work and in August 1991, less than a year after he had been put on the project, he was able to present an articulated proposal. The proposal consisted of a comprehensive evaluation scheme. First came a selection of four indicators that were to be common to all units so that they could be compared with one another. These four indicators were: number of square meters per visit, number of visits per fulltime equivalent staff members, ratio among visitors of borrowers and nonborrowers, and turnover of the book stock. According to Robertsson's intention, these indicators were to assess how each unit was performing in terms of what could be regarded as the basic task of a municipal library—being open for visitors and lending out material—while recording how the three main resources of the library—staff, premises, and stocks—were employed. Secondly, Robertsson proposed that each unit develop its own measures of its activities along with these four indicators. Yet, he did not go far in describing how such indicators would look. He simply stated that the measures would have to be designed so as to fit the specific profile of each unit, which gave some room for creativity. To him, this scheme was an instrument of dialogue between the parties involved. (Some examples of the computations were attached to the proposal.)

The proposal provided a precise definition of the role indicators were to play. It provided an answer, moreover, to both of the two major concerns that had accompanied the project thus far: first, the search for something that would enable one to compare one unit with another—a matter which particularly interested the county librarian—and secondly, that one be able to assess how each unit was performing in terms of its specific profile, a concern that Norman shared with the client-contractor project group. These concerns were in part irreconcilable, and Robertsson had dealt with the incompatibility of the demands of both a general and a specific set of performance indicators by decoupling them and splitting the project of developing performance indicators into two.[20] This decoupling proved to be a skillful measure that put an end to many contradictions among the demands the process had prompted. Indicators for comparisons did not need any longer, for example, to account with precision for the specificity of a branch; they could thus be fewer in numbers, and information overflow could be avoided. Neither did indicators of profile need to permit comparisons. They could thus be customized and be as numerous as needed. Many criticisms lost their relevance when redirected at only one of the two subprojects. Technical solutions seemed much easier to find and this increased the strengths of the proposal considerably.

Robertsson's proposal, though, presented operational solutions for only half of the evaluation scheme, the one oriented to comparison. Actually, Robertsson has never compensated for this imbalance: he did not develop further the part of the evaluative scheme that was to permit an assessment of how well the library branches attained their specific goals. He stranded this part of the scheme, which, as Hatch (1995) pointed out, can be an indication that, for him as for Norman, performance might have been more a matter of providing a sense of end-result than a matter of maintaining a good feeling about what is done—the performing side of performance. And when much of this subproject was carried out, it was within the client-contractor project, and in a rather different form than the one Robertsson had imagined.

Robertsson's proposal was to be accepted without change by the managerial staff of the library on a meeting on 12 September. Norman had clearly stated that this would be the last meeting at which the indicator set design was to be discussed before a choice was to be made and attempts at implementing were to be carried out. The meeting gave Robertsson the opportunity to present the logic of his project at length and to answer questions. The deputy city librarian, for example, asked how these measures came into being. To that, Robertsson replied that he had seen many measures, but that none that he found could readily describe the basic activity of the library. He also recounted how he had imagined that the standard performance indicators and the profile performance indicators should be articulated, that he had been working under the constraint of keeping the amount of standard performance indicators under half a dozen, and how he had tried to relate resources and performance.

Robertsson presented the technical aspects of the indicator set and these were discussed. He emphasized the practicality, the independence, and the ability of indicators to complement each other. He pointed out the balance these achieve between visitors, collection, and premises, and the comparisons these provide. He explained that he preferred avoiding monetary indicators, so as to avoid bringing about "less creative" discussions on how to save money. That the traditional indicator loan per inhabitant was not among them was emphasized, as was that these indicators could be influenced by actions that were within the reach of the library.

Various criticisms were advanced. Robertsson himself regretted that the set did not take into account how many hours the library was open. He also noted that it ignored the characteristics of the population served. The deputy city librarian added that it did not account either for the social activities of the library. The sharpest criticisms, however, were to come from Norman, who wanted the set to include as an indicator the number of hours worked per hours open. I found it surprising at first that Norman came in so late with such strong criticisms. Later, I changed my mind and took it as an indication that Norman had been quite far from the indicator project for a while and that the proposal was much more Robertsson's own than something elaborated on in collaboration between the two.

The meeting also dealt with how these indicators were to be used. Several questions were asked about how indicators were to influence the staff policy. In response to these, Robertsson, and Norman at times, emphasized repeatedly that these indicators were to foster the emergence of a discussion—a "dialogue," the word was used on several occasions—regarding the work of the library units. They specified that the indicators were not to be used as central decision devices, which was, and in my eyes still is, a very disputable standpoint.

The meeting turned out to be more informative than filled with debates. Its tone was positive and inquiring. At no time has the proposal been seriously called into question, either from a technical point of view or as regards its assumed social implications. Without any hammer hitting the deliberation board, the proposed performance indicator set had been formally adopted.

With this meeting, the process entered a phase of solidification. From then on, the design of the set was not to be modified. What were to change were the arguments used to make the set attractive to people who had not been involved in its elaboration. At this stage, the project had lost most of its malleability and was to become more solid every day.

A program concerned with the implementation of these indicators had been attached to the proposal and, according to it, the set was to be presented to the head librarians of the county, and to be tested by November 1991. This was done in due time. Several computations—some of them going back in time, according to a suggestion I had made at an early stage of the process—had already been undertaken when the set was presented for the staff of the Storköping Public Library. The set was to be presented to the chief librarians of the county at their 1991 meeting in November. I was not allowed to participate in this meeting, but from the documents that were distributed I could reconstruct that the set was presented there in approximately the same form as during the meeting at the Storköping Public Library the month before. According to Robertsson, the set was met by broad interest and reception was almost unanimously positive. The only criticism that was expressed was that the set seemed more adequate for urban than for rural libraries, which Robertsson found ungrounded. To him, the idea of performance measurement seemed to be accepted, though with no guarantee as to how much of it would be translated into acts.

With this presentation to the county's head librarians, the indicator set had been made available for collective scrutiny and had become something public. This public status was accentuated even further when Robertsson and Norman together wrote "Take the Pulse of Your Library," a paper presenting the set, which was published in the *Swedish Library Journal*, the main library journal in Sweden. The paper was Norman's idea. He wanted it to prevent the project from "running into the sand."

The most remarkable thing about this paper is that it emphasizes quite different aspects than those that Robertsson had in his presentation to the managerial staff of the Storköping Public Library. The paper does not mention, for example, the set having been developed in relationship to the theme of decentralization and to a client-contractor model. Neither does it mention that the four indicators were part of a two-sided evaluation scheme that also encompassed tailor-made indicators. Instead, the paper repeatedly emphasized the themes of efficacy and of defense of the library, two themes that, to be sure, had been present during the shaping process, but not at all to the extent suggested in "Take the Pulse of Your Library." By toning down some aspects and emphasizing others, the paper radically redefined the context in which the indicator set had been invented. As compared with earlier (e.g., the meetings with the working group at the Storköping Public Library, or the meeting of the Storköping county libraries), even though the design of the set was unchanged, it is quite a different reading of these four indicators that "Take the Pulse of Your Library" invites one to make.

The paper aimed at making the set irresistible. It opens, for example, with a denunciation of the loan per inhabitant ratio, a denunciation that is a very federative theme within the library world. In addition it emphasizes the work having been carried out by librarians—to be understood as persons friendly to the library—and it also mentioned researchers from the University of Lund having collaborated in the shaping process, suggesting hereby that this endowed the result with some sort of academic guarantee of quality. The authors also stress that practical use of the indicators requires neither large investments nor complicated computations, and that the indicators are easy to put into practice, requiring at most that one set up a person counter. The sensitive topic of how appropriate the philosophy of measurement was to cultural activities was carefully avoided.

It was indeed essential, for the vigor of the indicator set, that this paper be convincing and that it lead to the set being put into practice. To really exist, the set had to be used and be put into practice. Thus far, the set did not exist, other than on paper. The best way for it to exist "for real" was to be integrated into the managerial practice of Swedish librarians. As Latour and Woolgar (1986) have observed regarding machines designed for laboratory use, managerial tools do not really exist unless they have been adopted by a large share of the community to which they are addressed. Before they are adopted, they are virtual objects, prototypes with an uncertain future. This is why, in its last lines, the paper so explicitly encouraged librarians to put the indicator set to use. Any adoption of the set *outside* the Storköping Public Library could only reinforce the position of the set *inside* the library, where it had been thus far exclusively dependent upon certain high-ranking managers. This is why the paper by Norman and Robertsson in the *Swedish Library Journal* was a part of the shaping process, an important step toward the materialization of the set.

With the first implementation having been carried out at the Storköping Public Library, and the set having been advertised in Storköping County, as well as nationwide, a new managerial tool had been launched. For the record, only a few of the libraries in Storköping County began making use of the indicators. In contrast with this, other Swedish libraries showed a warmer interest, twenty public libraries requesting further information about the indicator set that Norman and Robertson described in their *Swedish Library Journal* paper. At the Storköping Public Library itself, indicators came to be used on a yearly basis only, since they proved to be too insensitive to change to be used more frequently. Despite their less than imagined frequency of use, they were nevertheless to play an important role for the library. As Norman observed about two years after the close of the case, several projects have been initiated or been intensified on the basis of the information provided by the first computations that were based on these indicators. The client-contractor was of course among these projects, as was a project concerning premises that led to considerable reallocation of space and to a few removals. So too was a systematic weeding policy aimed at easing stock rotation and stock maintenance.

On the whole, these indicators have had a rather noticeable impact on the evolution of the Storköping Public Library. In particular, the indicators have initiated significant changes in the way key actors in the library perceive the activities they carry out as organizational actors and the activity of the library as an organization. Through their work on performance indicators, Norman, Robertsson and the other managers of the library came to increasingly view themselves as managers whose task was to turn the library into a superior achiever. Accordingly, the library's activity was redefined perceptibly so as to fit the agonetic logic of performance.

The Crafting of Indicators

This is where I close the case. With the initial implementation trials, the indicators became public. They had become something solid enough to be offered to people who had nothing to do with its development, for them to accept or refuse it. The history of the set does not end here. Indeed, it will continue for as long as there is someone who uses it or chooses to speak of it.

The process: from a topic, to an issue, to a project, to a managerial tool. The preceding pages have depicted the process of developing a performance indicator set at the Storköping Public Library. This process started with performance indicators being first born as a topic, that is to say, as something worthy of interest, although of only vague and hardly defined shape. A vague idea had been advanced that it might be interesting to have access to indicators, but reflections regarding indicators as such were very slight.

The topic was given progressively greater weight and gained in substance. One became more discerning and developed ad-hoc categories of analysis, such as the feasibility of an indicator or how an indicator might contribute to the operation of the organization. The indicator set was formulated as a problem requiring attention in order to be solved. These ideas were not ordered, and were very much of a jumble, but a first outline was designed and the first checkpoints were established. At this stage, the project had become an issue.

A person was appointed to deal with this particular issue. With this, the developing of performance indicators had been acknowledged as something important. A public commitment was made to achieving results, and a deadline was established for completion of the task. With these gains in formalization and structuring, the process had become a project.

Thereafter, the project evolved through systematic experimentation. Ideas about the project that had previously been quite free of constraints—such as that the set should enable every branch to express its specificity—had now to comply with technical conditions of expressiveness so as to avoid being removed. Other ideas were introduced into the project and were given a strong position—for example, that the indicators of the set should be compatible with each other. Preliminary results were dispatched and were discussed; some were abandoned and others were kept. The importance of technical requirements increased as the project went ahead and toward the end of the process they functioned as very decisive criteria of selection. One of the craftsmen presented a proposal that was accepted. The set had become a sustainable proposition.

Then, within the space of several months, the set was made public to broader and broader audiences, audiences that had not participated in the elaboration of the set and were cut off from the history of its being produced, but were likely to make use of it. The set had been turned into something real. In two and a half years, performance indicators had evolved from half a line in a planning document to a managerial tool.

A sense-making process. The developing of performance indicators was not based on a clearly defined result that was aimed at. It was not supported by any theoretical knowledge, and has never been—at least until it was presented in the professional press—a coherent project. On the whole, the process has been a momentary and occasional activity in the professional lives of the persons involved, one that will not be reproduced, at least in any such form.

In its departure from a means-ends relationship and from a rational model of decision making, together with its corresponding nonlinearity, in its relying upon the combination of existing elements, in its progressive materialization of the solution idea, and in its being carried out by nonprofessional people, the process can be seen as a *bricolage* (French) (English) (Levi-Strauss 1962:32; Linstead and Grafton-Small 1990). It can be seen, as well, as a case of muddling through (Lindblom 1959), illustrating again that: "Policy-making is a process of successive approximation to some desired objectives in which what is desired itself continues to change under reconsideration" (Lindblom 1959:86).

At the heart of this *bricolage* were two connoisseurs, Norman and Robertsson. In contrast to a planned endeavor, the developing of indicators was a matter of reacting to impulse—for example, the need for

change—in a creative manner. It involved shuffling and reshuffling existing elements, creating new ones, and inventing intelligent combinations
of them in order to permanently renew and increase the repertory of what
it was possible to achieve. The process was a sense-making operation. It
represented an effort to assemble disparate knowledge into an articulated
view of fragments of reality.

What characterizes this sense making is that sense only appears at the
very end of the process. Until a final result is achieved, the sense of it
seems to be waiting, as if suspended. It is through the result that the
various efforts that have paved the way to process become endowed with
meaning—which I experienced myself in not becoming aware of having
gathered material for a case until after the case was written—other end
results providing these efforts with other meanings.

What also characterizes this sense making is that it intimately inter-
twines knowledge with practice. Theoretical and practical knowledge
cohabit with the practice of random attempts and errors and of stubborn
efforts. As a result, actors become parts of the process in an unmistak-
able manner and the result unmistakenly bears their signature.

Linking processes. Making sense of and through performance indicators implied for Norman and for Robertsson their continually reformulating the project—as a story, I would say—so as to link it to other
projects. Performance indicators were born in relation to the notions of
planning and change. As the project forged ahead, the notion of roles
was introduced. The notion of efficacy came then, formulated as being a
coupling of resources and activity. Change remained important, but roles
had to give way some to decentralization, introduced in the form of a
client-contractor model. Efficacy and the defense of the library were
mentioned, though only occasionally. Better relationships between politicians and civil servants were alluded to. The defense of the library
gained ground with the arrival of Robertsson, and the role lost some
ground when Norman left the topic, letting it live a life of its own elsewhere. Decentralization had become more important, which for a while
featured profiles and comparisons as the main themes of the project. At
least until the project was presented to the professional press, and efficacy and defense of the library were propelled as the central themes. At
this stage of the process, roles had disappeared and so had planning,
although the latter in appearance only, since indicators remained at the
heart of several projects aimed at better planning of the library's activity.

New concerns hardly eliminated earlier ones. Linkages, instead, were continually reorganized. To replicate the reasoning of Latour (1987) about the nature of scientific knowledge, one could say that the success of the process depended on Norman's and Robertsson's ability at keeping at every moment the developing performance indicators within the ever-changing network of the library's worth-of-interest concerns. By adequate moves between such concerns, the indicator project managed to always remain within the tail of important issues. Not unlike what Cohen et al. (1972) describe as a garbage can model of organizational choice, though in a more systematic and more intentional manner than those authors intend, the process consisted of a stream of problems that met a stream of solutions, and involved too a stream of energy from participants and a rate of flows of solutions. Indicators left various concerns on their way down and joined other concerns on their upward curve, for example, when the move from planning to decentralization occurred. Thanks to such moves and the changes in their nature these involved, performance indicators remained permanently interesting. This judicious game of changing alliances secured strong ties with important (and continually renewed) allies, most of them belonging to the sphere of managerialism. Developing performance indicators never fell to the level of an unimportant or uninteresting project.

The set was defined over and over again through these continual reorganizations and redefinitions. The nature of the indicators changed again and again. A dynamic and confused game was played that continually modified the purpose the indicators were to serve, how they were to be designed, and which ones they should be, as new persons or new issues entered or left the developing process, endowing indicators with a "variable ontology" (to re-use an expression coined by Latour 1992:144).

Indicators were not, however, mere *products* of an environment. Even before their coming into existence as potentials, indicators participated in *shaping* their environment, that is, the library's life. They contributed to making some issues potentially important for the library, and thus kept these issues part of the library's agenda. Indicators have contributed decisively, for example, to providing an expression and thus a substance to the idea of roles. They have also contributed to making the functioning of the client-contractor model credible and thus to its being worthy of interest and efforts. Indicators have likewise prompted a new language for accountability and consequently fostered a new form of advocacy of the library's claims for a larger budget. The virtual existence of indicators has made other concerns thicker, more possible, more worthy of being dealt with, and thus a part of those concerns that receive attention. By the mere possibility of their existence, performance indicators have contributed to turning planning, decentralization, and accountability into issues worthy of attention. Indicators have helped make it possible for such concerns to continue to exist. The indicator set and its context of birth were involved in a dynamic multidimensional process of interaction and support.

Performance Indicators as Instances of Narration

The multiple combinations that the people involved had to invent along the way in the process involved elements that varied in nature. The crafting process was not simply a matter of judiciously linking the project of developing indicators with other projects and ideas within and outside the library. The actors also had to associate and conciliate concerns that belonged to different fields, particularly to the technical, social, and narrative fields.[21] It was through these successful associations and conciliations of heterogeneous concerns that meaning was produced.

Most prominent were the technical aspects of the process, that is to say, issues pertaining to the choice, generation, computation, and presentation of statistics, including issues of computer mainframe and the customization of external softwares. Norman and Robertsson spent quite some time identifying and finding a solution to these issues.

These were not the only issues the actors had to find a solution to, however. Indicators had to be socialized into the organization as well. Each indicator had to obtain the support of Norman, of Robertsson, and of the rest of the working group. Even though the project benefited at its start from a diffuse support by the managerial staff, the solutions had to be accepted still by the staff. To be successful, indicators had to align the interests of the many different people involved (cf. Latour 1992). They had to appear to be a solution to many people's problems. They had to interest, enroll, and mobilize the population (Callon 1985). The project thus needed to be not only technically satisfying, but also socially seducing. To agree with the ideas of the moment and to match the top management of the organization was important, but indicators had, in addition, to be accepted and supported by the people directly affected by them. An acceptance by the latter was a condition for the set's existence. This is why, for example, the set had to pass beyond the worries that were expressed concerning the impact of indicators upon the staff policy.

There is also a third range of issues, narrative ones. Indicators had to tell something. "Few measures that tell much" had been Norman's guideline. They were to be telling for the public at large as well as for specialists. They were to cover all the library's activities, but not be so many that they could not be read in a single glance. Above all, they were to tell something. Performance indicators were defined, in this regard, as narrative instances.

Selectors, Collectors, and Inscriptors

Performance indicators *select*. They serve as filters. They act as screens that strain the organization's activity. What passes through the holes of the sieve becomes visible—in a literal sense according to the Latin etymology: capable of being seen. What is made visible can be taken into account later in the evaluation process, while what does not pass the holes will most probably not. Indicators make the difference between what is heard and what is kept silent. They are gatekeepers. They are expressions of what is to be regarded as important; by way of contrast they proclaim the rest of the activity to be less important. Thus, they represent—in the sense that they make it present in a very concrete manner—a perspective, a certain way of looking at the organization's activity. They are materialized expressions of criteria. Seen within the perspective of the various constituencies of an organization, they are political expressions.

Performance indicators also *collect* the information that is used in performance assessment. This role involves a technical as well as a social dimension. Performance indicators are technical items in the sense that they function as any other form of meter, such as height gauges or Geiger counters. They rely upon specific technologies; they make use of and give life to particular theories; they exist with various specificities of scale, precision, design, or price. Yet performance indicators also have a social dimension in the sense that their functioning requires constant human intervention. They have first to be installed, which is no simple operation. The Storköping Public Library performance indicator set, though uncomplicated in its use, requires for its functioning, for example, the installation of new technical devices (visit meters), an intervention in the computerized information system, the computation of new variables (the surface area of the library units) and the preparing of the staff for the implementation of the set (something that can be very demanding). Second, performance indicators have to be calibrated: deciding whether a pupil running back and forth five times in one hour between the classroom and the school library for a single assignment is to be computed as taking part in one or in five visits, or deciding what is to be considered as a single reference question. Third, indicators have to be read; this requires the determination of a periodicity of reading, the attribution of responsibility, and hence a modification of someone's task. Fourth, indicators have to be controlled, for example in order to ascertain whether the visit counter is still working correctly or whether two different units, the results for which are to be compared, effectively compute reference inquiries on so similar a basis that they measure the same thing. Finally, indicators have to be maintained in a technical sense, for example, through cleaning the mirror that sends back the light beam of the visit counter, as well as in their social aspects. In many regards, performance indicators contain moving parts.

Performance indicators not only *select* and *collect*, but they also *inscribe*.[22] Their function is to turn the organization's activity into signs, signs imprinted somewhere, for example, in a computer's memory or on an evaluation sheet. They record and list the organization's activity into registers of signs. They are not just any signs, but standardized and usually quantitative ones. They are signs that aim at presenting concentrated information,[23] and which themselves can be read, allowing the activity, in turn, to be read. Performance indicators are not inscriptors in exactly the same sense as a Gamma counter, though, since they lack the capacity themselves of ensuring the materiality of the sign as ink on paper or light on a screen spot. They are not machines in a concrete sense. They are inscriptors in the sense that they are the very point—the black box, I am tempted to say—where the organization's activity leaves the realm of human interactions to become a sign. We have seen above that performance indicators are expressions of what is to be regarded as important and that at the same time, by contrast, they proclaim the rest of the activity to be less important. Actually, their role of emphasizing some aspects of the organization's activity at the expense of others is more decisive than this. It is performance indicators that, by granting some particular aspects of an activity the privilege of being expressed, confer upon them the priority of being acknowledged. That something is regarded as important is not a sufficient condition to its acknowledgment, but that which is caught by indicators is most likely to become acknowledged.

Textualizing the Activity

To summarize the triple function of indicators of being selectors, collectors, and inscriptors, one could say of performance indicators that they textualize an organization's activity. What indicators do is to arrange an organization's life into signs organized in a text. All the efforts that made it possible for the Storköping Public Library to lend 1.8 million items last year—among other things, ordering the books, putting them on the shelves, keeping the library open, recording loans, paying the wages of the librarians, indeed nearly every single action undertaken within the library that year—are turned into a mere "In 19xx, the Storköping Public Library lent 1.8 million items." No matter what the library's activity consists of—in my view, mostly socio-technical interactions involving various practical and symbolical overtones—performance indicators turn this activity into a series of signs and characters.

Just as novelists do, performance indicators operate on the passage from life to text. Their function is to make possible the encoding of the organization's actual life into written accounts. Book loans and visits cannot in themselves speak. To exist, especially for whoever is not directly involved with the lending or with the visiting activities, loans and visits need to be narrated. It is performance indicators that fulfill this function, making it possible for the organization's activity to be arranged in a story available for intelligible reading.

The difference between the signs that performance indicators produce and the activity they describe is thus important. The statement that 1.8 million books were lent by the Storköping Public Library last year is by its very nature completely different from that which it depicts. Performance indicators neither lend books nor answer telephone inquiries; they tell how many books are borrowed (and possibly how the books are borrowed). The difference between the action of narrating (the narration) and the action narrated (the narrative) is a significant one.

Characteristically, the texts that indicators produce consist mostly of figures. Indicators narrate the activity in digits. Just like the game in which children draw a picture by following a series of numbers with a pen on a paper, performance indicators draw the organization's activity "by numbers." The crux is that there will be as many "numbers" portraits as there are indicators or sets of indicators. It is all a matter of criteria—and the above case has shown how varied and discretionary these can be, or, to re-use a sports metaphor, a matter of rules, performance indicators being much akin to the rules in sports that determine how one is to compute a score.

Conclusion

Acting as selectors, collectors, and inscriptors of an organization's activity, performance indicators translate into figures the social relationships that make up the organizational activity. Performance indicators occupy a privileged position at the point where the social relationships and artifacts that together constitute the organization become texts. In this respect, they play a key role in the process of textualizing the organization's activity into the narrative of the organization's performance, and they accomplish this role with considerable brilliance.

The present chapter has focused on the process of developing a set of performance indicators. Describing the historicity of performance measures, insisting upon the discursive nature of calculation, and unfolding the ensembles of practices and rationales that have led to the formation of that particular way of accounting for the organization's activity has provided, on a local level, what Miller and Napier (1993) have called a genealogy of calculation. The focus of the chapter has been on the *developing* of indicators so as to elucidate where these key elements of performance stories come from.

The process has been shown to be mostly nonlinear and subject to the whims of disorders, contingencies, and hazards of a technical, social, and narrative nature. Discretion and ad-hocness have been two main engines in the process, as have been, as well, trials, errors, invention, the recycling of ideas, learning, compromises, interpretation, experiences, and replications.

Tracing how performance indicators have been developed shows how performance accounts are caught in the confused interaction of ideas, people, and techniques that guides the development and the choice of performance indicators. Something that the mere analysis of indicators as managerial tools can readily miss—if, for example, one only studies presentations of indicators that are cleansed of the disordered and chaotic features of developing them—and which the present case study endeavors to show, is that the narration of an organization's performance is not a matter of necessity, but instead has a solid history.

The history of the narration of an organization's performance can in part be traced back to the history of the indicators used in performance accounts. By excavating the history of a set of indicators, and by showing that much of what these invite one to consider as the performance of the organization is indeed the product of specific events in the history of the indicators, the case illustrates that *how* the organization's activity is narrated has a history of its own, one subject to influences of its own. An organization's performance has a narrative history, but this history is only loosely coupled with the history of the organization's results.

That an organization's performance has a narrative history, in turn, demystifies the issue of the objectivity of performance indicators and performance accounts, and of the objectivization of an organization's performance. Far from being true to some objective organizational reality, what performance indicators and performance accounts appear to be true to is their own history as narrative instances and narrative products.

Performance, again, appears to represent the encounter between a telling and a reading. The case in the chapter illustrates how, prompted by a concern for accountability, performance texts reduced here to being performance indicators are bearers and activators of an agonetic vision of an organization. Depicting concerns for how the library can best uphold its interests in competition with other municipal services, and searching for commensurable grounds for fair comparison and ranking of the library's various units took us through the main dimensions of modern agon. The present case thus confirmed that speaking of performance supposes that organizational events are organized in sequences of actions aimed at convincing the audience of the superiority of the organization's achievements.

Notes

1. In Mary Paley Marshall, *What I Remember* (Cambridge: Cambridge University Press, 1947). Quoted in Pierre Guillet de Monthoux, *Läran om företaget—Från Quesnay till Keynes* (Stockholm: P.A. Norstedts & Söner förlag, 1983).
2. See Childers and Van House 1989; Lancaster 1988; Moore 1989; O'Connor 1982; Revill 1983; Van House et al. 1987; for a review see, e.g., Corvellec 1991.

3. E.g, "Bibliotek i större kommuner 1964" [Libraries in larger municipalities 1964], *Biblioteksbladet—The Swedish Library Review* 3 (1966); and the discussion that followed in *Biblioteksbladet* 7 (1966): 446–47.
4. Examples from K. Knutsson, "Att budgetera för ett bibliotek" [Budgeting in a Library], *Biblioteksbladet—The Swedish Library Review* 54, no. 19 (1969): 977–89; Gösta Ottervik, "Bibliotekens budgetsituation i dyrtid" [Library Budgets in Harsh Times], *Biblioteksbladet* 57, no. 2 (1972): 38–40.
5. Examples from S. Möhlenbrock, "Organisation av folkbibliotek i storstäder" [The Organization of Public Libraries in Large Cities], *Biblioteksbladet* 52, no. 1 (1967): 17–28; T. Edbom, "Mål i bibliotekens sikte" [Goals in Libraries], *Biblioteksbladet* 54, no. 5 (1969): 451–57; L. Bergh, "Rationalisera biblioteken—En kulturpolitisk fråga?" [To Rationalize Libraries¾A Cultural Policy Issue?], *Biblioteksbladet* 54, no. 9 (1969): 878–79.
6. E.g., the report from E.S.O., *Produktivitetsmätning av Folkbibliotekens utlånings-verksamheten* [Productivity Measurement of Public Libraries's Lending Activities] Ds 1989:42 (Stockholm: Finansdepartementet, 1989).
7. See, e.g., M. Thomas, "Effektivitet, rationalisering och målformulering" [Efficacy, Rationalization and Goal Formulation], *Biblioteksbladet* 11, no. 11 (1981): 208–209, for an older example, and the special issue of *Svensk Biblioteksforskning* 3 (1991): "Effektivitet och Kvalitet [Efficacy and Quality]," for a more recent one.
8. E.g., Anna Lena Höglund, "Högre kvalitet i bibliotekets verksamhet = Ökad produktivitet och effektivitet" [Higher Quality in Library Activities = Higher Productivity and Efficacy], paper awarded for excellence at the conference Kvalitet i Kommuner och Landsting, Göteborg, 2–3 September 1991.
9. E.g., the Storköping county conference, Målstyrning, Uppföljning, Effektivisering, Versamhetsförändring [Management by Objectives, Effication, and Organizational Changes], presented in the case below, October 1990.
10. E.g., the conference Folkbibliotek under 90-talet—verksamhetsförändring och styrformer [Public Libraries in the 90s—Activity Changes and Management], organized by SAB (Sveriges Allmänna Biblioteksförening [The Swedish Association of Libraries]), Stockholm, 19 November 1990.
11. E.g., Staffan Parnell, "Bibliotekens framtid—Intryck från den svenska biblioteksdebatten" [The Future of Libraries—Impressions from the Swedish Library Debate], in *Biblioteken och framtiden* [Libraries and the Future], edited by Romulo Enmark (Centrum för biblioteksforskning: Göteborg, 1991).
12. E.g., the conference Bibliotek som service företag [Libraries as Service Companies], FRN (Forskningsrådsnämnden) and Företagsekonomiska Institution, Lund, 6–8 April 1992.
13. E.g., M. Thomas, "Effektivitet, rationalisering och målformulering [Efficacy, Rationalisation and Goal Formulation]," *Biblioteksbladet* 11 (1981): 208–209; Barbro Blomberg, "Konsten att mäta biblioteksverksamheten" [The Art of Measuring Libraries' Activities], *Biblioteksbladet* 11–12 (1983): 231–32; P. Marner and G. Renborg, "Bibliotekens mål och mått?" [Goals and Measures of Libraries?] *Biblioteksbladet* 2 (1982): 34–35; *Att mäta den uppsökande verksamheten* [To Measure Outreach Activities], Rapport från Statens Kulturråd 1986:10; S. Von Flitner, "Evaluering av literaturbeståndet" [Stock Evaluation], *Biblioteksbladet* 6–7 (1986): 192; E. Andersson, "Metoder för utvärdering" [Evaluation Methods], *Biblioteksbladet* 13 (1986): 374; T. Nordström, "Nya mått på bibliotekseffektivitet" [New Efficacy Measures for Libraries], *Biblioteksbladet*

13 (1986): 395–96; C. Olausson, "Utvärdering av universitetsbibliotek—ett instrument för utveckling?" [Evaluation of University Libraries—A Tool for Development?], *Biblioteksbladet* 2 (1991): 56–58; A.-L. Höglund, "Mätmetoder och ledarskap måste utvecklas inom biblioteksväsendet" [Libraries Should Develop Methods of Measurement and Leadership], *Biblioteksbladet* 9 (1990): 280–82; O. Miletic and R. Tymark, "Hur mäter man information? [How to Measure Information?]," *Biblioteksbladet* 5 (1991): 134–35; A.-L. Höglund, *Mäta för att Veta* [Measuring for Knowing], Rapport från Statens Kulturråd, (1992): 4.

14. Few libraries, however, actually made use of such measurement, according to Ford (1989), no more than 10 percent in the United States. "It is about the same percentage in Sweden," says A.-L. Höglund (telephone interview, 2 September 1992), an active promoter of activity measurements for the last twenty years, who affirms that, thus far, most Swedish libraries have paid very little attention to figures on activity and that many chief librarians have known neither the key figures regarding their activities nor the corresponding national averages.

15. The discrepancy between what librarians experience as desirable and what they actually do is important. A survey (n=237, N=284) I made of Swedish public libraries showed, for example, that whereas 87 percent of the respondents believed it important to assess libraries' performance, only 37 percent of them had made any effort in that direction (November 1992).

16. I asked Robertsson, on a later occasion, if it had been the very controversial study on the productivity of the loaning activity of public libraries (E.S.O 1989) that had prompted the idea of the paper. He declared, however, that he had not known of this publication at the time.

    Also, Robertsson pointed out that this paper had been written before the discussion on the topic had been fully developed within the Storköping Public Library, something that was quite in accordance with the deadline for the manuscript, indicated in the publication to have been 15 August 1990.

    The reference to the quotation used cannot be provided in order to preserve anonymity.

17. In a survey conducted by *Kommun Aktuellt* 1 (16 January 1992): 2 and 3, a weekly devoted to municipal economy, in December 1991, 61 municipalities out of 265 that had answered the survey were working with a client-contractor model.

18. For one of the earliest presentations of the model, see Andersson and Hansson (1989). For a detailed study of the rise and fall of the model, see Blomquist (1996).

19. The terminology is mine. After having read the case, Norman and Robertsson pointed out that they never regarded the developing of activity indicators as a project. Projects, they said, are for them much larger undertakings, such as planning for a new location of the main library or introducing a new computer system.

20. Decoupling issues so as to solve them one at the time is indeed a frequently used procedure, not the least when demands are irreconcilable, as Czarniawska-Joerges (1992:288) has observed.

21. Indicators in this regard are hybrids. The etymology of the term—Latin *ibrida*: mixed blood—evokes the idea of a cross between races, breeds, or species that differ in their genetic traits. Indicators, too, cross and combine technical, social, and narrative concerns. They are among those strange "objects" that can be regarded neither as purely cultural nor as purely natural, and tend, according to Latour (1991:7), to proliferate today, such as ecological issues, frozen embryos,

or new technologies such as virtual reality. Performance indicators are at one and the same time real, collective, and narrated.

22. The notion of inscription, originally from Derrida, is discussed by Latour and Woolgar (1987:45). It has been aptly actualized in the context of accounting by Robson (1992).

23. According to a tradition described by Mossberg (1977:224)

6

Narrating Performance: Activity Reports

The previous chapter, with its study of performance indicators, em-
barked on a discussion of the textualization of an organization's activity.
The present chapter pursues this discussion further and examines how a
particular type of organizational texts—annual or activity reports—narrate an organization's activity and through this narration compose the
organization's performance. Again, this chapter deals with public libraries. The aim is to examine one of the surfaces at which the discourse
emerges and to intercept the modes of constituting that discourse before
these have sunk too deeply into the organization's logic, as may be the
case, for example, in industrial organizations.

Activity reports, in particular in the form of annual reports, are meant
to be important documents. They are produced at regular intervals, are
readily available to anyone who is interested, sometimes receive considerable publicity, and are of an official character. They are also the most
articulated and comprehensive documents available on a given organization, its activity, its results, and its achievements. For people outside the
organization, whether the public or specific political bodies, and for most
of those within the organization, activity reports are of crucial importance for assessing the organization's outcomes. Thus, more generally,
they are of crucial importance for what is to be regarded as the organization's performance, just as financial analyst reports are important ele-

ments in the construction of an organization's identity and of its environment, as observed by Boland and Bricker (1995).

Section 1 describes the study and section 2 presents library activity reports, detailing who it is that speaks (the narrator), to whom (the audience), and how (the language). Section 3 focuses on the narrative structure of these reports, describing how activity reports provide positive accounts of the organization's activity, how these accounts are organized as multiplot stories, and how they appear in a serialized manner. The concluding section restates how activity reports narratively construct an organization's performance.

The background of such an approach to annual and activity reports is to be found in the growing interest that organizational studies have shown in organizational texts (Fiol 1989), organizational stories (Martin et al. 1983), organizational narratives (Mumby 1987), narratives of organizational actors (Clair 1993), organizations as texts (Czarniawska-Joerges 1992), fictions regarding organizations (Czarniawska-Joerges and Guillet de Monthoux 1994), the rhetoric of administration (Sköldberg 1994), and fictions as heuristic devices applicable to organizational studies (Marini 1992).

Interest in these matters provides strong support for a theory of organizations in which an organization is regarded as a storytelling system (Boje 1991), and illustrates the relevance and fruitfulness of textual approaches within organization studies (Gephart 1993; Hummel 1991; Silverman 1994), the present chapter aiming too at illustrating the relevance of such approaches.

Description of the Study

Open a library activity report. It tells us how the buildings involved have been renovated. It lets us enter the office of the head librarian to estimate whether the budget has been adhered too. It takes us to the information desk to reckon how often patrons get right answers to their queries. It lets us count how many items are left on the bookshelves after the latest weeding-out campaign was completed. It takes us out of the main library to the different outreach activities. Just before that, we are taken to the main hall of the library to see how many people above twenty-five years of age cross its threshold. We are then taken back to the head librarian's office, where we are reminded of the goals that have been set for the library. On the way there, we take a look at the new integrated computer system. A glimpse at the work of the city council is also provided. We are allowed to test the latest on-line database concerning the European Union. In the background we hear children laughing (again and again) at hearing how Emil from Lönneberga got his head stuck in the soup tureen, while we hear the rustle of dozens of daily newspapers being skimmed through in the newspaper room. Just as there are dozens of activities in parallel that constitute the activities of a library, activity reports recount dozens of stories in parallel.

Their purpose is to present the organization's activities in a meaningful way, and to do that they organize the library's activities in stories. Activity reports select which events are to be presented at the end of the year as representative of the library's activities and provide a specific account of these events. Each in its own manner, they deliver stories about the library and its activities.

This is, in any case, how activity reports are approached in this study: as presenting organizational stories. The study does not investigate whether activity reports are objective and accurate, what use is made of them, or what theoretical function they may have in an organization. What is focused upon are the narrative features of the stories that activity reports recount.

Activity reports are analyzed here with the help of an analytical framework that uses categories of analysis which narratology—the field of literature studies that deals with narrative structure—has identified as central to the analysis of narratives, such as who the story is told to, how intrusive the narrator is, what the traits and attributes of the characters are, how time runs in the text, or how the plot is organized.[2] The framework employed uses categories that Stegman (1987) selected in his study of the rhetoric of annual reports, and discusses the outlook and arrangement of such reports, the use of positive and diminishing words, and the presence of a table of contents, of highlights, and of multi-years analysis. (See Appendix 2 for a more detailed description of this framework.)

The reports come from thirteen municipal libraries: Eskilstuna, Eslöv, Gävle, Helsingborg, Hässleholm, Höör, Kristianstad, Landskrona, Lund, Malmö, Partille, Trelleborg, and Umeå. I first chose libraries I had visited when doing previous work, considering it an advantage having seen the actual places. I then looked for other places that might be producing interesting activity reports, consulting here the professional press, peers, and contacts within the library world; this led me to approach Gävle, Eskilstuna, and Partille. Two other places I had in mind blankly refused to send me anything. From another one, I received a twenty-page paper prepared for a library conference, describing an activity measurement project they had conducted; because of the unusual character of the text, I opted, after much hesitation, for leaving it out. A few more places were too late in sending me material for me to make use of it. This late material, however, just as with other reports I have gathered since, proved to be quite like the material I had collected. The thirteen libraries provided me with more examples that I could ever use.

The libraries were contacted by phone and were asked to send documents that in one way or another accounted for the library's 1993 activities and results. Some sent the library's annual activity report, or some other form of report on the library, whereas others sent the annual activity report of the municipality (see section below for further details; see also Appendix 3 for a list of the documents used in this chapter). Which of these it turned out to be depended on which documents they deemed to best correspond to my request and which documents were available at the time (February-April 1994).

Narrative Features of Activity Reports

Appearance, Titles, and Content

Library activity reports are quite simple documents. Cover pages, if any, are plain and only rarely make use of pictures. They are unadorned documents that are far distant from the glamorous brochures that listed companies hand out to their shareholders. There are some exceptions, though. The report of the Eskilstuna Public Library, for instance, uses many drawings and illustrations. Also, the activity report for 1993 of the cultural administration of the Kristianstad municipality reminds one of a magazine, with its pictures of people attending and participating in various cultural events (Verksamhetsberättelse 1993). On the whole, however, activity reports are texts that display no sophisticated layouts.

The titles that are given to activity reports can differ considerably. At the library level, the standard title is *verksamhetsberättelse* (annual activity reports of the library), and at the municipal level it is *årsredovisning* (municipal annual report). Still, other designations are used as well.

Malmö prints a yearly *Verksamhetsplan* (activity plan) and an *Årsanalys* (annual analysis). Similarly, the staff at the library in Umeå speaks of their *Planeringsdokument* (planning document). Helsingborg Public Library has produced a document entitled *Uppföljning av mål—93* (goal assessments—93), whereas the document sent by the Höör Public Library to the library board is labeled *Resultatanalys* (result analysis).[3] As indicated by these titles, the intention of these documents is to account (*redovisa, redovisning*) for the activity (*verksamhet*) in question and possibly to provide an analysis (*analys*) of it. Likewise, reports speak of planning (*planering*) of goals (*mål*) or of results (*resultat*). These are documents purposely written to tell us what the library has done and achieved, the two main dimensions of performance.

This does not mean, however, that activity reports deal with library activities only. Let me, for example, present some of the terms used to recount the library's activity in the reports of the libraries in Partille and in Eskilstuna—two reports that resemble many of the others in this respect.

Terms from the Activity Report of the Partille Cultural Board (Section 47: Library Activities, in Order of Appearance):

circulation
library branch
adult students
discontinuation
teenagers
in-house use of material
fiction
information queries
genealogical research
stock
women
registered patrons
commissioned activities
staffing
resources
research library
interlibrary loans
information technologies

main library
unemployment
rotation of stock
children
sick or disabled persons
nonfiction
information center
video rentals
fees
sophisticated requests
visits
local associations
school administration
hours of opening
library network
loan orders
acquisitions
Bibliotekstjänst AB
(Library Service Inc.)

international databases
tourism
collaboration
competence

regional databases
outreach activities
vocational education
education

**Terms from the Eskilstuna Public Library Report
(Verksamhetsberättelse 1993, from the Highlights Presented on
the First Two Pages of the Report, in Order of Appearance):**

activity
main library
loans
public
schools
information services
junior information services
possibilities
teenagers
training abroad
the European Union
voting
job-development programs
public lectures
pleasure (of reading)
Arbetslivsfonden[4]
high school
university
priorities
renovation
goal document

circulation
adults department
visits
exhibitions
popular studies federations
staff resources
queries
studies
work
network
The Swedish Foreign Office
citizens
professional competence
women
criminal novels
front office
college
unemployment
rebuilding
public space

These two lists of terms illustrate quite well that activity reports, although they focus primarily on internal library matters, also touch upon
matters that lie outside librarianship, such as municipal policy, economy,
management, and administration. Reports deal with the network of the
organization's contacts. The Malmö report takes one, for example, on a
trip far outside the library, to the European Union Embassy in Stockholm,
to the Assembly of European Regions, and to Catalonia, via issues of
cultural policy and trends in contemporary architecture (Årsredovisning
1993).

Reports provide highly comprehensive descriptions of the library's total field of activity. These descriptions encompass not only the activities of the library per se, but also the conditions under which the activities take place and the priorities that are set, both within and surrounding the organization. Moreover, as a comparative reading of the two lists above shows, such universes that reports describe are quite different from one report or one library to the other since different types of events are being presented and the various aspects of activity receive differing degrees of attention.

The descriptions that activity reports provide of a library's activity can be made in large strokes, as when it is indicated in a one-line sentence that there has been a 33 percent rise in the efficacy of the library over the past five years (Lund, Årsredovisning 1993), or when it is stated in only a few lines that the library has achieved its goals for the year satisfactorily (Malmö, Årsredovisning 1993).

Description can also be very detailed. The 1992 activity report of the Lund Public Library (Verksamhetsberättelse 1992), for example, relates how a cultural evening dealing with "the America of the American Indians" was organized with "music, dance, food and myths from South America." It tells us that the library organizes cultural activities outside office hours, that the library is an opening to the whole world, that the library aims at fulfilling the role of calling forth awareness of contemporary cultural trends (in this case, a re-evaluation of American history from the perspective of the American Indian), and that the library is much more than books alone, indeed that it is a comprehensive cultural center for the community, with culture being understood in more of an anthropological than a fine arts sense. Likewise, when the same report states that "by tradition, story telling sessions are held at 10 A.M. and they are usually attended by a large audience" and that "from the autumn onwards, the adult department first opened at 11 A.M., whereas the children's section opened at 10 A.M.," it tells us that the library has a tradition of the oral transmission of children's literature, that this is an activity that is appreciated by the public, that children's activities are given a high priority, but also that it may be difficult to keep such a tradition alive in its present form, since it may be necessary to delay the opening of the children's department by an hour, as is already the case for the adult department (observe the word "first"), which hints at the danger of the library not being open to children at the traditional time for this activity. Through this, the reader is informed of the activities the library undertakes, of the priorities that have been set, and also, though in discrete form, of the long-run consequences that budget reductions might have upon the activity.

Library activity reports deliver such descriptions on a yearly basis. Some reports, such as that in Kristianstad (appendix to the Verksamhetsberättelse 1993), provide the reader with detailed lists of the various cultural events that have been staged, and a report such as Malmö's specifies that the final stages of discussions on the building of an extension on the main library occurred in the first half of the year, and even more precisely, that promotion of poetry reading on local trains occurred in May (Årsredovisning 1993). Most reports, though, provide only aggregated accounts of the year that has been. Rare are statements of the type "whereas the first X months showed a decrease in A [something], the remainder of the year showed an increase in it," or vice versa.[5] Activity reports are yearly publications, and this is the time frame they use to present the organization's activity.

Library activity reports are usually unpretentious. Still, behind their unassuming facades and their somewhat dull titles, one can find a remarkable capacity to portray complex pictures of the organization's performances.

Language

Library activity reports are written in a plain language, which is, roughly speaking, somewhere between spoken Swedish, official Swedish and newspaper Swedish. There are noticeable local differences, however. The report of Kristianstad, for example, leans more expressly toward reportage (Verksamhetsberättelse 1993). Management jargon is scattered through the one from Helsingborg, there being expressions such as: "the good encounter," "market evolution," "entrepreneurship," "pre-school customers," and "a decentralized, modern, need-driven and customer oriented organization." Most reports are somewhere in between, however. They are written in what could be termed casual administrative Swedish.

As was already touched upon in connection with the lists of nouns and expressions presented above, activity reports take one across a wide range of topics. Reading them thus mobilizes a wide range of specific knowledge. It mobilizes, first of all, knowledge of librarianship. Readers are supposed to be able to understand such terminology as: main library, library branches, circulation, information desk, outreach activity, stock, posts in databases, front and back office, library stands at workplaces, orders, interlibrary loans, delayed loans, in-house use of material, and indexed items. Some reports use specialized library terminology with parsimony—for example, Malmö and Eslöv (Årsredovisning 1993)— but most do not, simply assuming that the reader knows what terms of librarianship designate.

Reports also take us into the local geography of municipalities, which presupposes some acquaintance with the demographic and social pro- files of the places mentioned, as well as an acquaintance with the speci- ficities of the library, as, for example, when the report in Trelleborg speaks without further explication of The Pleasant Mondays Lectures *(Sköna måndag föreläsningar)* (Årsredovisning 1993). One is also required to master the basic principles and the terminology of business economics, involving such terms as running expenses, investments, and nontenured appointments. Last but not least, activity reports usually assume that readers are acquainted with the rules governing the Swedish municipal sector, such as the formal decision processes in a municipality. In the language they use, activity reports clearly indicate their belonging to the municipal administrative sphere.

A language that all the reports consulted tend to use abundantly is that of numbers, digits, and figures. Figures, as we saw in the context of sports, are master signs of performance stories. Figures are also master signs of the practice of accounting. Their swarming through activity re- ports can thus hardly come as a surprise. True enough, some reports are quite restrictive in their use of quantifiers (e.g., the 1993 Eslöv Munici- pal Annual Report on the library, Årsredovisning 1993). Yet about one fourth of the sentences in the report of Malmö (Årsredovisning 1993), half of them in the case of Landskrona (Årsredovisning 1993) and of Hässleholm (Årsredovisning 1993), two-thirds in the case of Partille (Verksamhetsbeskrivning 1993) and of Helsingborg (Årsredovisning 1993), and almost all the sentences in the appendix of the activity report of Kristianstad (appendix to the Verksamhetsberättelse 1993) are based on figures. It can also be observed that some reports, such as that of Höör, hardly use figures at all but use instead figure-like words such as "to increase," "to double," "half," or "third" (Årsredovisning 1993). Thus, aside from local differences, and for that matter differences between two separate texts produced in the same library,[6] the pervasiveness of the rhetoric of quantification in performance reports, once again, is clearly illustrated.

If one turns to performance indicators, about the same picture emerges. Various places and various documents differ considerably in the use they make of such indicators and the degree these are commented on. Some use no performance indicators, whereas Partille lists twenty-seven of them (Verksamhetsbeskrivning 1993). Also, indicators are sometimes commented upon and sometimes not. One can observe that it is nearly always about the same traditional indicators that are used: opening hours, visits, circulation, stocks, and acquisitions (these being usually computed either as gross for the year, as a percentage of the previous year, or per person). This is far removed from the hundreds of performance indicators that have been identified in literature on library management generally.

Most of the figures and performance indicators are used to establish comparisons, but, as far as the sample is concerned, usually not direct comparisons between libraries. Most comparisons involve the library itself, and concern year n versus year n-1, or goals versus achievements. When libraries compare themselves with others, it most often involves comparing their score on the traditional loan per inhabitant ratio against the national average. Public libraries performance stories tend to remain a matter of internal comparisons that make only few references to outside competitors.

Eventually, the performance stories, besides being rendered in casual administrative Swedish, are largely structured around figures that are available and that are deemed interesting. The traditional accounting ideal is never very far removed, since figures stand for precision and exactitude. It would undoubtedly be possible to summarize the history of the library's performances in long series of figures indicating how well the library scores on circulation, visits, entry, items, processing capacity, and so forth. True enough, activity reports are not composed exclusively of figures, but figures and comparisons are unquestionably key rhetorical features of the performance stories they recount.

Narrator and Point of View

From a formal point a view, reports are usually signed by the chief librarian (e.g., Eskilstuna, Verksamhetsberättelse 1993), or by the chief librarian and the chairperson of the library board (e.g., Lund, Årsredovisning 1993), or, when the library is a part of an integrated cultural administration, the name of the cultural director and of the chairperson of the cultural board appear (e.g., Helsingborg, Verksamhetsberättelse 1993; Höör, Årsredovisning 1993).

In some places, reports are expressly collective works in the sense of different sections of the text being signed by different persons (Landskrona, Verksamhetsberättelse 1992; Kristianstad, appendix to Verksamhetsberättelse 1993). Statements made by users can also be found (Eskilstuna, Verksamhetsberättelse 1993:4), but these seem to be rare. On the whole, activity reports lend their voice to the leadership involved, most often two-person leadership consisting of the manager and the chairperson of the board, which confers both an administrative (professional) and a political (democratic) legitimacy on the text.

Still, it is difficult to determine who, in practice, writes the report. One can often find significant differences in style and content between the successive drafts that pass the various administrative levels. The texts of activity reports receive impulses from different people during the process of being written. Annual library reports are in this regard similar to annual corporate reports, regarding, which Stegman has observed, that drafts of ideas are discussed by managers all the way to the boardroom, that texts are written and rewritten, and that pictures too are ordered to be retaken before the final version is approved, usually by the chief executive officer, the person who actually signs the letter to shareholders (1987:22). Of course, it can be different people from one year to the other.

Since several different persons can thus in formal terms be regarded as the author of the text, and since the writing itself cannot necessarily be traced to one or even to several specific persons, one should stress that, despite a report's being presented as though it were delivered by a single or a double voice, it is an all-hands evolution and it represents a multiindividual construction. This is why I choose to follow Stegman's (1987:22) suggestion to call the author, the originator, the writer, the initiator, the composer, the creator, or the producer of an annual report for its narrator.

A narrator writes from a given point of view, that is, from a given angle from which things are to be seen, where "seen" is to be interpreted here in a broad sense, not in the strict optical-photographic sense of what is visually perceived. This point of view (or focalization as it is also sometimes called) can lie with one or several characters, or it can be either inside or outside the story (the point of view cannot then be bound with that of any character, which tends to give the narrator a more neutral and detached position). In many stories, the point of view varies from one section of the text to another. In all cases, the point of view is an essential condition for the reader's understanding of a text since any given point of view entails a given way of looking at it (from Prince 1982:50; and Toolan 1988:67).

The issue is from which point of view are the performance stories that activity reports present written. The name or names attached to the text and the absence of any external author suggest that it is the point of view of some insider. The tone of reports, however, is generally quite detached. The degree of intrusiveness of the narrator is low. Pronouns such as we or I are rare, as are terms that express an opinion—for example, good or satisfactory—or that evaluate an observation—for example, important or successful. Activity reports thus seem to endeavor to tell as from the outside something that is known from the inside, as if they were to stand for both objective factuality and inside knowledge.

Metaphorically speaking, activity reports could be said to be written from the point of view of some little demons that observe and that have the unusual capacity of being at one and the same time both a part of the library's life (insiders), and external observers of this life (outsiders). They are insiders in the sense that they look at the activity with involvement and personal knowledge, and take account of the best and most relevant information available. They are outsiders too, however, in that they deliver their report in a detached and impersonal manner, as if they were seeing things from above or outside.

These demons happen to know exactly what management knows. However, they are neither the leadership nor the board, as indicated by the use of the third person to describe what the managers or board members do. In this sense, they regard all of the organization's members with the same external detachment.

The demons are on an outside that is in fact the inside.[7] They can be viewed as imaginary citizens who lend their eyes to real taxpayers. This is exemplified best in Malmö's report, where one can find the following observation of what visitors could see (as depicted from the point of view of a third party) when the Limhamn branch re-opened on new premises: "The new premises of the Limhamn branch were opened in March 1993. Visitors who came into the library at street level met a completely new library environment, with light wood flooring, blue shelves, each with its own lighting appliance, and a see-through front facing Linnégatan" (Malmö, Årsredovisning 1993:20). What the demons focus on is the library as such. In the sample studied, the verbs usually have the library as their subject. Likewise, it is the library that is the most frequent complementary agent of passive verbs, whether this is expressed or not. It is the library that does, that buys, that changes, that opens, that improves, that closes, that acquires, that presents, or that lends. The people who do these things tend to disappear behind what the organization is allegedly doing; few people are mentioned by name. Activity reports intensively reify and personify the library. In activity reports, the library is a human-like body that thinks, plans, acts, and sees. It is a Super-Person to use Czarniawska-Joerges' expression (1993:60).

The stories of an organization's performance in activity reports are delivered by demons who are unspecified and ambiguous narrators. Yet should we believe these demons? Well, we hardly have any other choice if we are to read activity reports. We in fact have scant possibilities of countering what is claimed. Even though we might be regular users of the library, we are there only now and then, and we use only a limited part—mostly the same part—of its services. Thus, our knowledge and impressions of its activities cannot help but be fragmented, biased, unsystematic, and under-informed. Unless there is a comprehensive auditing of the organization and a counter-report is available, our possibilities are very limited to discern whether or not that which the activity report says is relevant. We have only limited possibilities of determining whether the report is so reliable and so reasonably free of error and bias that it faithfully represents what it purports to, and thus adheres to the ideals of the traditional accounting paradigm. Our possibilities of checking the coherence of the text (do the comments match the figures?), of listing the weaknesses of presentation, or of being suspicious of the text in a systematic way are indeed small. We remain highly dependent upon what the report says. Our possibilities of resisting its hegemonic control of what is to be viewed as constituting the performance of the organization are minimal. Activity reports catch us up in their performance stories.

Audience

Not only is it difficult to ascertain who the narrator is, but it is also difficult to assess, from what the text says, who its audience is. The performance stories in activity reports are delivered largely unaddressed. Formally speaking, of course, activity reports are addressed to the certified accountants involved and to the citizens at large, the former in the name of generally accepted accounting practices and the latter in the name of democracy. (I wonder, however, how many citizens actually do read annual municipal reports). One can suppose, moreover, that they also interest people inside the organization, as well as politicians, journalists, and other people who are eager to inform themselves about the municipality's activities. Still, signs of the audience are scarce in the material studied. Some speak of writing "to the library board" or "to the municipal board," but most do not expressively say whom they are intended for.

That potential audience(s) can belong to groups that differ from each other drastically in their knowledge, interest, assumptions, political agendas, and institutional positions is a matter of significance. As discussed in chapter 3, performance is not simply what the text of the performance says it to be. The construction of performance requires and involves a reader as well. It is when the text of a performance meets its readers that the performance is actually completed. Since audiences of very differing background read the text of a performance, several different readings of the text are likely to occur. Thus, several different constructions of the organization's performances are likely to emerge. Still, nothing transpires in what activity reports say indicating whom the narrator has in mind as an audience(s). Anyone, indeed, can regard herself/ himself as the audience of their story.

By not revealing the identity of its audience(s), activity reports thus allow for the possible coexistence of multiple readings and thus multiple constructions of the organization's performance, constructions that can all be considered as equally legitimate, and indeed valuable, at least as viewed from within the text of the report. Uninvolved as they are, narrators do not enter into possible conflicts of interpretation. They therefore leave such conflicts unsolved, making it impossible for conceivable contradictions between how different groups read and thus construct the organization's performance to be solved from within annual reports as texts. Conflicts of interpretation must be solved outside them, for example within the organization or in the political arena.

Because of their silence as to the identity of their audiences, and because different audiences produce different readings, activity reports permit a pluralist construction of the organization's performances. The stories they present resist being read unidimensionally and this invitation for opinions to diverge is encouragingly democratic.

The Narrative Structure of Activity Reports

The previous section has described how activity reports deliver, in an administrative language and to an unspecified audience, detailed stories of achievements that are written from both internal and external points of view. The present section focuses on the narrative structure of these reports. It describes their positive character, their presenting multiplot stories, and their being serialized. The purpose is to describe further what sorts of stories annual reports present us to read.

Positive Accounts

A major feature of activity reports is their positiveness. To some, it may well seem that Swedish public libraries went through particularly difficult times in 1993. That year saw, for example, the closing down of several library branches. Many libraries lost their administrative independence when they were grouped in boards with other cultural activities or sports activities. Few recruitments were made and the population of librarians became older. Also, the overall economic situation of libraries was strained, even if the pressure on them was possibly less than on other municipal services.

Still, according to library activity reports and municipal activity reports in general, 1993 was a good year for Swedish public libraries. The decrease in circulation that started in 1987 gave way to an increase in the number of loans in many libraries. There were never so many people who visited the libraries as there were in 1993. Information desks answered more inquiries than ever before. Audiences of all sorts were offered the traditional flora of cultural programs. All over the country many positive organizational changes (e.g., computerization and automation, and space utilization changes) could be observed. A few warning signs only could be noted, in particular that the rise in activity was accompanied by a corresponding rise in spending. To put it briefly, according to the year's activity reports, 1993 was a year of increasing performance for Swedish public libraries, despite these being times of economic hardship.

Activity reports are written in a positive tone. If one lists positive and negative terms and expressions,[8] the former systematically outnumber the latter. The reports of Landskrona (Årsredovisning 1993) and of Höör (Årsredovisning 1993), for example, contain mostly positive words. That of Malmö is less positive but still shows a clear majority of positive words (Årsredovisning 1993). At most, negative terms are nearly as numerous as positive ones, such as in Lund (Årsredovisning 1993) or in Trelleborg (Årsredovisning 1993). In no case are there more negative terms than positive ones. "It won't take you anywhere to be whining," a chief librarian told me upon my sharing with her this observation. From how activity reports are written it seems that her analysis is shared by many in the profession.

Pessimistic allusions are not totally absent from activity reports, though. The reports of Malmö (Årsredovisning 1993), Helsingborg (Uppföljning), and Lund (Årsredovisning 1993), for example, end with an apocalyptic prophecy that public libraries will be unable to serve more and more people, with more and more sophisticated services, without receiving additional resources. The report of Partille refers explicitly to the long-range threat of diminishing acquisitions lessening the library's ability to serve their patrons' needs, especially when these needs become increasingly sophisticated (Verksamhetsbeskrivning 1993). Pessimist remarks, however, are formulated in a low key, as an undertone, and they do not take up more than a marginal share of the total text. Just as in other performance discourses (e.g., in sports), activity report stories tend to focus upon successful achievements and to ignore failures. This is confirmed by the total lack of statements of the type "we did not manage to...," or "we failed to...." Problematic results are, indeed, minimized. What is recounted is that which has been working, been successful, been attended, or been completed: activity reports end rather far from the traditional accounting ideal of a fair and true view of the activity.

To use Stegman's terminology (1987), public libraries are most often equivocators in the sense that they provide ambiguous and partial statements, and are often vaunters in the sense that they readily report on how well they are doing. Only a few of them are inventors, in the sense of providing rationales that differ markedly from those of most others. Similarly, only few of them are futurists that promise magnificent tomorrows, or even satisfiers that claim to have achieved their goals. Hardly any mention poor results. Libraries thus definitely avoid being blamers and try to place the responsibility for poor results on external factors. In annual reports, performances are the good things the library has done.

Multiplot Stories

As regards how they are arranged or organized, activity reports tend to cover many heterogeneous and unrelated topics. This leads them to be composed of sections of very differing nature. The activity report of the Umeå Public Library, for example, features paragraphs and sections as different in their nature and content as a section on circulation, one on visits, and one on improvements in the library as a working place, one on the enlarging of its information activities concerning the European Union, one on outreach activities, one on school libraries, one on activities specifically directed at youth, and one on cultural programs (Årsredovisning 1993). A standard library activity report thus consists of the following:

- the depicting of different activities (circulation, visits, inquiries),
- the depicting of the services provided for different types of clients (e.g., young people, and those covered by outreach activities),
- a section on economic matters,
- the depicting of specific projects (e.g., information on the European Union, computerization, and building repairs and improvements),
- a section on each local library branch and on the mobile library (if any),
- a comparison of past and future activities.

This does not mean that, in practice, all reports include all these sections. Whereas some topics such as circulation and visits are mentioned in all the reports, others such as the comparison of the past and the future are less frequently addressed. All reports in the sample nevertheless tend to show a similar blend of sections of rather differing nature. They freely take in sections of quite differing rationale, such as the rationale of activities, a geographical rationale and a thematic rationale. Each section tells its own story about the library.

The Malmö annual report (Årsredovisning 1993), for example, presents the story of a monumental library and the story of a reforming library. It also features stories of an effective library, a networking library, and a library as a key actor in the municipal cultural policy. It depicts, as well, the story of how the library is managed.

Yet there are only few attempts to link these stories. They are usually kept separate and it is only occasionally that explanations combine several of them. One can find in the Partille report, for example, the line of reasoning that since nonfiction items circulate more today than fiction items, and do so to an increasing degree, a growing number of users make use of the library as an information center, which reinforces the need for the library to be strong on recent technical literature. Such an analysis brings together circulation statistics, purchase policy, and developments in both economic resources and environmental variables (Verksamhetsbeskrivning 1993). One can find, as one does in Landskrona (Verksamhetsberättelse 1992; Årsredovisning 1993) or in Eskilstuna (Verksamhetsberättelse 1993), allusions to the relationship between the rise in circulation and the rise of unemployment. This is an analysis that links the roles of the library as a community center and as a training center with its activities concerning circulation and visits. These are rare examples, however. Results achieved in one area of the library's activity are usually not related to those achieved in another. Different sections tend to remain isolated from each other. As a result, activity reports resemble laundry lists, detailing what has been done in the organization within the past year.

Several features reinforce this impression of events and sections being piled one upon another rather than being ordered in a coherent chain of statements. Reports in the sample hardly ever make it clear why a particular section comes first and another last. Neither do they specify whether the results achieved in one section are more, or are less, important than the results achieved in another. Hardly any of them, by the way, have any regular tables of contents (Lund, Verksamhetsberättelse 1992 being a notable exception). Only a minority have a section highlighting the important events of the year (three in the sample: Lund, Årsredovisning 1993; Landskrona, Verksamhetsberättelse 1992; Hässleholm, Årsredovisning 1993).[9] Serious attempts to produce a synthesis of what is reported are virtually nonexistent.

Activity reports are collections of different sections based upon different rationales that simply exist side-by-side, each in its own right. To tell us the story of the library's performance, they tell us more than one story. As accounts, activity reports are split up into different substories. Each substory is told in a manner of its own, in its own terms and, in particular, in reference to its own past and its own future. Computerization is such a substory. Circulation, visits, children's activities, acquisitions, collections, and budget are others. Substories are crossed over and wrapped around each other in intricate though nonexplicit patterns.

Activity reports recount the performance of the library step-by-step, one activity or story at a time, through multiple stories that coexist as distinct lines of narration. The performance stories they present are not mono-narratives but multiple ones. Performance is constructed as a multidimensional narrative consisting of parallel subplots that maintain only loose relationships with one another. What ensures the unity of the performance story is that all these substories, in one way or another, are about what has been done and achieved by the library that year, and it is together that they constitute the performance of the organization.

Serialized Stories

What activity reports do is invite us each year to follow the positive progression of a selection of substories. They tell us for each activity what has happened during the year that has gone. Each annual report takes the reader *in medias res*—into the midst of things—which endows the organization's performance with an immediate contemporaneity. Step-by-step, one substory at a time, reports take us a few events ahead in the history of their library. The performance of an organization thus meets the definition of a serial story given by Hughes and Lund (1991:2) in their work on Victorian literature, of a continuing story over time with enforced interruptions. Reports are episodes in a serial. This has a major impact upon how we are invited to read performance stories.

Serialization fosters an approach to narrative as a gradually developing story consisting of patterns of significance, with pauses between parts for reflection and for speculation, rather than as a finished product to be read and considered as a whole all at once (after Hughes and Lund 1991:7). The period during which the reading occurs is noticeably longer, for example, than for an article or a monograph. In turn, the length of time between two installments—a year for activity reports—influences the perception readers have of the story delivered by the serial. Many things are likely to happen between two installments that can influence readers. The world, the country, the sector, the economic climate or the organization are all likely to change. The reading of a serial of activity reports is automatically intertwined with the reading of a considerable amount of other texts of diverse nature—not the least other activity reports—that all modify the readers' apprehension of the world. During the time between two installments, readers have time to forget details, substories, or even the main of previous episodes. The diachronic continuity of the organization's performance story, as delivered in successive activity reports, is thus threatened by the slow pace governing the separate installments of activity reports, as is the continuity of the story of the organization's performances.

Yet, activity reports are not constructed as episodes with an end (which would make them episodes of series instead of serials). By no means do activity reports consist simply of statements regarding what has gone on exclusively that year. Reports make references to past reports, and are much concerned with what is going to happen. Promises, announcements, plans, or previews are legion and ensure suspense and anticipation. Their narrative structure is a permanent reminder of their serial nature.

Activity reports obviously assume that the organization will exist the following year (and, by recurrent induction, all the years after that, precisely as in the accounting hypothesis of the going concern) and that the audience will be interested the next time too in knowing what has happened, so that it will have reasons to attend to the next installment. In so doing, activity reports assume a loyalty to the serial, and an acceptance by the audience of the periodicity and extended duration of the story's deliverance, and thus an acceptance that the performance story will go on toward a virtually infinite time horizon.

Underestimated cliff-hangers, activity reports tend to close with a "To be followed." In this way, activity reports acknowledge that for the organization the basic performance is that of survival. They also invite readers and reviewers to engage in what Hughes and Lund (1991:8) have called "provisional assumptions and interpretations," and leave the very performance during a given year a matter to view and assess both in the present and in the light of the future, which, like in sports, is an indication of the ambiguous relationships with time the notion of performance entertains.

Activity reports leave the story they present without closure, which casts an interesting light on the absence of a bottom line in public and in nonprofit organizations. In narrative terms, a bottom line would be a closure, whereas activity reports, with their split open-ended narrative structure, do not offer their readers closure. True enough, this absence of

closure allows them to leave contradictions unresolved, which is a convenient way of avoiding delicate assessments, as Fiske (1987:195) notes,
regarding the serial drama. At the same time, the absence of closure
isolates activity reports from the feeling of efficiency and the feeling of
legitimacy that closure entails (from a study by Bass 1985). In terms of
pleasure, activity reports, through their lack of closure, cannot provide
the reader with complete satisfaction—at least in the case of the mascu-
line goal-end-oriented reader (from an observation by Calhoun-French
1992). Rather, through noncompliance with the traditional Western desire for closure, activity reports endanger the unity of the subject they
present (Archer 1992), that is to say, the organizations themselves.

The issue is whether demands for a bottom line are not both unrealistic and superfluous. They are unrealistic in that one hardly sees how one
could manage to fit all the different dimensions of a library's activity into
a single story. They are also superfluous in the sense that organizations
indeed already do produce a sort of bottom line. This, of course, is not a
single-dimensional one, such as profit can be, but rather is a multidimensional one that consists of the point that each and every one of the
substories that comprise the serial of the organization's performances
has reached.

Demands for bottom lines are aesthetic demands. They are demands
that rest on a major aesthetic assumption, namely, that mono-narratives
are to be preferred to multiple ones, probably because they communicate
better. However, the stubborn success of serials as a genre—either the
Victorian serial novel, the *följetongsroman* (Swedish), the *roman-
feuilleton* (French),[10] the Fantomas films by Feuillade, or today's comic
strips and television drama serials—challenge such an assumption. Serials do communicate with their audience.

By evading closure, activity reports allude to an aesthetics of seriality
that, according to Eco (1990:97), wholly escapes the "modern" idea of art
and literature and relies upon the infinity of the text. Activity reports come
close, in this regard, to the infinite variations of sense making that are
possible. As serials, they invite their readers to return to the continuum, to
the cyclical, the periodical, or the regular (after Eco 1990:96), and they
invite one to a corresponding reading of the organization's activity.

Complaining about the absence of a bottom line is a matter of taste. On
the basis of the existence of profit in privately owned organizations, this
aesthetic preference is in the process of making its way into public man-

agement. Yet it has never been formulated in aesthetic terms. It has been dressed, instead, in the clothes of economic rationality. Driven by a taste for closure, the demand for a bottom line has been masked behind rationalistic argumentation. The study of the narrative structure of activity reports emphasizes, however, this being merely a matter of aesthetic taste.

Conclusion: Administrative Serials

Organizational lives, as Czarniawska-Joerges (1997) suggests, are analogous to serials in their being repetitive and open-ended; each episode of an organization's life, she argues, is a skillful mix of problems that are solved and problems that arise (ibid.). Activity reports depict, correspondingly, these lives episode by episode. Borrowing from both the narrative tradition of accounting and the tradition of literary serials, activity reports could be said to constitute a genre in itself: *the administrative serial.*

The administrative serial is very clear regarding the spatial aspects of performance: although the main library and its branches may be the most conspicuous part of the scene, they are definitely not the entire scene of library activity. Much of a library's performance is said to depend on conditions that lie outside the organization itself. When activity reports take us outside the library walls—for example, to homes for the elderly, to prisons, to outreach activities, to the city hall or to the virtual space of Internet—what they tell us is that what is happening in the library has to be considered in the light of what is happening outside. Activity reports effectively narrate the performance of a modern library as involving much more than the library itself: they make ambient economic ideas, political decisions, and geographical features part of the library's results and achievements. Activity reports repeatedly remind us that much of the performance of an organization depends on how the organization evolves in its environment. The architectural manifestation of a library is misleading in this respect. The physicality it bestows on the organization is illusive.

As texts that describe what has been done and achieved in the organization, administrative serials present their organization's performance. They not only reflect what has happened within the organization, but also participate actively in the shaping of what is to be considered as the organization's activities and performance. By naming, describing, ordering, and qualifying individual events, administrative serials let some of these events emerge from anonymity, gain meaning or signification, and become visible. Activity reports not only tell the story of what tasks have been defined as being those of the library and which have been identified as being worth mentioning, but they also reflect organizational choices and indicate both how the organization views its mission and how it views its accomplishments. Reports shape activities, tasks, priorities, choices, missions, and accomplishments, and provide them with a name, a history, and a *raison-d'être* (and sometimes even a price).

What activity reports recount of year n becomes a part of the reality of year n+1 and of the years thereafter. This is independent of the truth value (in the traditional sense) of what is said: any statements would play a part in the construction of the organization's reality. The reality of an organization's performance is what performance texts, such as activity reports, say of performance. Hines (1988) says about accounting that in communicating something, you create it. Similarly, one could say of organizational performance that activity reports create what they communicate.

Notes

1. Edward Sapir, *Selected Writings in Language, Culture and Personality*, edited by David G. Mandelbaum (Berkeley: University of California Press, 1949), 162.
2. These categories are common to Prince (1982; 1990), Rimmon-Kenan (1983) and Toolan (1988), and are debated at length in Martin (1986). The use of narratology outside literature studies follows a suggestion made by Bal (1990).
3. Höörs bibliotek, *Resultatsanalys 1993*, internal note.
4. *Arbetslivsfonden*, The Swedish Worklife Fund, is a state-funded foundation in Sweden, the purpose of which is to support initiatives that may improve safety at work and/or reduce occupational diseases.
5. In the Partille report, one can read , for example: "The introduction of a fee for genealogical researches has...induced a noticeable decrease in the demand for this service, namely from 17 500 crowns per half year before the fee was introduced to 2 300 crowns for the second half of 1993" (Verksamhetsbeskrivning: 4).
6. In Eskilstuna, for example, the activity report of the library makes only a moderate use of figures, but there is a special brochure that consists only of statistics (Eskilstuna stads och länsbibliotek, Södermanlands län, 1993, *Fakta om biblioteksverksamheten i Eskilstuna* [Facts about the Eskilstuna Library's Activity]). In Trelleborg, nearly all the sentences in the municipal annual report are centered around figures (Årsredovisning 1993), whereas no figures at all appear in the brochure that presents the library to the public (Trelleborg Bibliotek, Brochure).

7. "What about the author of these lines, then?" one could ask. "He observes the demons," one could say.

8. Examples of positive terms: a good year, a rise, an augmentation, an increase, a positive reception, collaboration, amelioration; rapid, productive, broad, well-visited; to inaugurate, to open, to improve, to reach, to initiate. Examples of negative terms: a problem, a decrease, a plunge, a danger, a threat, a deficit; to hollow out, to pull down, to limit, to stop. Neutral terms: to map, to study, to observe. True enough, one can regard a *reduction* in current costs as something positive and a *rapid augmentation* of these costs as something negative. The counting of positive and negative words that is referred to here is thus purely indicative.

9. Library annual reports differ significantly in this regard from corporate annual reports. As Stegman (1987:32) has observed, most corporate annual reports contain a letter to the shareholders and nearly all contain a financial highlights section that summarizes the important events of the year.

10. Although they experienced their strongest popularity at about the same period of time and indeed share a pattern of publication by installments, Victorian serial novels, Swedish *följetongsromaner* and French *romans-feuilleton* do not refer to exactly the same phenomena as Oscarsson's (1980) historical review of the genre in the Swedish press indicates, not the least because of national differences in literary traditions and the decisive roles played by individual newspaper editors such as François and Louis Bertin, or Lars Johan Hierta.

Conclusion: Meaningful Accounts

Innombrables sont les récits du monde.

—Roland Barthes[1]

In a somewhat paradoxical way, by telling us that the narratives of the world are numberless, Roland Barthes (1966) invites us to itemize them. If it were impossible to distinguish among stories, his statement would be nonsensical. This may be why Barthes emphasizes immediately thereafter both the prodigious variety of genres that exist, each branching out into media of various kinds, as well as the variety of narrative vehicles—written, in pictures, either still or moving, gestures, or a mixture of all these elements—these narratives can take.

Indeed, by affirming there to be an endless variety of narrative forms in the world, Barthes seems to maintain it is to be our duty to track this variety, to follow it with our attention. Barthes' emphasis on the innumerableness of stories also signifies how important it is that we understand what these stories tell. He enjoins us to investigate both what these stories have in common and what they have in particular. In so doing, he engages us in a Sisyphean pursuit. Yet it is the very impossibility for such a pursuit to come to an end that makes it akin to the pursuit of life itself and thus something worth striving for.

In response to Barthes' urging, the present book focuses on one particular form of stories: those of organizational performance. Viewed in a simplified way, organizational performance *stories* can be said to be nonfiction accounts of an organization's achievements, ones that, strongly influenced by both sports and accounting traditions, recounts what has been going on and what has been attained within an organization during a given period of time.

Like the myths analyzed by Greimas (1966), stories of performance are organized around dichotomies and oppositions. The first of these is that performance stories can be stories of actions as well as stories of results. This is a trait that has been found in the lexical content of the term, in the management literature, in the discourse of sports, in activity reports, and which is echoed by how differently connoisseurs and performance-focused spectators read performances. As Hatch (1995) observed, performing can be converted into a result at any time during the process. The nature of the results, likewise, is to be found in the history of the performing. One might agree with Baudrillard (1986:25) that there is a bias today in favor of defining performance simply as a result. Much of the notion's dynamism still comes from this ability to designate both action and outcomes. Ignoring that important trait would overthrow most of the notion's attractiveness.

The second pair of opposites upon which performance stories are constructed is the contrast of one process and outcome to other processes and outcomes. A deed is made into a performance in contrast to another deed. This presupposes the commensurability of the two, and the existence of an adequate—read precise, valid, and reliable—means of quantification. These contrastive oppositions are staged either as competitions or as comparisons, such as when two organizations are compared with each other, or when outcomes are compared with plans, which has been discussed at some length above. The nature of the opposition—be it competition or comparison—however, is not as important as the integration into a meaningful account of the terms that are contrasted.

The third pair of opposites that structures performance stories is that of success and failure. Success presupposes failure, just as a record performance presupposes an inferior result. Performance stories are stories of success, of records, and of feats, all of them more or less outstanding, yet they are just as much stories of nonachievements, however much the latter are systematically avoided in the explicit practice of performance discourse. Performance stories are stories that participate in the modernist belief in the possibility of separating with scientific certitude what is right from what is wrong, and in the progression of human conduct toward progress.

These three oppositions constitute the basic configuration upon which the local stories of organizational performances are produced. They constitute the elementary configuration of what I have labeled modern *agon* (see chapter 4). Yet, as collective creations of organizational actors, organizational performance stories follow the highly specific rules—the formal hierarchical order, for example—that organizations set up for communicating. Every single story elaborates on that configuration, for its own needs and according to its own premises. This is why the interpretation of performance stories cannot be detached from an understanding of the intersociability of the context of production of the stories, especially since such an understanding of the local context of the performance stories is the condition for understanding how a particular story defines what is a performance.

The present chapter recaps the most central narrative features of organizational performance tales. It emphasizes again organizational performance being narrative productions, and it aims at clarifying the distinctive features of such stories. Not every story represents an organizational performance story. The lexical content of the term, the use made of the notion in management literature, and the idea that organizational actors have of the performances of their organization, all contribute to delineating what one can reasonably regard a performance story to be.

Organizational performance stories are countless in number and in types. For any given event—a business transaction, for instance—one can adopt different judgmental criteria, different ways of writing, and different ways of reading. For each of the choices involved, a different performance is produced. Multiplying in one's imagination the number of possible criteria—going as far as creativity can take one—in the number of possible ways of recounting an event—in a written, oral, gestural, or other manner—and in the number of readings anyone can make of a text—now and later—provides one with an idea of the vertiginous number of performance stories that potentially exist in connection with any given event. If one takes into account, moreover, how many aspects of social life are currently viewed in terms of performance, one can easily agree that there is virtually an infinite number of performance stories. This should not deter us, nevertheless, from trying to identify the specificities of performance stories.

Organizational Performance Stories

My original aim was to study, in the particular context of organizations, the "contemporary cult" that performance represents, as Ehrenberg (1991) puts it. This aim has led me to present a study that peregrinates into etymology, sports history, management literature, Swedish public libraries, and literary serials. Some might think this a somewhat erratic way of presenting things, believing one should stay within one's academic field. That I chose, however, to present the study as I did, is because of my repeated feeling during my work of the need to go outside the disciplines of management and organization studies to grasp the use that is made of the notion of performance within organizations. Understanding both what performance means for an athlete and how the term can be translated to other languages from English turned out to be necessary for comprehending the use of the notion by organizational actors. The chapter structure adopted for the study's presentation reflects my path to understanding (even though the order of presentation of the chapters does not correspond exactly to the order in which these chapters were conceived). Indeed, I regret that I could not plunge into still more contexts where the notion is used. I wish, for example, that I had contrasted the use made of the performance notion in theater studies or in anthropology with its use in engineering or in work assessment, since I suspect all impinge in some way upon how performance is told in organizations. However, one can well understand that no individual can master such a wide array of academic disciplines, not to mention the disastrous impact that an accumulation of areas could have on the clarity and, indeed, the aesthetics of the study.

As I went ahead, I became increasingly convinced of the adequateness of seeing performances as being stories. This gradually evolving conviction of mine was not foreign, of course, to the increasing acceptance, within social sciences in general (e.g., Polkinghorne 1987), and within management studies in particular (e.g., Czarniawska-Jeorges 1997), of a narrative approach to understanding human activities. What convinced me most, however, was how well the approach to performance in terms of a story catered to fundamental aspects of organizational performance. Considering performance as a story—in a literal sense, not a metaphorical one—fitted, for example, Norman's (my respondent at the Storköping Public Library) recurrent concern with adequate ways of interpreting and explaining the library's activity. My interest grew stronger when I realized that an activity report is called in Swedish a *verksamhetsberättelse*, which in a word-for-word translation stands for the story of the activity. Later, focusing on the narrative character of performance opened innovative insights into the role that measurement plays in management literature on performance. Increasingly, the idea of performance being a story not only organized the observations I had gathered, but also pointed to a new and exciting direction for my research.

To me, viewing an organization's performance as a story emphasizes that a performance is not what an organization does and achieves, but rather something that is recounted about what an organization does and achieves. It thus indicates that performance is a matter of telling. Considering the way that most texts within management literature on performance approach performance (see chapter 2), and saying that performance is a story, thus involves a dramatic displacement of performance from the realm of action and results to the realm of accounts. Such a displacement from what is done to what is said (is done) has major consequences for the study of performance: it propels to the fore, as the central issue in the study of performance, the question of meaning and sense making. This displacement is one from the question "What is performance?" to the question "How is it that performance accounts are meaningful?"

The answer to this question is that the very organization of events into stories turns these events into something meaningful. Take, for instance, a statement such as "Astra's sales of Losec in 1993 amounted to SEK 7,115 (4,347)m., up 64 percent" (Astra's 1993 annual report, page 6).[2] It is when reported—and compared with 4,347—that sales of 7,115 acquire their meaning. Through this comparison, sales are turned into part of a story: the story of how sales during that period rose to more than 7 billion Swedish crowns, 64 percent above the previous year's sales. Comparison binds the two figures together and it is from this that meaning emerges.

By contrasting the two figures, comparison organizes the budget and the outcome into a progression. This progression goes from state A—1992 year's sales of 4,347—to state B—1993 year's sales of 7,115—the passage from A to B being the passage between two states of equilibrium. The 1992 sales become a before, and the 1993 sales an after, with a year of sales activity intervening between the two. The sales for 1992, the budget for 1993, the selling efforts of that year, and total sales for 1993 are put into a chain of events. Every single act of anyone in the sales department or the company at large that year is framed within that story of the move from 4,347 (1992) to 7,115 (1993). Once inserted into their slot in a time progression, events are made part of a story. This is how they become meaningful, and also how and why people can remember them and identify with them (as when a salesperson describes a day's or a year's efforts as an effort to meet the budget's target).

If the organization of events in a temporal progression is a process of creation, it is because from progression one easily moves on to explanation. Narrative accounts do not simply organize events in a chronology, they also tend to organize them in terms of causality. Take, for instance, such comments as: "Although our sales trend was influenced by the weakened Swedish Krona, the *increase in volume* was on the order of 20 percent" (ibid., 2, emphasis original), or a statement such as: "The strong growth now shown by Astra is largely an effect of the exceptionally competent work performed, in stiff competition, by Astra's international marketing organization" (ibid., 2).

By sharing successes and failures, such comments translate single events into elements of blame and credit. Because they tell how one moved from the state of before to the state of after, these comments provide meaning to individual sales events. Variance analysis can then take the causal analysis further and detail how much of the year's result is due to a volume effect and how much is due to a price effect. Strategy tales, in turn, come into play—at the discretion of the narrator—in celebrating the daring current CEO or bitterly criticizing the former top management team. Here, for instance, is how the 64 percent rise in sales for Losec was introduced in the report:

> The antipeptic-ulcer agent Losec, Astra's largest-selling product, represents an important medical advance in the treatment of ulcers in the duodenum, stomach and esophagus. Losec is the dominant product in the *gastro-intestinal* area. This product has now been approved in about 80 countries for short-term therapy. Losec has also been approved for long-term therapy of poorly responsive peptic ulcer and esophageal ulcer in more than 20 countries. In 1993, this product was also approved for the first time for general long-term therapy in certain countries. (ibid., 6)

There is no doubt, from what the annual report says, that Losec's market success involved an adequate strategic approach to human biology and to national legislation on medical treatment, one involving a skillful mix of commercial and research efforts. Because of its associating with one another elements of differing nature, the passage on Losec succeeds in being a meaningful causal account of a 2.8 billion rise in sales for a single product. And so on, with accountants keeping the story going, entry by entry, in the general ledger for any interpretation to come.

It is not my aim here to provide a theory of how stories produce meaning. I simply want to restate, in line with Gumbrecht (1992:45), for example, that narration represents a basic means of sense formation (without, for that matter, making any claim as to alternative modes of experience).

Boland (1993) has shown how organizational actors give meaning to accounting texts by organizing their interpretation into stories that provide a context for these texts and make it possible for the actors to go beyond the "surface" or "obvious" meaning of these texts into a deeper, more subtle and more sophisticated reading. What I want to illustrate here is how it is the organization of events into tales that provides these events with meaning and that ultimately enables one to speak of organizational performance. The linearity of a narration creates meaning. So does the translation of one event into another, such as when the development of a performance indicator set becomes a means for implementing a client-contractor model (chapter 5). So does the inserting of events into a set of rules that govern them, as in sports (chapter 3). Relating one notion to another—for instance when performance evaluation becomes part of a well-functioning democratic machinery (chapter 2)—produces meaning too. The meeting of a performance text with its readership (chapter 3) is likewise an instance of meaning production. So are the use of fashionable metaphors (chapter 4), techniques for presenting annual reports (chapter 6), choice of a split narrative structure (chapter 6), preference for (or rejection of) well-established measures of performance (chapter 2), the adoption of a nonintrusive all-knowledgeable point of view in activity reports (chapter 6), and the inscribing of a given performance within a tradition (chapter 4). As this enumeration suggests, the sense in stories is everywhere: in their rhetoric, their coherence, their duration, and their context.

Get the Story Straight!

The specific features of performance stories are constraints on them in the sense that individual stories cannot deviate much from the features generally associated with the genre of performance stories without the risk of their failing to be identified as performance stories.

There is, for example, a ban on pure invention in performance stories. Performance stories have to give the impression of providing a faithful and trustworthy rendering of the organization's activity. Even though performance stories may involve creative presentation of activities—we saw that creativity is an integral part of the work of developing performance indicators, and we know that financial accounting can prove to be a very creative endeavor—invention is not allowed to be the main vector of performance stories. Novelists can imagine any sort of managerial exploit—such as in Gower novels[3]—but performance writers cannot declare just any given drug to be "an important medical advance in the treatment of ulcers in the duodenum, stomach and esophagus" (Astra's Annual report, page 6) or just any particular organization to be "among the fastest-growing pharmaceutical companies in the world market" (ibid., 2), as Astra's annual report is entitled to do. In this regard, advertisements can come much closer to fiction than performance stories do.

Likewise, performance stories have to be explicit. Ideally, they have to provide an immediate and integral access to what is an outcome and at least implicitly to what is not, to the context of competition, to the terms of the comparison, to background information and to causal links. Clarity is for performance stories a requirement, something witnessed, for example, by the impressive amount of notes appended to the financial statements of private companies.

Still, countless performance stories are possible for any given single event. One can tentatively adopt highly different judgmental criteria. The performance literature provides an extensive selection of performance measures. Each of these is an expression of performance criteria, such as that when one prefers return on equity to return on sales; what counts is financial or commercial success. Organizations add to these measures other customized measures that fit their own premises. The choice of a criterion is decisive in that it indicates the direction of achievement: in sports this corresponds to the choice of a discipline, and in organizations to the choice of which aspects of the activity are to be regarded as important.

It is remarkable that, whereas performance is caught between the criteria adopted and the conditions of their being put into operation, in discussions of performance the choice of criteria is usually left out. This is the case, for example, when authors of management literature fail to inform their readers of their motives for preferring the use of some particular criterion of performance. This leaving out of the motives for performance criteria from performance stories can also be found in the differences in the concerns of Norman and of Robertsson in the Storköping Public Library while working on the development of indicators, and in the presentation they made of them in the professional press (chapter 5). It is also to be found in sports, where discussing performance criteria is discussing the foundations of the sports discipline in question.

Differences in criteria lead, anyway, to the adopting of different points of view, different strategies of selection, collection, and inscription, and the production of differing performance texts. The point is that, even with a given criterion, writing leads to extensive variation in how an event can be recounted. The choice of words, the order of arguments, and the choice of tropes are decisive. I remember a company's share dropping several points, for example, when a press release announcing the third quarter report stated that earnings that year would be *twice* those of the previous year. The drop was because of the second-quarter report having promised that earnings would be *at least twice* those of the previous year: several million kronor disappeared with what—for the company—was an unfortunate choice of words. Think, also, of how different the various comments may be upon the publication of national budget figures or of an OECD report on a country's economy. Writing strategies are important when it comes to the textualization of an organization's activity. The company world seems well aware of this, in view of the care that is taken in the writing of corporate annual reports.

The reading of stories, then, increases still further the number of stories that are possible. Organizational performance stories are, in this regard, like sports performance stories. Think of the difference between a connoisseur and a performance-focused spectator reading a sports game (chapter 3), or of an audience reading a serial (chapter 6): reading is an individual sense-making process, there being as many stories as there are readings, by different people at the same time, by the same people at different times, or when the two are combined.

As stated in the chapter's introduction, if one multiplies the number of social life events one can consider in terms of performance by the number of possible criteria one can use to judge an event, then multiplies that by the number of possible ways of recounting the event, and finally multiplies that in turn by the number of readings one can make of this account, one ends up with a very considerable number of potential performance stories indeed. There are so many of them, in fact, that any event at all can end up being performance. If the criteria, the way of writing, or the way of reading are adjusted appropriately, virtually any event can be told as performance. It is simply a matter of imaginative narration!

In this view, anything can be turned into a performance. Performance being a story that is akin to a performative (Austin 1962), one needs simply to get the story straight, for example, through finding a favorable angle, imagining an engaging way of writing, and addressing oneself to a benevolent audience. This is no provocation on my part, but the mere observation that, provided you respect the rules of the genre and make use of your imagination in creating the story, any event can be conceived in a way that will fit within the narrative framework of a performance story.

Accounts of Significance

Performance stories are accounts of significance. They are significant in organizations because they recount the organization's achievements (or achievements undertaken in the name of the organization) and confirm the organization's being an instance of production. By celebrating outcomes and purposiveness, performance stories help individual actors to make sense of their daily individual efforts. They also gather organizational actors, presenting the superiority of the organization today compared with its own past and with other organizations. Performance stories participate in the making and holding together of organizations. (A direction for future research would be to study the role taken by performance stories in the institutionalization of organizations, for example, as organizational myths.)

Performance stories are also significant at the societal level in that they voice and echo the inclination of modern societies to seek efficacy as a means, end, and justificatory mode, a concern that Lyotard (1979) designates as specific to our times. Performance stories, through their explicit elevation of competition to a universal yardstick of value, their repeated affirmation of the necessity of measurement, and their glorification of champion performers, belong to the mythologies that we and our contemporaries cherish in order to, among other things, convince ourselves of our own superiority.[4] Performance tales are here to make such a belief in our superiority possible.

Organized in endless patterns of repetitions and redundancies, performance stories fulfill a need we have to reassure ourselves of our operative capacity to face the problems we identify as being important but which we have no effective solution to. I think here of problems such as poverty and illiteracy, pollution, fair access to drinking water and to medicine, as well as crime and wars: all of these pressing problems with no solution in sight. Faced with such problems and their repeatedly demonstrated resistance to solution, our societies need to be confirmed in their capacity to achieve. This, I believe, is what makes performance stories potent. Each performance connotes a little progress and signals one's having achieved something here and now that is better than that achieved at earlier times or other places.

Performance stories are practical attempts to prove the capacity of our societies to operationalize progress. They try to indicate that, despite daily signs to the contrary, we are indeed moving toward progress. Not being simply modernist stories, performance stories are stories that keep the modernist dream afloat.

Notes

1. R. Barthes, "Introduction à l'analyse structurale des récits," *Communication*, no. 8 (1966): 1. "The narratives of the world are numberless," translation by Stephen Heath, in "Introduction to the Structural Analysis of Narratives," *Image-Music-Text* (London: Fontana/Collins, 1977), 79.
2. AB Astra, S-151 85, Södertälje, Sweden, telephone: + 46-8-553 260 00.
3. Gower novels are management textbooks disguised as works of fictions. E.g., Eliyahu Goldtratt and Jeff Cox, *The Goal* (Hants, United Kingdom: Gower, 1989); or Alan Warner, *Beyond the Bottom Line* (Hants, United Kingdom: Gower, 1992).
4. In the sense given the term *mythology* by Roland Barthes (1957:194): a system of signification; a mythology is a form of expression for a set of beliefs considered meaningful by a given population during a given period.

Appendix 1:
List of Dictionaries Consulted for Chapter 1

English Language

The Barnhart Dictionary of Etymology. 1988. R. K. Barnhart, editor. S. Steinmetz, managing editor. New York: The H.W. Wilson Company.

Collins COBUILD English Language Dictionary. 1987. London: HarperCollins Publishers. (COBUILD: Collins Birmingham University International Language Database)

Collins English Dictionary. 1991. Third Edition. J. M. Sinclair, general consultant. London: Harpers Collins Publisher.

A Comprehensive Etymological Dictionary of the English Language. 1967. By E. Klein. Amsterdam: Elsevier Publishing Company..

A Dictionary of Contemporary American Usage. 1957. By Evans B. and C. Evans. New York: Random House.

Dictionary of Scientific and Technical Terms. 1974. Lapedes D. N., editor in chief. New York: McGraw-Hill Book Company.

International Dictionary of Management. 1986. Third Edition. Johannsen H. and G. T. Page. London: Kogan Page.

Longman Dictionary of Business English. 1982. Adam J. H. Harlow: Longman and York Press.

Management Glossary. 1968. Compiled by H. Johannsen and A. Robertson. Edited by E. F. L. Brech. London: Longman.

The New Palgrave Dictionary of Money and Finance. 1992. Newman P., M. Milgate and J. Eatwell, editors. London: McMillan.

New Practical Standard Dictionary of the English Language. 1955. Britannica World Language Edition. C. E. Funk, editor. New York: Funk and Wagnalls Company.

Oxford Advanced Learner's Dictionary of Current English. 1992. Encyclopedic Edition. Cowie A.P., chief editor. Oxford: Oxford University Press.

The Oxford Encyclopedic English Dictionary. 1991. J. M. Hawkins and R. Allen, editors. Oxford: Clarendon Press.

The Oxford English Dictionary. 1989. Second Edition, prepared by J.A. Simpson and E.S.C. Weiner. Oxford: Clarendon Press.

The Oxford Thesaurus: An A—Z Dictionary of Synonyms. 1991. Urdang L. Oxford: Clarendon Press.
The Random House Dictionary of the English Language. 1987. Second Edition, Unabridged. Flexner S. B. New York: Random House.
Roget's International Thesaurus. 1992. Fifth Edition. R. L. Chapman, editor. London: Harper Collins Publishers.
Webster's Third New International Dictionary of the English Language. 1966. Unabridged. P. B. Gove, editor in chief. London: G. Bell and Sons, ltd.

French Language

Dictionnaire de la langue française. 1957. Littré E. Paris: Gallimard—Hachette.
Dictionnaire des synonymes de la langue française. 1947. Par R. Bailly sous la direction de M. de Toro. Paris: Librairie Larousse.
Dictionnaire historique de la langue française. 1992. Sous la direction de A.Rey. Paris: Dictionnaires le Robert.
Encycloplédie du bon français dans l'usage contemporain—Difficultés, subtilités, complexités, singularités. 1972. Dupré P. Comité de rédaction sous la présidence de F.Keller avec la collaboration de J.Batany, Paris: Editions de Trévise.
Grand Larousse de la langue française. 1976. Paris: Librairie Larousse.
Le grand Robert de la langue française, Dictionnaire alphabétique et analogique de la langue française de Paul Robert. 1985. Deuxième édition. Par A. Rey. Paris: Le Robert.
Nouveau dictionnaire des difficultés du français moderne. 1987. Deuxième édition. Hanse J. Paris: Ducuclot.
Trésor de la langue française—Dictionnaire de la langue du 19è et du 20è siècles (1789–1960). 1988. Publié sous la direction de P. Imbs. Paris: Centre National de la Recherche Scientifique et Gallimard.

Swedish Language

Bonniers svenska ordbok. 1986. S. Malmstöm, I. Györki, and P. Sjögren. Stockholm: Bonniers.
Facklig ekonomisk ordbok. 1980. Utarbetad av en arbetsgrupp inom Landsorganisationen. Stockholm: Landsorganisationen Tidens förlag.
Norstedts svenska ordbok. 1990. Utarbetad vid Språkdata Göteborgs Universitet: Norstedts.
Nusvensk Ordbok. 1938. Av O. Östergren. Stockholm: Wahlström and Widstrand.

Ordbok över svenska språket. 1954. Utgiven av Svenska akademien. Lund: Gleerupska universitets bokhandel.

Ord för ord—Svenska synonymer och uttryck. 1992. Fjärde reviderad upplaga. Reviderad av H. Blomqvist. Lillemor Swedenborg, redaktion. Stockholm: Norstedts.

Svensk ordbok. 1986. Utarbetad vid Språkdata Göteborgs Universitet. Vetenskaplig ledare S. Allén. Solna: Esselte Studium.

Svenska akademiens ordlista över svenska språket. 1986. 11 upplagan. Stockholm: Norstedts Förlag.

French-English and English-French

Collins and Robert French-English, English-French Dictionary. 1987. Second Edition. By B. T. Atkins, A.Duval, and R. C. Milne. London: Collins, Paris: Dictionnaires Le Robert.

Dictionnaire Anglais-Français et lexique Français-Anglais des termes politiques, juridiques et économiques. 1978. Chaudesaigues-Deysine A.E. and A.E. Dreuilhe. Paris: Flammarion.

Dictionnaire commercial de l'Académie des Sciences commerciales. 1987. Paris: Conseil international de la langue française et Entreprise moderne d'Édition.

Dictionnaire de l'anglais économique et commercial. 1980. Par M. Marcheteau et al. Paris: Presses Pocket.

Dictionnaire économique et juridique—Economic and Legal Dictionary. 1989. Baylete J. et al. Paris: Navarre.

Dictionnaire français-anglais des affaires—Dictionnaire anglais-français des affaires. 1968. Péron M. avec la collaboration de W. Withnell et de M. Péron. Paris: Librairie Larousse. 1968.

Glossary of French and English Management Terms—Lexique de termes Anglais Français de gestion. 1972. By/Par J. Coveney and/et S. J. Moore. London: Longman.

Harrap's Standard French and English Dictionary. 1962. With supplement. J. E. Manson, editor. London: Harrap.

English-Swedish and Swedish-English

A Concise English-Swedish Glossary of Legal Terms—Kortfattad Engelsk-Svensk juridisk ordbok. 1980. A. Bruzelius, E. Wångstedt, and/och M-L. Norking. Lund: Liber Läromedel.

Ekonomi ordbok—Engelks-svensk fackordbok för ekonomifunktionen med begreppsförklaringar. N. F. Edström, L. A. Samuelson, and O. K. Böök. Stockholm: Norstedts Ekonomi.

Engelsk-Svensk ordbok. 1988. Utarbetad av E. Gomer et. al. Stockholm: Prisma.

Engelsk-Svensk teknisk ordbok. 1971. Tolfte upplagan. Av E. Engström. Stockholm: AB Svensk Trävaru tidning förlaget.

English Business Dictionary—engelsk-svensk-engelsk. 1989. P. H. Collin, translated by Lars Malmström and Roy Fox. Stockholm: Esselte. (First published in Great Britain by Peter Collin Publishing Ltd with the title *English Business Dictionary.*)

English-Swedish Business Dictionary-Engelsk Svensk Affärslexikon. 1982. St. Anne, United Kingdom: J. G. Sanders.

Merkantil ordbok: Svensk, Engelsk, Amerikansk, Tysk, Fransk, Spansk. 1951. O. Vidaeus et al. Stockholm: Strömbergs Förlag.

Norstedts stora Engelsk-Svenska ordbok—A Comprehensive English-Swedish Dictionary. 1992. Second Edition. Har utarbetats av V. Petti. Stockholm: Norstedts.

Svensk-Engelsk fackordbok för näringsliv, förvaltning och forskning. 1977. Andra reviderade upplagan med supplement. Av I. E. Gullberg. Stockholm: P. A. Norstedts and Söner Förlag.

Appendix 2: Analytical Framework Referred to in Chapter 6

The framework presented here consists of the main categories of analysis that narratology has identified as being pertinent to the analysis of narrative structures (Bal 1990; Prince 1982, 1990; Rimon-Kenan 1983; Toolan 1988), and of categories that Stegman (1987) uses in his rhetorical study of corporate annual reports.

I.   Outlook of the report
      A. General presentation
      B. Format
      C. Cover
      D. Pictures
II.   The narrator and focalization
      A. The narrator
         i.   Signs of the narrator
         ii. Grade of intrusiveness of the narrator
         ii. Distance of the narrator
         iv. Reliability of the narrator
      B. Focalization
         i.   Angle from which things are seen
         ii. Identity of the focalizor(s)
         iii. Unrestricted point of view, internal point of view, objective point of view, or else?
III. The narratee/The audience: Signs of the narratee (who and why)
IV.   Arrangement
V.   Rubricing
      A. Name given to the report
      B. Name given to other performance reports
VI.   Table of contents: Overview of the structure the text is given
VII. Highlights
      A. Presence of highlights
      B. What is highlighted
VIII. Multi-years analysis: Presence of summary

IX.   Text and time
    A. Order
    B. Duration
    C. Frequency
    D. Signs of the spatio-temporal orientation of the text

X.   Style

XI.   The language of activity report
    A. Technical terminology
    B. Positive and diminishing words

XII.   The practice of naming and of nomalizations

XIII. Verbs
    A. Are verbs of active or passive voice?
    B. If passive voice is the agent explicated?

XIV. Types of speech presentation
    A. Free direct discourse
    B. Normal direct discourse
    C. Free indirect discourse
    D. Normal indirect discourse

XV.   The place given to figures

XVI. The place given to performance indicators

XVII. The place given to diagrams

XVIII. The practice of quotation

XIX. Organization of the narration

XX.   Plots
    A. Events
    B. Presence of functionally equivalent events (relevance of events)
    C. Order of presentation (among which temporal axis of the events)
    D. Duration of events and speed of the narration
    E. Causal relations
    F. Organization of the events into a plot
    G. Multiple sequences of narration
    H. Homogeneity of the narratives

XXI. Character
    A. Traits and attributes
    B. Articulation of the traits
    C. Categorizations of characters
    D. Portraits and portraying technique (means of characterization)
    E. Characters who are and characters who do

XXII. Settings: Indication of the spatio-temporal complex

XXIII. Explicit/implicit information and presupposed information

XXIV. Themes

XXV. Comments

Appendix 3: Municipal Activity Reports (Årsredovisning) and Public Library Activity Reports (Verksamhetsberättelse) Referred to in Chapter 6

Eskilstuna

* Verksamhetsberättelse 1993, Eskilstuna stads—och länsbibliotek, Södermanlands län.
* *Fakta om biblioteksverksamheten i Eskilstuna*, Eskilstuna stads och länsbibliotek, Södermanlands län, 1993.

Eslöv

* Årsredovisning 1993, Eslöv kommun.

Gävle

* Bokslut och verksamhetsberättelse 1993. Errand number 10 for the cultural board meeting of April 14th, 1994.
* *Arbetsplatsprogram för kultur, Gävle bibliotek 1993/94—Ansökan till Arbetslivsfonden*, Gävle maj 1993.

Helsingborg

* Uppföljning av mål-93 (Sammanfattning). Intern note. Introduced by the chief librarian as a report to the cultural director and the board for culture (Uppföljningsrapporter från verksamhetschefer till förvaltningsledning och styrelse).
* Årsredovisning 1993, Helsingborgs stad.

Hässleholm

• Årsredovisning 1993, Hässleholms Kommun

Höör

• Årsredovisning 1993, Höör kommun.

Kristianstad

• Kulturnämnden, Kristianstad kommun, Verksamhetsberättelse 1993, with appendix.
• Kristianstad länsbibliotek, Statistik 1993, stencil.

Landskrona

• Landskrona stadsbibliotek, Verksamhetsberättelse 1992.
• Årsredovisning 1993, Landskrona kommun.

Lund

• Lund stadsbibliotek, Verksamhetsberättelse 1992.
• Årsredovisning 1993, Lund kommun.

Malmö

• Årsredovisning 1993, Malmö stad, with appendix.

Partille

• Verksamhetsbeskrivning, Kulturförvaltningen, Partilles kommun, 1993, stencil.

Trelleborg

• Årsredovisning 1993, Trelleborg kommun.
• Trelleborgs bibliotek, brochure of presentation produced by the Trelleborg public library.

Umeå

- Marianne Svennerstam. 1990. *Kultur i Umeå*, Umeå: Kulturförvaltningen.
- Årsredovisning 1993, Umeå kommun (draft of the section on the culture board)

References

Abernethy, Margaret A., and Johannes U. Stoelwinder. 1991. "Budget Use, Task Uncertainty, System Goal Orientation and Subunit Performance: A Test of the 'Fit' Hypothesis in Not-For-Profit Hospitals." *Accounting, Organization and Society* 6, no. 2: 105–20.

Ahlstedt, Valter. 1952. *Biblioteksproblem—Några synpunkter på biblioteksarbetets organisation och rationalisering* (Library Problems—Reflections on Library Organization and Rationalization). Stockholm: Natur och Kultur.

Alexander, John. 1991. *Televersions—Narrative Structure in Television.* Pyrford, United Kingdom: Intermedia Publications.

Alvesson, Mats. 1993. "The Play of Metaphors." In *Postmodernism and Organizations,* edited by John Hassard and Martin Parker, 114–31. London: Sage.

Andersson, Johnny. 1989. *Morgondagens idrott—Framtidsstudien* (Tomorrow's Sport—Future Study). Stockholm: Framtidsgruppen, Riksidrottsförbundet.

Andersson, Per-Magnus, and Lennart Hansson. 1989. *Beställare-Utförare—Ett alternativ till entreprenad i kommuner* (Client-Contractor—An Alternative to Contracting in Local Governments). Ds 1989:10. Stockholm: E.S.O (Expertgruppen för studier i offentlig ekonomi).

Anell, Anders. 1991. *Prestationsbaserad Ersättning i Hälso—och Sjukvården* (Performance-based Payment System in Health Care Services). Ds 1991:49. Stockholm: E.S.O. (Expertgruppen för studier i offentlig ekonomi).

Anthony, Robert N., John Dearden, and Norton M. Bedford. 1989. *Management Control System.* Fifth edition. Homewood, Ill.: Irwin.

Archer, Jane. 1992. "The Fate of the Subject in the Narrative Without End." In *Staying Tuned—Contemporary Soap Opera Criticism,* edited by Suzanne Frentz, 89–95. Bowling Green, Ohio: Bowling Green State University Popular Press.

Asplund, Johan. 1987. "Idrott och samhällsordning" (Sport and the Social Order). In *Den sociologiska fantasin—Teorier om samhället* (The Sociological Fantasy—Theories on Society), edited by Ulla Bergryd, 11–32. Stockholm: Rabén och Sjögren.

———. 1989. *Rivaler och Syndabockar* (Rivals and Scapegoats). Göteborg: Korpen.

Audit Commission, The. 1985. *Good Management in Local Government—Successful Practice and Action.* Luton, United Kingdom: Local Government Training Board.

———. 1989. "Managing Services Effectively—Performance Review." *Audit Commission (UK)—Management Papers,* no. 5, December.

Austin, John Langshaw. 1962. *How to do Things with Words,* edited by J. O. Urmson and Marina Sbisà. Second edition. Cambridge, Mass.: Harvard University Press.

Autrement. 1987. *L'excellence—Une valeur pervertie* (Excellence—A Perverted Value). Série Mutations No. 86. Paris: Editions Autrement.

Baguley, Philip. 1994. *Improving Organizational Performance—A Handbook for Managers.* Maidenhaid, Berkshire: McGraw-Hill Book Company Europe.

Bal, Mieke. 1990. "The Point of Narratology." *Poetics Today* 11, no. 4: 727–53.

Barre, Raymond. 1975. *Économie Politique* (Economics), Tome 1. Paris: Presses Universitaires de France.

Barthes, Roland. 1957. *Mythologies* (Mythologies). Paris: Éditions du Seuil.

———. 1966. "Introduction à l'analyse structurale des récits" (Introduction to the Structural Analysis of Narratives). *Communication*, no. 8: 7–33. (Translated and edited by Stephen Heath in *Image-Music-Text*, 79–124. London: Fontana/Collins.)

Bass, Jeff D. 1985. "The Appeal to Efficiency as Narrative Closure: Lyndon Johnson and the Dominican Crisis, 1965." *The Southern Speech Communication Journal* 50, Winter: 103–20.

Baudrillard, Jean. 1986. *Amérique* (America). Paris: Grasset et Fasquelle. (The page numbers are that of the pocket edition in Le livre de poche, Biblio essais LP6.)

Bell, R. A., and R. C. Morey. 1994. "The Search for Appropriate Benchmarking Partners: A Macro Approach and Application to Corporate Travel Management." *Omega* 22, no. 5: 477–90.

Bengtsson, Erik. 1979. *Marathon—En bok för barn och dårar, lidingölöpare och poeter* (Marathon—A Book for Children and Mad People, Lidingö Runners and Poets). Nacka: Författarförlaget.

Bengtsson, Lars. 1993. *Intern Diversifiering som strategisk process* (Internal Diversification as a Strategic Process). Lund: Lund University Press.

Betts, John Rickards. 1981. "The Technological Revolution and the Rise of Sport, 1850–1900." In *Sport, Culture Society*, edited by John W. Loy, Jr., Gerald S. Kenyon, and Barry D. McPherson, 273–86. Second revised edition. Philadelphia: Lea and Febiger.

Bialot, Irène. 1987. "Corps et décors (Bodies and Settings)." In *Organisations et management en question(s)* (Questions on Organizations and Management), edited by Salvador Juan, 47–63. Paris: L'Harmattan.

Biblioteksarbete—En översyn av verksamheten vid kommunala bibliotek (Library Work. A Review of Municipal Libraries Activities). 1972. Betänkande avgivet av 1970 års rationaliseringsutredning vid folkbiblioteken. Lund: Bibliotekstjänst.

Blanchard, Kenneth, and Spencer Johnsson. 1982. *The One Minute Manager*. New York: William Morrow and Company.

Blomquist, Christine. 1996. *I marknadens namn—Mångtydiga reformer i svenska kommuner* (In the Name of the Market—On the Ambiguity of Reforms in Swedish Municipalities). Stockholm: Nerenius & Santérus.

Boje, David M. 1991. "The Storytelling Organization: A Study of Story Performance in an Office-Supply Firm." *Administrative Science Quarterly* 36, March: 106–26.

Boland, Richard J., Jr. 1993. "Accounting and the Interpretative Act." *Accounting, Organizations and Society* 8, no. 2/3: 125–46.

———. 1996. Comments delivered at the occasion of the oral defense of the dissertation, Department of Business Administration, University of Lund, Sweden, 15 February 1996.

Boland, Richard, Jr., and Robert J. Bricker. 1995. "Financial Analyst Reports as the Social Construction of Corporate and Management Identities." (Weatherland School of Management, Case Western University, Cleveland, Ohio 44106-7235). Paper presented at the 18th Congress of the European Accounting Association in Birmingham (United Kingdom), May 1995.

Borges, Jorge Luis. 1981. "Pierre Menard, Author of the Quixotte." In *Borges: A Reader*, edited by E. R. Monegal and A. Reid, 96–103. New York: E.P. Dutton.

Bouet, Michel. 1968. *Signification du sport* (The Signification of Sport). Paris: Editions Universitaires. (Thèse pour le doctorat ès-lettres présentée devant la Faculté des Lettres et Sciences Humaines de Paris-Sorbonne.)

Bourdieu, Pierre. 1984. "Comment peut-on être sportif?" In *Questions de sociologie*, 173–95. Paris: Minuit. (Translation by Richard Nice: "Sport and Social Class." In *Rethinking Popular Culture-Contemporary Perspectives in Cultural Studies*, 1991, edited by Chandra Mukerji and Michael Schudson, 357–73. Berkeley: University of California Press.)

Bourguignon, Annick. 1994. "Au pays des mots-valises—L'exemple de la performance" (In the World of Polysemous Words. An example: Performance). *Document de recherche du CERESSEC* (No. 94042), Cergy-Pontoise, France.

Boyd, Brian K. 1991. "Strategic Planning and Financial Performance: A Meta-Analytic Review." *Journal of Management Studies* 28, no. 4: 353–74.

Boyer, Luc, and Noël Equilibrey. 1990. *Histoire du management* (A History of Management). Paris: Les éditions d'organisation.

Boyne, George, and Jennifer Law. 1991. "Accountability and Local Authority Annual Reports: The Case of Welsh Districts Councils." *Financial Accountability and Management* 7, no. 3: 179–94.

Brohm, Jean-Marie. 1992. *Sociologie politique du sport* (Political Sociology of Sport). Nancy: Presses Universitaires de Nancy.

Bromiley, Philip. 1991. "Testing a Causal Model of Corporate Risk Taking and Performance." *Academy of Management Journal* 34, no. 1: 37–59.

Bruner, Jerome. 1986. *Actual Minds—Possible Worlds*. Cambridge, Mass.: Harvard University Press.

Calhoun-French, Diane M. 1992. "Soap and Serials—The Transformation of Daytime Drama Into Romance Literature." In *Staying Tuned—Contemporary Soap Opera Criticism*, edited by Suzanne Frentz, 128–35. Bowling Green, Ohio: Bowling Green State University Popular Press.

Callon, Michel. 1985. "Some Elements of a Sociology of Translation: Domestication of the Scallops and the Fishermen of St Brieuc Bay." In *Power, Action and Belief*, edited by John Law, 196–233. Sociological Review Monograph, no. 32. London: Routledge and Kegan Paul.

Calori, Roland, and Philippe Sarnin. 1991. "Corporate Culture and Economic Performance: A French Study." *Organization Studies* 12, no. 1: 49–74.

Caves, Richard E. 1980. "Industrial Organization, Corporate Strategy and Structure." *Journal of Economic Literature* 18: 64–92.

Chandler, Alfred D., Jr. 1990. *Scale and Scope—The Dynamics of Industrial Capitalism*. Cambridge, Mass.: The Belknap Press of the Harvard University Press.

Childers, Thomas, and Nancy Van House. 1989. "Dimension of Public Library Effectiveness." *Library and Information Science Research*, no. 10: 275–301.

Clair, Robin Patric. 1993. "The Use of Framing Devices to Sequester Organizational Narratives: Hegemony and Harassment." *Communication Monographs* 60, June: 113–36.

Clarkson, Max B. E. 1995. "A Stakeholder Framework for Analyzing and Evaluating Corporate Social Performance." *Academy of Management Review* 20, no. 1: 92–117.

Cohen, Michael D., James G. March, and Johan P. Olsen. 1972. "A Garbage Can Model of Organizational Choice." *Administrative Science Quarterly* 17, March: 1–25.

Columbia Dictionary of Modern Literary and Cultural Criticism. 1995. Edited by Joseph Childers and Gary Hentzi. New York: Columbia University Press.

Corvellec, Hervé. 1991. "Trend, Weaknesses and Perspectives of Performance Evaluation in Public Libraries." *Swedish Library Research,* no. 3, 19–28.

Covin, Jeffrey G. 1991. "Entrepreneurial Versus Conservative Firms: A Comparison of Strategies and Performance." *Journal of Management Studies* 28, no. 5, 439–62.

Covin, Jeffrey G., Dennis P. Slevin, and Randall L. Schultz. 1994. "Implementing Strategic Missions: Effective Strategic, Structural and Tactical Choices." *Journal of Management Studies* 31, no. 4, 481–505.

Crozier, Michel. 1990. *L'évaluation des performances pédagogiques des établissements universitaires—Rapport au ministre d'État ministre de l'Éducation nationale de la Jeunesse et des Sports* (Pedagogical Performance of Universities—Report to the State Minister of Education, Youth and Sports). Paris: La documentation française.

Czarniawska-Joerges, Barbara. 1992. *Styrningens paradoxer—Scener ur den offentliga verksamheten* (Paradoxes of Management—Scenes from the Public Sector). Stockholm: Norstedt.

———.1993. *The Three Dimensional Organization—A Constructionist View.* Lund: Studentlitteratur.

———. 1997. *Narrating the Organization—Dramas of Institutional Identity.* Chicago: The University of Chicago Press.

Czarniawska-Joerges, Barbara, and Pierre Guillet de Monthoux, eds. 1994. *Good Novels—Better Management.* Chur, Switz.: Harwood Academic Publishers.

D'Elia, George, and Sandra Walsh. 1985. "Patron's Use and Evaluation of Library Service: A Comparison Across Five Public Libraries." *Library and Information Science Research* 7: 3–30.

Datta, Deepak K., Nandini Rajagopalan, and Abdul M. A. Rasheed. 1991. "Diversification and Performance: Critical Review and Future Directions." *Journal of Management Studies* 28, no. 5: 529–58.

Delort, Robert. 1972. *La vie au moyen-âge* (Life in the Middle Ages). Lausanne: Edita. (Reprinted as Point-Histoire No. 62, Paris: Éditions du Seuil). (Translated by Robert Allen. 1983. New York: Greenwich House.)

Denzin, Norman K. 1992. *Symbolic Interactionism and Cultural Studies—The Politics of Interpretation.* Oxford: Blackwell.

Diakoulaki, D., G. Mavrotas, and L. Papayannakis. 1992. "A Multicriteria Approach for Evaluating the Performance of Industrial Firms." *Omega* 20, no. 4: 467–74.

Didriksson, Mats, and Niclas Mogensen. 1993. *Resultatansvar inom kommunal förvaltning—En (o)möjlig styrform?* (Profit Centers in Local Government—A Possible Form of Management). KEFU Skriftserie, 1993:3. Lund: KEFU (Kommunal Ekonomisk Forskning och Utbildning).

Drucker, Peter F. 1989. "What Business Can Learn from Nonprofits." *Harvard Business Review,* July-August: 88–93.

Duby, Georges. 1984. *Guillaume le Maréchal ou le meilleur chevalier du monde* (William Marshal, the Best Knight in the World). Paris: Fayard.

Duby, Georges, and Robert Mandrou. 1968. *Histoire de la civilisation française* (History of the French Civilisation), Tome 1: Moyen-âge—XVIᵉ siècle (Tome 1: Middle Ages to Sixteenth Century). Paris: Armand Collin.

Duncan, Margaret Carlisle, and Barry Brummett. 1987. "The Mediation of Spectator Sport." *Research Quarterly for Exercise and Sport* 58, no. 2: 168–77.

————. 1989. "Types and Sources of Spectating Pleasure in Televised Sports." *Sociology of Sport Journal* 6: 195–211.

Dvir, Dov, Eli Segev, and Aaron Shenhar. 1993. "Technology's Varying Impact on the Success of Strategic Business Units Within the Miles and Snow Typology." *Strategic Management Journal* 14: 155–162.

Eccle, Robert G. 1991. "The Performance Measurement Manifesto." *Harvard Business Review*, January-February: 131–37.

Eco, Umberto. 1962/1965. *L'oeuvre ouverte* (The Open Work). 1965. Translation Chantal Roux de Bézieux and André Boucourechlier. Paris: Éditions du Seuil. (Original title: *Opera Aperte*. 1962. Milan: Bonpiani.) (English translation by Anna Cancogni. 1989. Cambridge, Mass.: Harvard University Press.)

————. 1969/1985. "Le bavardage sportif (Chatter on Sport)." In *La guerre du faux*, 172–77. Paris: Grasset. (Originally published for *Quindici* 1969).

————. 1990. *The Limits of Interpretation*. Bloomington and Indianapolis: Indiana University Press.

Ehrenberg, Alain. 1991. *Le culte de la performance* (The Cult of Performance). Paris: Calman-Levy.

Eilon, Samuel. 1992. "Key Ratios for Corporate Performance." *Omega* 20, no. 3: 337–43.

Emmanuel, Clive, David Otley, and Kenneth Merchant. 1990. *Accounting for Management Control*. Second edition. London: Chapman and Hall.

Engström, Lars-Magnus. 1989. *Idrottsvanor i förändring* (Changes Attitudes on Sports). Rapport 1/1989. Stockholm: Avdelning för idrottspedagogik, Högskolan för Lärarutbildning i Stockholm.

E.S.O. (Expertgruppen för studier i offentlig ekonomi). 1989. *Produktivitetsmätning av Folkbibliotekens utlåningsverksamhet* (Productivity Measurement of Public Libraries' Lending Activities). Ds 1989:42. Stockholm: E.S.O.

Fernandez-Castro, A., and P. Smith. 1994. "Towards a General Non-parametric Model of Corporate Performance." *Omega* 22, no. 3: 237–49.

Fiol, C. Marlene 1989. "A Semiotic Analysis of Corporate Language: Organizational Boundaries and Joint Venturing." *Administrative Science Quarterly* 34, June: 277–303.

Fish, Stanley. 1980. *Is There a Text in This Class?—The Authority of Interpretative Communities*. Cambridge, Mass.: Harvard University Press.

Fisher, Walter R. 1987. *Human Communication as Narration—Toward a Philosophy of Reason, Value, and Action*. Columbia: University of South Carolina Press.

Fiske, John. 1987. *Television Culture*. London and New York: Routledge.

Ford, Geoffrey. 1989. "Approaches to Performance Measurement—Some Observations on Principles and Practice." *British Journal of Librarianship* 2, no. 4, 74–87.

Ford, Jeffrey D., and Deborah A. Schellenberg. 1982. "Conceptual Issues of Linkage in the Assessment of Organizational Performance." *Academy of Management Review* 7, no. 1: 49–58.

Foucault, Michel. 1966. *Les mots et les choses*. (The Order of Things—An Archeology of the Human Sciences). Paris: Gallimard, Bibliothèque des sciences humaines. (1974. London: Tavistock).

————. 1975. *Surveiller et punir* (Discipline and Punish—The Birth of the Prison). Paris: Gallimard, Bibliothèque des sciences humaines. (Translation Alan Sheridan. 1979. Harmondsworth: Penguin).

Frykman, Jonas. 1993. "Becoming the Perfect Swede—Modernity, Body Politics and National Processes in Twentieth-Century Sweden." *Ethnos*, no. 3–4: 259–74.

Fryxell, Gerald E., and Sidney L. Barton. 1990. "Temporal and Contextual Change in the Measurement Structure of Financial Performance. Implication for Strategy Research." *Journal of Management* 16, no. 3: 553–69.

Gephart, Robert P., Jr. 1993. "The Textual Approach: Risk and Blame in Disaster Sensemaking." *Academy of Management Journal* 36, no. 6, 1465–1514.

Giddens, Anthony. 1990. *The Consequences of Modernity*. Cambridge, United Kingdom: Polity Press.

Goffman, Erving. 1959. *The Presentation of the Self in Everyday Life*. Garden City, N.Y.: Doubleday Anchor Books.

Gomez-Mejia, Luis R., Henry Tosi, and Timothy Hinkin. 1987. "Managerial Control, Performance, and Executive Compensation." *Academy of Management Journal* 30, no. 1: 51–70.

Gordon, George G., and Nancy DiTomaso. 1992. "Predicting Corporate Performance from Organizational Culture." *Journal of Management Studies* 29, no. 6: 783–98.

Gordon, Lawrence A., and Kimberley J. Smith. 1992. "Postauditing Capital Expenditures and Firm Performance: The Role of Asymmetric Information." *Accounting, Organizations and Society* 17, no. 8: 741–57.

Gore, Al. 1993. *From Red Tape to Results—Creating a Government that Works Better and Costs Less*. Report of the National Performance Review. Washington, D.C.: National Performance Review. (Electronic reference @ National Performance Review).

Graves, Samuel B., and Sandra A. Waddock. 1994. "Institutional Owners and Corporate Social Performance." *Academy of Management Journal* 37, no. 4: 1034–1046.

Greimas, Algirdas Julien. 1966. "Eléments pour une théorie de l'interprétation du récit mythique (Elements of a Theory of Interpretation of Mythic Narratives)." *Communication* 8: 34–65.

Gruneau, Richard. 1993. "The Critique of Sport in Modernity—Theorising Power, Culture, and the Politics of the Body." In *The Sport Process—A Comparative and Developmental Approach*, edited by Eric G. Dunning, Joseph A. Maguire, and Robert E. Pearton. Champaign, Ill.: Human Kinetics Publishers.

Gumbrecht, Hans Ulrich. 1992. *Making Sense in Life and Literature*. Translation Glen Burns. Minneapolis: University of Minnesota Press.

Guthrie, James. 1993. "Critical Issues in Measurement and Indicators." In *The Australian Public Sector—Pathways to Change in the 1990s*, edited by James Guthrie, 69–74. Sydney, Australia: IIR Conferences.

Guttmann, Allen. 1977. *From Rituals to Records—The Nature of Modern Sport*. New York: Columbia University Press.

Habermas, Jürgen. 1981/1985. Modernity—An Incomplete Project. In *Postmodern Culture*, 1985, edited by Hal Foster, translation Seyla Ben-Habib, 3–15. London: Pluto Press. (Originally published in *New German Critique* 22, Winter 1981.)

Hamburg, Morris. 1974. *Library Planning and Decision-Making Systems*. Cambridge, Mass.: MIT Press.

Hannabuss, Stuart. 1987. "The Concept of Performance: A Semantic Review." *Aslib Proceedings*, no. 5: 149–58.

Hargrove, Erwin C., and John C. Glidewell, eds. 1990. *Impossible Jobs in Public Management*. Lawrence: The University Press of Kansas.

Harris, Janet C., and Laura A. Hills. 1993. "Telling the Story: Narrative in Newspaper Accounts of a Men's Collegiate Basketball Tournament." *Research Quarterly for Exercise and Sport* 64, no. 1: 108–21.

Hatch, Mary Jo. 1995. Comments delivered at the occasion of the preliminary defense of the dissertation, Department of Business Administration, University of Lund, Sweden, 25 September 1995.

Hatry, Hary P., James R. Fountain, Jonathan M. Sullivan, and Lorraine Kremer, eds. 1990. *Service Efforts and Accomplishments Reporting: Its Time Has Come—An Overview.* Norwalk, Conn.: Governmental Accounting Standard Board.

Haveman, Heather A. 1992. "Between a Rock and a Hard Place: Organizational Change and Performance under Conditions of Fundamental Environmental Transformation." *Administrative Science Quarterly* 37, no. 1: 48–75.

Heikkala, Juha. 1993. "Discipline and Excel: Techniques of the Self and the Body and the Logic of Competing." *Sociology of Sport Journal* 10: 397–412.

Hines, Ruth D. 1988. "Financial Accounting: In Communicating Reality, We Construct Reality." *Accounting Organization and Society* 13, no. 3: 251–61.

Hitchens, D. M. W. N., and P. N. O'Farell. 1988. "Comparative Performance of Small Manufacturing Companies in South Wales and Northern Ireland." *Omega* 16, no. 5: 429–38.

Hughes, Linda K., and Michael Lund. 1991. *The Victorian Serial.* Charlottesville: University Press of Virginia.

Huizinga, Johan. 1938/1966. *Homo Ludens—A Study of the Play Element in Culture.* London: Beacon Paperbacks. (Originally published in Dutch as *Homo Ludens.* 1938).

Hummel Ralph. P. 1991. "Stories Managers Tell: Why they are as Valid as Science." *Public Administration Review* 51, no. 1: 31–41.

Isaac-Henry, Kester. 1993. "Development and Change in the Public Sector." In *Management in the Public Sector—Challenge and Change*, edited by Kester Isaac-Henry, Chris Painter, and Chris Barnes, 1–20. London, United Kingdom: Chapman and Hall.

Jackall, Robert J. 1988. *Moral Mazes—The World of Corporate Managers.* New York and Oxford: Oxford University Press.

Jauss, Hans Robert. 1982. *Toward an Aesthetic of Reception.* Translation Timothy Bahti. Brighton: Harvester Press.

———. 1990. "The Theory of Reception: A Retrospective of Its Unrecognized Prehistory." In *Literary Theory Today*, edited by Peter Collier and Helga Geyer-Ryan, translation John Whitlam, 53–73. Cambridge, United Kingdom: Polity Press.

Jeu, Bernard. 1987. *Analyse du sport* (An Analysis of Sport). Paris: Presses Universitaires de France.

Johnson, Edward. 1993. "The Challenge to the Public Sector: Changing Politics and Ideologies." In *Management in the Public Sector—Challenge and Change*, edited by Kester Isaac-Henry, Chris Painter, and Chris Barnes, 21–36. London, United Kingdom: Chapman and Hall.

Johnson H. Thomas and Robert S. Kaplan. 1987. *Relevance Lost—The Rise and Fall of Management Accounting.* Boston, Mass.: Harvard Business School.

Kalleberg, Arne L., and Kevin T. Leicht. 1991. "Gender and Organizational Performance: Determinants of Small Business Survival and Success." *Academy of Management Journal* 34, no. 1: 136–61.

Kanter, Rosabeth Moss. 1989. *When the Giants Learn How to Dance—Mastering the Challenges of Strategy, Management, and Careers in the 1990s.* London: Unwin Paperbacks.

Kanter, Rosabeth Moss, and David V. Summer. 1987. "Doing Well While Doing Good: Dilemmas of Performance Measurement in Nonprofit Organizations and the Need for a Multiple-Constituency Approach." In *The Nonprofit Sector—A Research Handbook*, edited by Walter W. Powell, 154–66. New Haven, Conn.: Yale University Press.

Kantor, Paul B. 1976. "The Library as an Information Utility in the University Context: Evolution and Measurement of Service." *Journal of the American Society for Information Science*, March-April 1976: 100–12.

Kaplan, Robert S., and David P. Norton. 1992. "The Balanced Scorecard—Measures that Drive Performance." *Harvard Business Review*, January-February: 71–79.

Ketchen, David J., Jr., James B. Thomas, and Charles C. Snow. 1993. "Organizational Configurations and Performance: A Comparison of Theoretical Approaches." *Academy of Management Journal* 36, no. 6: 1278–1313.

Kihlberg, Morgan. 1983. *Idrottshistoria—Hur olika sporter uppstod och utvecklades* (Sport History—The Birth and Development of Various Sports). Göteborg: Zindermans.

Koch, James V., and Richard J. Cebula. 1994. "In Search of Excellent Management." *Journal of Management Studies* 31, no. 5: 681–99.

Konkurrensverket. 1993a. *Go'Morgon Sverige!* (Good Morning Sweden!). Stockholm: Konkurrensverket. (Brochure.)

———. 1993b. *Daghemsverksamhet—Kostnader och konkurrensförutsättningar* (Kindergartens—Conditions of Costs and Competition). Stockholm: Konkurrensverket.

Kristeva, Julia. 1988. *Etrangers à nous-mêmes* (Stranger to Ourselves). Paris: Fayard. (1991. London: Harvester Wheatsheaf.)

Lamont, Bruce T., Robert J. Williams, and James J. Hoffman. 1994. "Performance During 'M-Form' Reorganization and Recovery Time: The Effect of Prior Strategy and Implementation Speed." *Academy of Management Journal* 37, no. 1: 153–66.

Lancaster, F. Wilfrid. 1988. *If You Want to Evaluate Your Library*. London: London Library Association.

Latour, Bruno. 1986. "The Power of Association." In *Power, Action and Belief—A New Sociology of Knowledge?*, edited by John Law, 264–80. London: Routledge.

———. 1987. *Science in Action—How to Follow Scientists and Engineers Through Society*. Milton Keynes: Open University Press.

———. 1991/1993. *Nous n'avons jamais été modernes—Essai d'anthropologie symétrique*, Paris: La Découverte. (English translation by Catherine Porter. *We Have Never Been Modern*. 1993. New York: Harvester Wheatsheaf.)

———. 1992. *Aramis ou l'amour des techniques* (Aramis or the Love of Techniques). Paris: La Découverte.

Latour, Bruno, and Steve Woolgar. 1986. *Laboratory Life—The Construction of Scientific Facts*. Second edition, with a new postscript by the authors. Princeton, N.J.: Princeton University Press.

Levine, Marylin M. 1980. "The Circulation/Acquisition Ratio: An Input-Output Measure for Libraries." *Information Processing and Management* 16: 313–15.

Levi-Strauss, Claude. 1962. *La Pensée Sauvage* (The Savage Mind). Paris: Plon. (1966. Chicago: University of Chicago Press.)

Lindblom, Charles E. 1959. "The Science of 'Muddling Through'." *Public Administration Review* 19, no. 2: 79–88.

Linstead, Stephen A., and Robert Grafton-Small. 1990. "Organizational Bricolage." In *Organizational Symbolism*, edited by Barry A. Turner, 291–308. Berlin and New York: Walter De Gruyter.

Lipovietski, Gilles. 1987. *L'empire de l'éphémère—La mode et son destin dans les sociétés modernes* (The Empire of the Ephemeron—Fashion and its Destiny in Modern Societies). Paris: Gallimard.

Lothian, Niall. 1987. *Measuring Corporate Performance—A Guide to Non-Financial Indicators*. Occasional Paper Series. London: CIMA (Chartered Institute of Management Accountants).

Loveday, Barry. 1993. "Management and Accountability in Public Services: A Police Case Study." In *Management in the Public Sector—Challenge and Change*, edited by Kester Isaac-Henry, Chris Painter, and Chris Barnes, 133–50. London, United Kingdom: Chapman and Hall.

Lowe, Benjamin. 1977. *The Beauty of Sport—A Cross-Disciplinary Inquiry*. Englewoods-Cliffs, N.J.: Prentice-Hall.

Lowe, Tony, and Tony Puxty. 1989. "The Problems of a Paradigm: A Critique of the Prevailing Orthodoxy in Management Control." In *Critical Perspectives in Management Control*, edited by Wai Fong Chua, Tony Lowe, and Tony Puxty, 9–26. London: Macmillan.

Loy, John W., and Graham L. Hesketh. 1984. "The Agon Motif: A Prolegomenon for the Study of Agonetic Behavior." In *Contribution of Sociology to the Study of Sport—In Honour of Kalevi Heinilä*, edited by Kalevi Olin, 31–49. Jysväskylä: University of Jyväskylä.

Lubatkin, Michael, and Sayan Chatterjee. 1991. "The Strategy-Shareholders Value Relationship—Testing Temporal Stability Across Market Cycles." *Strategic Management Journal* 12: 251–70.

Lubatkin, Michael, Hemant Merchant, and Narasimhan Srinivasan. 1993. "Construct Validity of Some Unweighted Product-Count Diversification Measures." *Strategic Management Journal* 14: 433–49.

Lubatkin, Michael, and Ronald E. Shrieves. 1986. "Toward Reconciliation of Market Performance Measures to Strategic Management Research." *Academy of Management Review* 11, no. 3: 497–512.

Lüschen, Günther. 1967. "The Interdependence of Sport and Culture". *International Review of Sport Sociology*, no. 2: 127–39. (Reprinted in *Sport, Culture Society*, 1981, edited by John W. Loy, Jr., Gerald S. Kenyon III, and Barry D. McPherson, second revised edition, 287–95. Philadelphia: Lea & Febiger.)

Lyotard, Jean-François. 1979. *La condition postmoderne* (The Postmodern Condition—A Report on Knowledge). Paris: Minuit (English Translation by Geoffrey Bennington and Brian Massumi. 1984. Manchester: Manchester University Press).

Maher, Michael W., Clyde P. Stickney, and Roman L. Weil. 1994. *Managerial Accounting—An Introduction To Concepts, Methods and Uses*. Fifth edition. Fort Worth, Texas: The Dryden Press.

Marini, Franck. 1992. "The Uses of Literature in the Exploration of Public Administration Ethics: The Example *Antigone*." *Public Administration Review* 52, no. 5: 420–26.

Martin, David E., Herbert W. Benario, and Roger W. H. Gynn. 1977. "Development of the Marathon from Pheidippides to the Present, with Statistics of Significant Races." In *The Marathon: Physiological, Medical, Epidemiological, and Psychological Studies*, edited by Paul Milvy, 820–52. Annals of the New York Academy of Science, volume 301. New York: The New York Academy of Sciences.

Martin, Joanne, Marths S. Feldman, Mary Jo Hatch, and Sim B. Sitkin. 1983. "The Uniqueness Paradox in Organizational Stories." *Administrative Science Quarterly* 28: 438–53.

Martin, Wallace. 1986. *Recent Theories of Narrative*. Ithaca, N.Y.: Cornell University Press.

McClure, Charles R., Amy Owen, Douglas L. Zweizig, Mary-Jo Lynch, and Nancy Van House. 1987. *Planning and Role Setting for Public Libraries—A Manual for Options and Procedures*. American Library Association: Chicago

McGuire, Jean, Thomas Schneeweis, and Joanne Hill. 1986. "An Analysis of Alternative Measures of Strategic Performance." *Advances in Strategic Management* 4: 127–54.

Metcalfe, Les, and Sue Richards. 1990. *Improving Public Management*. Second edition. London: European Institute of Public Administration and Sage Publications.

Meyer, Marshall W., and Lynne G. Zucker. 1989. *Permanently Failing Organizations*. Newbury Park, Calif.: Sage Publications.

Michener, James A. 1976. *Sports in America*. New York: Random House.

Miles, Grant, Charles C. Snow, and Mark P. Sharfman. 1993. "Industry Variety and Performance." *Strategic Management Journal* 14: 163–77.

Miller, C. Chet, and Laura B. Cardinal. 1994. "Strategic Planning and Firm Performance: A Synthesis of More than Two Decades of Research." *Academy of Management Journal* 37, no. 6: 1649–65.

Miller, Peter, and Christopher Napier. 1993. "Genealogies of Calculation." *Accounting Organizations and Society* 18, no. 7/8: 631–47.

Miner, John B., Timothy M. Singleton, and Vincent P. Luchsinger. 1985. *The Practice of Management*. Columbus, Ohio: Charles E. Merill Publishing Company.

Moe, Terry M. 1990. "The Politics of Structural Choice: Toward a Theory of Public Bureaucracy." In *Organization Theory—From Chester Barnard to the Present and Beyond*, edited by Oliver E. Williamson, 116–53. Oxford: Oxford University Press.

Möhlenbrock, Sigurd. 1953. "Rationalisering genom arbetsundersökning" (Rationalizing by studying work). *Biblioteksbladet*, no. 10: 490–500.

———. 1956. "Biblioteksarbetsorganisation" (Library Organization). *Biblioteksbladet*, no. 8: 513–18.

———. 1959. "Två organisatoriska undersökningar" (Two Studies on Organizations), *Biblioteksbladet*, no. 2: 90–94.

Molinero, C. Mar, and M. Ezzamel. 1991. "Multidimensonal Scaling Applied to Corporate Failure." *Omega* 19, no. 4: 259–74.

Moore, Nick. 1989. *Measuring the Performance of Public Libraries—A Draft Manual*. UNESCO and UNISIST: Paris.

Moores, Roger. 1994. *Managing for High Performance*. London: The Industrial Society.

Mossberg, Thomas. 1977. *Utveckling av nyckeltal* (Developing Key Numbers). Stockholm: EFI (Ekonomiska Forsknings Institut vid Handelshögskolan i Stockholm).

Mumby, Dennis K. 1987. "The Political Function of Narrative in Organizations." *Communication Monographs* 54, June: 113–27.

Nayyar, Praveen R. 1992. "Performance Effects of Three Foci in Service Firms." *Academy of Management Journal* 35, no. 5: 985–1009.

———. 1993. "Performance Effects of Information Asymetry and Economies of Scope in Diversified Service Firms." *Academy of Management Journal* 36, no. 1: 28–57.

Nelson, John S. 1993. "Account and Acknowledge, or Represent and Control? On Post-Modern Politics and Economics of Collective Responsibility." *Accounting, Organizations and Society* 18, no. 2/3: 207–29.

Newark, Peter. 1991. *About Translation*. Clevedon, United Kingdom: Multilingual Matters Ltd.

Newton, Ken M. 1990. *Interpretating the Text—A Critical Introduction to the Theory and Practice of Literary Interpretation.* New York: Harvester-Wheatsheaf.

Nilsson, Pea, and Torbjörn Wigg. 1982. *Marathonboken* (The Marathon Book). Visby: Manus Förlag.

OCDE/OECD. 1994. *Performance Management in Government—Performance Measurement and Results-Oriented Management.* Public Management Occasional Papers, no. 3. Paris: OCDE/OECD.

O'Connor, Daniel O. 1982. "Evaluating Public Libraries Using Standard Scores: The Library Quotient." *Library Research*, no. 4: 51–70.

Organisation och arbetsmetoder vid kommunala bibliotek—Betänkande avgivet av särskilda kommitterade (Organization and Methods of Work in Public Libraries—Report of a Special Committee). 1960. Lund: Bibliotekstjänst.

Osborne, David, and Ted Gaebler. 1992. *Reinventing Government—How the Entrepreneurial Spirit is Transforming the Public Sector.* Reading, Mass.: Addison-Wesley Publishing Company.

Oscarsson, Ingemar. 1980. *Fortsättning följer—Följetong och fortsättningsroman i dagspressen till ca 1850* (To Be Continued—Serial Publications and Serial Novels in the Daily Press up to 1850). Litteratur Teater Film No. 16. Lund: Liber Läromedel.

Ouchi, William G. 1981. *Theory Z—How American Business Can Meet the Japanese Challenge.* New York: Avon.

Painter, Chris, Kester Issaac-Henry, and Chris Barnes. 1993. "The Problematical Nature of Public Management Reform." In *Management in the Public Sector—Challenge and Change,* edited by Kester Isaac-Henry, Chris Painter, and Chris Barnes, 171–86. London, United Kingdom: Chapman and Hall.

Patriksson, Göran. 1982. *Idrott, tävling, samhälle—En jämförande analys av tävlingsidrotten i olika samhällen* (Sport, Competition and Society—A Comparative Analysis of Sport Competition in Various Societies). Örebro: Veje Förlag.

Pearce, John A., Elizabeth B. Freeman, and Richard B. Robinson, Jr. 1987. "The Tenuous Link between Formal Strategic Planning and Financial Performance." *Academy of Management Review* 12, no. 4: 658–75.

Perrow, Charles. 1986. *Complex Organizations—A Critical Essay.* Third edition. New York: Random House.

Petersson, Lars. 1988. *Det kulturella kapitalet—Kritik av kultursponsring* (The Cultural Capital—A Critique of Sponsoring in the Arts). Stockholm: Tidens Förlag.

Politt, Christopher. 1993. *Managerialism and the Public Services—Cuts or Cultural Change in the 1990s.* Second edition. Oxford, United Kingdom: Blackwell Business.

Polkinghorne, Donald E. 1987. *Narrative Knowing and the Human Sciences.* New York: State University of New York Press.

Prince, Gerald. 1982. *Narratology—The Form and Functioning of Narrative.* Berlin: De Gruyter.

———. 1990. "On Narrative Studies and Narrative Genres." *Poetics Today* 11, no. 4: 271–81.

Ragin, Charles C. 1987. *The Comparative Method—Moving Beyond Qualitative and Quantitative Strategies.* Berkeley: University of California Press.

Raiport, Grigori. 1990. *Red Gold—Peak Performance Techniques of the Russian and East-German Olympic Victors.* Los Angeles: Jeremy P. Tarcher, Inc.

Ranson, Stewart, and John Stewart. 1994. *Management for the Public Domain—Enabling the Learning Society.* London: McMillan.

Revill, D. H. 1983. "Some Examples and Types of Performance Measures." In *Do We Really Need Libraries?*, edited by John Blagden, 59–66. Cranfield, United Kingdom: Cranfield Institute of Technology.

Rey, Jean-Pierre. 1991. *Le contrôle de gestion des services publics communaux* (Management Control of Local Governmental Services). Paris: Dunod.

Richard, Jacques. 1989. *L'audit des performances de l'entreprise* (Auditing Corporate Performance). Paris: La Villeguerin éditions.

Rimon-Kenan, Schlomith. 1983. *Narrative Fictions—Contemporay Poetics.* London and New York: Routledge.

Roberts, Terence J. 1992. "The Making and Remaking of Sport Actions." *Journal of the Philosophy of Sport* 19: 15–29.

Robson, Keith. 1992. "Accounting Numbers as 'Inscription': Action at a Distance and the Development of Accounting." *Accounting Organization and Society* 17, no. 7: 685–708.

Rogers, Steve. 1994. *Performance Management in Local Government.* Harlow, Essex: Longman.

Roth, Kendall, and David A. Ricks. 1994. "Goal Configuration in a Global Industry." *Strategic Management Journal* 15: 103–20.

Rouse, John. 1993. "Resource and Performance Management in Public Service Organizations." In *Management in the Public Sector—Challenge and Change*, edited by Kester Isaac-Henry, Chris Painter, and Chris Barnes, 59–76. London, United Kingdom: Chapman and Hall.

Sage, George H. 1990. *Power and Ideology in American Sport—A Critical Perspective.* Champaign, Ill.: Human Kinetics Books.

Sandblad, Henrik. 1985. *Olympia och Valhalla—Idéhistoriska aspekter av den moderna idrottsrörelsens framväxt* (Olympia and Valhalla—Developments in Modern Sport Viewed from the Perspective of the History of Ideas). Stockholm: Almqvist and Wicksell.

Schefczyk, Michael. 1993. "Operational Performance of Airlines: An Extension of Traditional Measurement Paradigms." *Strategic Management Journal* 14: 301–17.

Schoenfeld, Hanns Martin W. 1994. "Management Accounting in Multinational Companies: Typical Data Adjustment and Unresolved Problems." *Advances in International Accounting* 6: 203–30.

Scholes, Robert E. 1989. *Protocols of Reading.* New Haven, Conn., and London: Yale University Press.

Silverman, David. 1994. *Interpreting Qualitative Data—Methods for Analysing Talk, Text and Interaction.* London: Sage.

Sköldberg, Kaj. 1994. "Tales of Change: Public Administration Reform and Narrative Mode." *Organization Science* 5, no. 2: 219–38.

Stegman, John Davis. 1987. *A Rhetorical Investigation of Selected 1982 Corporate Annual Reports.* Doctoral dissertation, Ohio State University.

Tan, J. Justin, and Robert J. Litschert. 1994. "Environment-Strategy Relationship and Its Performance Implications: An Empirical Study of the Chinese Electronic Industry." *Strategic Management Journal* 15: 1–20.

Terny, Guy, ed. 1990. *Performances des services publics locaux—Analyse comparée des modes de gestion* (Performance of the Local Services—Comparison of Managerial Modes). G.r.e.p.-U.n.s.p.i.c. (Place unknown): Litec.

Thomas, James B., Shawn M. Clark, and Dennis A. Gioia. 1993. "Strategic Sensemaking and Organizational Performance: Linkages Among Scanning, Interpretation, Action, and Outcomes." *Academy of Management Journal* 36, no. 2: 239–70.

Thompson, Grahame F. 1985. "Approaches to 'Performance'—An Analysis of Terms." *Screen*, no. 5: 78–90.

Toolan, Michael J. 1988. *Narrative—A Critical Linguistic Introduction.* London: Routledge.

Trujillo, Nick. 1985. "Organizational Communication as Cultural Performance: Some Managerial Considerations." *The Southern Speech Communication Journal* 50, Spring: 201–24.

Ulmann, Jacques. 1965. *De la gymnastique aux sports modernes—Histoire des doctrines de l'éducation physique* (From Gymnastics to Modern Sports—A History of Doctrines of Physical Exercises). Paris: Presses Universitaires de France.

Umiker-Sebeok, Jean. 1987. *Marketing and Semiotics.* Berlin: Mouton De Gruyter.

Van House, Nancy A., Mary-Jo Lynch, Charles R. McClure, Douglas L. Zweizig, and Eleanor Jo Rodger. 1987. *Output Measures for Public Libraries.* Second edition. Chicago: American Library Association.

Vargas, Yves. 1992. *Sur le sport* (On Sport). Série Philosophie, no. 34. Paris: Presses Universitaires de France.

Venkatraman, N., and Vasudevan Ramanujam. 1986. "Measurement of Business Performance in Strategy Research: A Comparison of Approaches." *Academy of Management Review* 11, no. 4: 801–14.

Virilio, Paul. 1977. *Vitesse et politique* (Speed and Politics). Paris: Galilée.

Williams, Raymond. 1976. *Keywords—A Vocabulary of Culture and Society.* London: Fontana/Croom Helm.

Williamson, Oliver E. 1985. *The Economic Institutions of Capitalism.* New York: The Free Press.

Wood, Donna J. 1991. "Social Issues in Management: Theory and Research in Corporate Social Performance." *Journal of Management* 17, no. 2: 383–406.

Index